Al-Fawz al-Kabīr fī Uṣūl at-Tafsīr

The Great Victory on Qur'ānic Hermeneutics

Al-Fawz al-Kabīr fī Uṣūl at-Tafsīr

The Great Victory
on Qur'ānic Hermeneutics

of

Shāh Waliyyullāh

Quṭbuddīn Aḥmad ibn 'Abdurraḥīm
al-Muḥaddith ad-Dihlawī
(1114 AH/1703 CE – 1176 AH/1762 CE)

A Manual of the Principles
and Subtleties of Qur'ānic Tafsīr

Translated, Introduced and Annotated by
Ṭāhir Maḥmood Kiānī

First Published in January 2014

Published by: Ta-Ha Publishers Ltd.
Unit 4, The Windsor Centre
Windsor Grove, London,
SE27 9NT

Website: www.tahapublishers.com
E-mail: support@tahapublishers.com

Translated by: Ṭāhir Maḥmood Kiānī

Edited and typeset by: Abdassamad Clarke

A catalogue record of this book is available from the British Library.

ISBN: 978 1 84200 134 9

Printed and bound by: Mega Printing, Turkey

Dedication

Dedicated for the conferral of its reward to

The Founder of Madrasah Raḥīmiyyah,
Co-author of *Fatāwā-e-'Ālamgīrī* and
Father of Shāh Waliyyullāh, namely

Shāh 'Abdurraḥīm
al-Qurashī ad-Dihlawī an-Naqshbandī
(d. 1131 AH/1719 CE)
(may Allah ﷻ have mercy on him)

Endorsement

Ṭāhir Maḥmood Kiānī has promoted the academic merits of *al-Fawz al-Kabīr fī Uṣūl at-Tafsīr* in a wonderful unique style of a much needed authentic English translation without losing the original flavour and essence. I am sure this translation will benefit all those who seek the scholarly wisdom contributed to the world by its eminent author, Shāh Waliyyullāh ad-Dihlawī, may Allah have mercy on him.

Prof. Imran Ahsan Khan Nyazee

Former Professor and Editor: Faculty of Shariah & Law, International Islamic University – Islamabad

Author of: *Murabaḥa and Credit Sale, Prohibition of Riba Elaborated, The Concept of Riba and Islamic Banking, Theories of Islamic Law, The Islamic Law of Business Organization: Partnerships, The Islamic Law of Business Organization: Corporations*

Translator of: *The Distinguished Jurist's Primer (Bidāyat al-Mujtahid)* of Ibn ar-Rushd, *The Guidance (Al-Hidāyah)* of al-Marghīnānī, *The Reconciliation of the Fundamentals of Islamic Law (Al-Muwāfaqāt)* of ash-Shāṭibī, *The Book of Revenue (Kitāb al-Amwāl)* of Abū ʿUbayd ibn Sallām

Contents

Dedication v

Endorsement vi

Shāh Waliyyullāh al-Muḥaddith ad-Dihlawī xv
- The Author xv
- Birth xv
- Further Education xvii
- Teaching xvii
- Achievements and Services xix
- Literary Career xxiv
- Death xxiv
- Family xxv
- Writings xxv
  - i. The Noble Qur'ān and Qur'ānic Exegesis (*Tafsīr*) xxvi
  - ii. Prophetic Traditions (*Ḥadīth*) xxvi
  - iii. Jurisprudence (*Fiqh*) xxvii
  - iv. Philosophy xxvii
  - v. Islamic Behavioural Spirituality (*Taṣawwuf*) xxvii
  - vi. History xxviii
  - vii. Biography xxviii
  - viii. Poetry xxviii
  - ix. Principles of Islamic Jurisprudence (*Uṣūl al-Fiqh*) xxix
  - x. Beliefs (*'Aqīdah*) and its Scholarly Science (*Kalām*) xxx
  - xi. Psychology xxx
- This Book xxxi

Al-Fawz Al-Kabīr 1

Preface 3

Part 1: The Five Fundamental Sciences that the Noble Qur'ān Contains 7

The Style of the Noble Qur'ān in Expressing the Five Sciences 10
Every *Āyah* Does not Need to Have a Cause of Revelation 11

Chapter 1: The Science of Polemic 12
A. Those who Associate Partners with Allah ﷻ 12
Rites of the Ibrāhīmic Way 12
Its Laws 13
Their Creed 14
The Deviation of Those who Associate Partners with Allah 14
Clarification of Association of Partners with Allah 15
Description of Anthropomorphism (*Tashbīh*) 16
Description of Alteration (*Taḥrīf*) 16
Dismissal of the Belief in the Hereafter 19
Considering the Message of the Prophet ﷺ Improbable 19
The Ones who Resemble Those who Associate Partners with Allah 19
Summary 21
Refutation of Association of Partners with Allah 21
Refutation of Anthropomorphism 21
Refutation of Their Alteration [of the Natural Revealed Way] 22
Response to Their Considering their Rising from the Dead and the Gathering Improbable 22
Refutation of Those who Deny the Message 22
B. The Jews 24
Clarification of [the Nature of] Alteration 25
Illustrations of the Alteration of Meaning 26
Clarification of [Their] Concealing *Āyāt* 28

Clarification of [Their] Fabrication (*Iftirā'*) 30
The Reasons Behind their Carelessness and Commission of Proscribed Actions 30
Reasons for [Their] Considering the Message of our Master Muḥammad ﷺ Improbable 31
Prophethood and Its Method of Reforming People 32
Differences in Sharī'ahs are Similar to Differences in Doctors' Prescriptions 32
Those Like the Jews 33
C. The Christians 33
The Doctrine of Trinity and its Refutation 33
First Problematic Issue [Those Texts in the Gospel that Refer to 'Īsā ﷺ as 'The Son'] 34
Second Problematic Issue [Those Texts in the Gospel in Which 'Īsā ﷺ Appears to Attribute Some Divine Acts to Himself] 34
Those Like the Christians 36
The Doctrine of the Crucifixion of 'Īsā ﷺ and its Refutation 36
Their Alteration of the Prophecy of the Paraclete 37
D. The Hypocrites 38
Hypocrisy in Creed and Hypocrisy in Action 38
The Objective Behind Mentioning the Hypocrites in the Noble Qur'ān 40
Examples of the Hypocrites 40
The Noble Qur'ān is the Book for All Times 40
Chapter 2: The Remainder of the Five Sciences 42
Clarifying the Reminder of the Favours of Allah ﷻ 42
Affirmation of the Divine Essence and Explanation of the Attributes 42
The Attributes of Allah ﷻ are Textual (*Tawqīfiyyah*) 43
The Favours of Allah ﷻ and the Signs of His Power 43
Celebrating the Days of Allah ﷻ 44
Mentioning the Purposes of Stories 45
Stories that are Oft-Repeated in the Noble Qur'ān 46

Stories Mentioned in the Noble Qur'ān Only Once or Twice 47
The Reminder of Death and What is After It 49
The Science of Rulings (*Aḥkām*) 52
The Role of Islamic Legislation in Reforming the Corrupted Primordial Way 52
Allusions Needing Explanation 53
Instances 54

Part 2: The Kinds of Meaning Hidden from the People of this Age in the Composition of the Qur'ān, and the Removal of their Concealed Nature by the Clearest of Explanations 57

Reasons Behind the Difficulty in Understanding the Intended Meanings of Speech 60

Chapter 1: Unusual Expressions of the Qur'ān (*Gharīb al-Qur'ān*) 62
The Early Generations Would Often Explain an Expression by its Most Obvious Meaning 64

Chapter 2: Abrogating (*Nāsikh*) and Abrogated (*Mansūkh*) *Āyāt* 65
The Meaning of Abrogation for the Early Generations 65
Number of Abrogated *Āyāt* 66
According to Earlier Scholars 66
According to Later Scholars 66
Sūrat al-Baqarah (2) 67
Sūrah Āl 'Imrān (3) 72
Sūrat an-Nisā' (4) 73
Sūrat al-Mā'idah (5) 75
Sūrat al-Anfāl (8) 77
Sūrat al-Barā'ah (9) 77
Sūrat an-Nūr (24) 78
Sūrat al-Aḥzāb (33) 79
Sūrat al-Mujādilah (58) 80
Sūrat al-Mumtaḥanah (60) 80
Sūrat al-Muzzammil (73) 81

Chapter 3: The Circumstances of Revelation (*Asbāb an-Nuzūl*) 83

Meaning of the Expression 'It was Revealed About Such-and-Such' in the First Generations 83
The Narrations of Hadith Scholars That Have no Connection to the Circumstances of Revelation 84
The Precondition for the Commentator in the Area of the Circumstances of Revelation 85
Stories of the Prophets Narrated by the People of the Book 85
Another Meaning of Their Saying 'It was Revealed About Such-and-such' 86
The Form of a Story Which has no Story 87
Sometimes They Would Assume a Question and Answer in *Tafsīr* 90
They May Mean Being Brought Forward or Put Back in Rank not in Succession 90
Two Preconditions for the Commentator 92

Chapter 4: Remaining Aspects of this Subject 98

Elements that lead to Obscurity 98
1. Omission (*ḥadhf*) 99
Examples of Omission 99
Omission of the Predicate of إِنَّ and the Main [Consequent] Clause of a Conditional Sentence, the Object of a Verb, the Subject of a Nominal Sentence and the Like Occur Very Often 103
There is No Need to Investigate the Word that Governs the Word 'When (إِذْ)' 104
Omission of the genitive of 'That (أَنَّ)' 105
2. Replacement or Substitution (*Ibdāl*) 105
3. Deferring and Advancing, and Remote Connection 116
4. Additional Wording 118
5. On the Decisive (*Muḥkam*), the Allegorical (*Mutashābih*), Indirect Expression (*Kināyah*), Allusion (*Ta'rīḍ*) and Conceptual Metaphor (*Majāz 'Aqlī*) 126
Picturing the Intended Meaning with a Sensory Image 128
Examples of that in common usage 129

Part 3: The Subtleties of the Qur'ān's Composition and Explanation of Its Marvellous Approach 133

Chapter 1: The Structure of the Noble Qur'ān and the Styles of the *Sūrahs* in it 135

The Beginnings and Conclusions of the *Sūrahs* are Like Royal Edicts 138

Poetic Format of the Beginning of Some *Sūrahs* 140

Concluding Parts of *Sūrahs* According to the Mode of Edicts 141

Interspersal of Eloquent Words in the Middle of the *Sūrahs* 141

Chapter 2: Division of the *Sūrahs* into *Āyāt* and Their Unique Mode of Expression 144

The Difference between *Āyāt* and Verses 144

What *Āyāt* and Verses Have in Common 145

Approximate Concordance is the Matter that Different Types of Composed Speech Have in Common 146

Indian Metres 147

Greek Tunes 147

Indian Tunes 147

Qur'ānic Observance of this Common Universal Beauty 148

Qur'ānic Rhymes 149

Suffixing an Alif 150

Concordance of the *Āyāt* on the Same Letter 150

The Secret Behind Harmonising Long *Āyāt* with Shorter *Āyāt* and Vice-versa 151

Qur'ānic *Āyāt* with Three Main Supports 152

Qur'ānic *Āyāt* with Two Metrical Feet 153

The Reason Behind a Longer *Āyah* Being with Other Short Ones 153

Other Modes of Expression in the *Sūrahs* 153

The Reason for Choosing New Metres and Rhymes 154

Chapter 3: The Logic Behind the Repetition of the
Five Sciences and the Lack of Order in Explaining Them   156

Chapter 4: The Inimitable Nature of the Noble Qur'ān   159

   Miracle of Qur'ānic Legislation   161

**Part 4A: The Varieties of Qur'ānic *Tafsīr* and the Differences
Between the *Tafsīr* of the Companions and the Successors 🌿 163**

Chapter 1: The Schools of the Commentators   165

   1. The *Tafsīr* of *Muḥaddithūn* (Hadith Scholars)   165

   2. The *Tafsīr* of Muslim Scholars of *Kalām*   165

   3. The *Tafsīr* of Experts in Juristic Principles   166

   4. The *Tafsīr* of Grammarians and Lexicographers   166

   5. The *Tafsīr* of Master Litterateurs   166

   6. The *Tafsīr* of Skilled Reciters   166

   7. The *Tafsīr* of the *Ṣūfīs*   166

   What Allah has Bestowed Upon me of Knowledge
      of *Tafsīr*   167

Chapter 2: The Reports in the Commentaries of the
Muḥaddithūn (Hadith Scholars)   169

   On the Saying 'كَذَا فِي الْآيَةُ نَزَلَت – the *Āyah* was
      Revealed About Such-and-such'   170

      Understanding the Backdrop of Revelations
         via Independent Reasoning (*Ijtihād*)   170

      Useless matters in *tafsīr*   170

   Qur'ānic *Tafsīr* by Means of the Noble Qur'ān   175

   Tafsīr of Unusual Expressions Used in the
      Noble Qur'ān   177

      Introduction of Independent Reasoning in
         Explaining Unusual Expressions   177

      The Differing Interpretations of the Earlier and
         Later Generations of the Meaning of Abrogation
         in Such a Way as Necessitate Different Views
         on the Number of Abrogated *Āyāt*   180

Chapter 3: Remaining Subtle Points in this Category   183

  Deducing Legal Rulings   183
  Tawjīh (Resolution of Apparent Problems)   183
    Sayings of the Companions ؓ on *Tawjīh*   184
    The Main Issue of *Tawjīh*   184
    Types of *Tawjīh*   185
  The Excesses of the Scholars of *Kalām*   185
  Polemic in the Qur'ān   186
  The Linguistic Usages of the Qur'ān   186
    The Syntax of the Qur'ān   186
    Declension of المقيمين الصلاة   187
    The Knowledge of Semantics and Rhetoric   187
    Sufic Indications (*Ishārāt*)   188

Chapter 4: Wonders of the Noble Qur'ān (*Gharā'ib al-Qur'ān*)   190

Chapter 5: The Outer and Inner States of the Noble Qur'ān   193

Chapter 6: Some Divinely-Gifted Sciences   195
  Interpretation of the Stories of the Prophets   195

Part 4B: Abbreviated Letters   197

Introduction   199

Glossary   207

Bibliography   222

Shāh Waliyyullāh al-Muḥaddith ad-Dihlawī

(1114 AH/1703 CE – 1176 AH/1762 CE)

THE AUTHOR

Birth

Shāh Waliyyullāh was born on 4th Shawwāl 1114 AH/10th February 1703 CE, in the town of Phulat (پھلت) in the district of Muẓaffarnagar, of the state of Uttar Pradesh, which lies in the division of Sahāranpūr in northern India.

He was named Quṭbuddīn Aḥmad by his father, reportedly after his birth was foretold to his father in a dream by the famous scholar and sufi, Quṭbuddīn Bakhtyār Kākī (568 AH/1173 CE – 632 AH/1235 CE) may Allah be merciful to him, when the former visited the mausoleum of the sufi. He later gained the title *Waliyyullāh,* i.e. Friend of Allah – by which he is more popularly and affectionately known – due to his *taqwā* and right behaviour. He hails from the Qurayshī lineage through his father, Shāh 'Abdurraḥīm (d. 1131 AH/1719 CE), linking him back to the second *khalīfah* of the Muslims, 'Umar ibn al-Khaṭṭāb ﷺ

(38 BH/586 CE – 23 AH/644 CE) through thirty generations.[1] Via his mother, his lineage is traced back to Mūsā Kāẓim (128 AH/745 CE – 183 AH/799 CE) – and thence to Sayyidunā al-Ḥusayn ibn 'Alī ﷺ (4 AH/626 CE – 61 AH/680 CE) and the beloved Messenger Muḥammad ﷺ.

His father, Shāh 'Abdurraḥīm, was a great sufi and religious scholar of twelfth century (AH) India, who established the Madrasah Raḥīmiyyah in Delhi. He had also played an important role in the compilation of the legal encyclopaedia, *Fatāwā-e-'Ālamgīrī*.[2]

Shāh Waliyyullāh received his early education from his father, who was also his spiritual guide, and he memorised the Noble Qur'ān by the tender age of seven. He was an adherent of the Ḥanafī school of *fiqh* and the Naqshbandī spiritual order.

1 Pīr Muḥammad Karam Shāh (1336 AH/1918 CE – 1418 AH/1998 CE), *Qaṣīdah Aṭyab an-Nagham fī Madḥ Sayyid al-'Arab wa'l-'Ajam* ﷺ of Shāh Waliyyullāh al-Muḥaddith ad-Dihlawī (Arabic/Urdu), (Lahore, 1978 CE/1399 AH), p.6, *Introduction*.

2 Also known as *al-Fatāwā al-Hindiyyah* in some parts of the world, *Fatāwā-e-'Ālamgīrī* is a compilation of Islamic law, principally in the Ḥanafī school of thought and legal methodology, authored by approximately five hundred jurists, three hundred of whom were from the Indian subcontinent that was under the rule of the Mughal empire, one hundred from the area that now includes Iraq, and one hundred from the Ḥijāz province of what is now Saudi Arabia. *Fatāwā-e-'Ālamgīrī* takes its name from the sixth Mughal emperor, Abu'l-Muẓaffar 'Ālamgīr Muḥyuddīn Muḥammad Awrangzeb, may Allah ﷻ have mercy on him, and it was at his insistence that this magnificent compilation was produced. The Emperor held the authors of *Fatāwā-e-'Ālamgīrī* in such high esteem that he would stand out of respect for them whenever any of them would enter his court. *Fatāwā-e-'Ālamgīrī* has been published by many publishing houses, including in Arabic under the title *al-Fatāwā al-Hindiyyah* by the Beirut based Dār al-Kutub al-'Ilmiyyah in six volumes containing 3,392 pages.

Further Education

He completed his primary studies in Arabic and Persian syntax and etymology within a year, followed by the study of philosophy, mathematics, Islamic creedal matters (*kalām*), Islamic behavioural spirituality (*taṣawwuf*), logic, medicine, oratory, algebra and *fiqh*, all of which he had mastered by seventeen years of age. His father then initiated him into the Naqshbandī sufi order, and authorised him to provide spiritual guidance to others.

Teaching

Shāh 'Abdurraḥīm, the father of Shāh Waliyyullāh, was a scholar in Islamic sciences, an adherent of Imām Abū Ḥanīfah's[3] school of *fiqh* and legal methodology, and a sufi of the Naqshbandī spiritual order. Shāh 'Abdurraḥīm died in the year 1131 AH/1719 CE when Shāh Waliyyullāh was hardly seventeen years of age. Thus, the latter took up the responsibility of teaching, as well as directing, at his father's seminary, the Madrasah Raḥīmiyyah in Delhi. He taught there for twelve years, providing guidance to fellow Muslims on spirituality and moral reform, together with the Islamic sciences. In 1143 AH/1731 CE, he decided to perform the *ḥajj*. After that, he visited the beloved city of Madīnah where he attended the lectures on *ḥadīth* by Shaykh Abū Ṭāhir Muḥammad al-Madanī[4] from whom he received a *khirqah* (a sufi

3 Imām Abū Ḥanīfah: He is an-Nu'mān ibn Thābit ibn Zuṭā ibn Marzūbān (80 AH/699 CE – 148 AH/765 CE). Of Persian origin, Imām Abū Ḥanīfah spent most of his life in Kūfa and Baghdād, studying and then teaching. His intelligence, wisdom and academic aptitude resulted in him becoming the founder of the largest school of *fiqh* and legal methodology in Islam – an adherent of this school is known as a *Ḥanafī*.

4 He is Shaykh Abū Ṭāhir Muḥammad ibn Ibrāhīm al-Kūrānī al-Kurdī al-Madanī (1081 AH/1670 CE – 1145 AH/1733 CE). He was the son and pupil of Shaykh Ibrāhīm ibn al-Ḥasan al-Kūrānī al-Kurdī al-Madanī, and was an erudite scholar, possessing encyclopaedic knowledge on creedal matters, *ḥadīths*, the inner sciences and Islamic law, holding the post of the Shāfi'ī *qāḍī* in Madīnah. He is said to have written approximately a

cloak denoting spiritual and/or academic authorisation). Under Shaykh Abū Ṭāhir Muḥammad al-Madanī, Shāh Waliyyullāh studied and was authorised to teach the following books of *ḥadīth*:

- *Al-Jāmi' aṣ-Ṣaḥīḥ* of Imām al-Bukhārī (194 AH/809 CE – 256 AH/869 CE)
- *Al-Musnad aṣ-Ṣaḥīḥ* of Imām Muslim (206 AH/821 CE – 261 AH/875 CE)
- *Jāmi' as-Sunan* of Imām at-Tirmidhī (200 AH/824 CE – 279 AH/892 CE)
- *As-Sunan* of Imām Abū Dāwūd (202 AH/817 CE – 275 AH/889 CE)
- *As-Sunan* of Imām Ibn Mājah (209 AH/824 CE – 273 AH/887 CE)
- *As-Sunan* of Imām an-Nasa'ī (215 AH/829 CE – 303 AH/915 CE)
- *Al-Muwaṭṭa'* of Imām Mālik (93 AH/711 CE – 179 AH/795 CE)
- *Al-Musnad* of Imām ad-Dārimī (181 AH/797 CE – 255 AH/868 CE)
- *Jāmi' al-Āthār* of Imām Muḥammad (749 AH/131 CE – 805 AH/189 CE)
- *Ar-Risālah* of Imām ash-Shāfi'ī (150 AH/767 CE – 204 AH/820 CE)
- *Al-Adab al-Mufrad* of Imām al-Bukhārī (194 AH/809 CE – 256 AH/869 CE)
- *Ash-Shifā' bi-Ta'rīf Ḥuqūq al-Muṣṭafā* of al-Qāḍī 'Iyāḍ (475 AH/1083 CE – 544 AH/1149 CE)

hundred treatises, including *Kanz al-'Amal fī Sunan al-Aqwāl* and *Shurūḥ al-Fuṣūṣ li ash-Shaykh al-Akbar* (explicating the doctrine of Ibn 'Arabī and thus reflecting the depth of Abū Ṭāhir's approach to *taṣawwuf*). Shāh Waliyyullāh made much mention of him in terms of his *taqwā*, independence of judgement and scholarly talents.

After performing another *ḥajj*, he studied the *Muwaṭṭa'* of Imām Mālik,[5] may Allah be merciful to him, under Shaykh Wafadullāh al-Mālikī al-Makkī, receiving an authorisation to transmit all its narrations. This study further enhanced Shāh Waliyyullāh's inclination towards, admiration and love for Imām Mālik. Shāh Waliyyullāh also studied the six *ṣaḥīḥ* collections[6] under Shaykh Tājuddīn al-Ḥanafī al-Qala'ī al-Makkī, and received authorisation to teach them. While in Makkah and Madīnah, Shāh Waliyyullāh studied under various other renowned scholars.

Shāh Waliyyullāh returned home, reaching Delhi on Friday 14th Rajab 1145 AH/1733 CE, where he continued to teach in the Madrasah Raḥīmiyyah and write for the remainder of his life. This was in compliance with a dream he is reported to have had during his stay at Makkah, wherein the beloved Messenger Muḥammad ﷺ instructed him to work for the organisation and welfare of the Muslims of the Indian subcontinent.

Achievements and Services

Shāh Waliyyullāh saw the academic, moral, educational and spiritual decay of the Indian people, which led him to establish several branches of the Madrasah Raḥīmiyyah in Delhi. He had diagnosed the malaise of his society at an early age as:

i. lack of faith,
ii. division among the Muslims, and
iii. collapse of moral values.

Without purification of the heart, it would be impossible to redress these problems, and so he advocated *taṣawwuf* in all spheres, recommending a generic and in-depth study of *ash-Shifā' bi-Ta'rīf*

5 He is Imām Mālik ibn Anas ibn Abī 'Āmir al-Aṣbaḥī al-Ḥimyarī (93 AH/711 CE – 179 AH/795 CE). He was born in and died in Madīnah, and is buried in the Baqī' cemetery. Imām Mālik was a Muslim scholar of great knowledge and founder of the Mālikī school of *fiqh* and legal methodology.

6 The six *ṣaḥīḥ ḥadīth* collections are the first six in the list above.

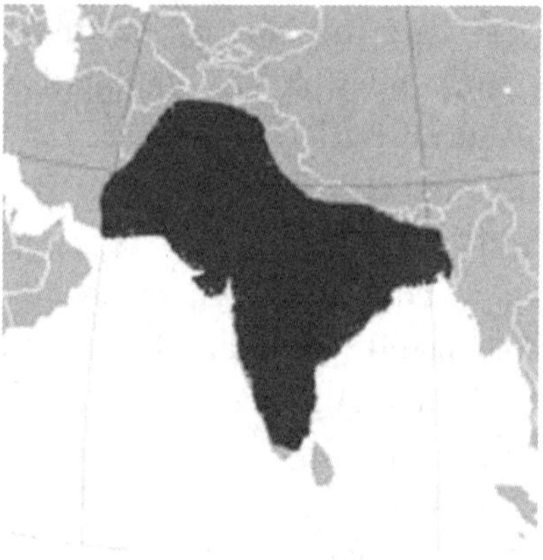

Extent of Mughal Empire under Awrangzeb
(image: Wikipedia, article: Mughal Empire (15/09/2012 CE))

Ḥuqūq al-Muṣṭafā of al-Qāḍī 'Iyāḍ (475 AH/1083 CE – 544 AH/1149 CE) in order to stem the widespread and multifarious decay. His father's attachment to the Naqshbandī sufi order encouraged his inclination to *taṣawwuf*. Through teaching and writing, Shāh Waliyyullāh also entered the political sphere in which the deterioration of Muslim rule in India had become a factor in destabilising Muslim cultural values, which he sought to rectify.

Shaykh Pīr Muḥammad Karam Shāh (1336 AH/1918 CE – 1418 AH/1998 CE) writes:

> "Shāh Waliyyullāh lifted the despairing spirits of the Muslims of the subcontinent. He blew fresh life into their hoary thoughts and ideologies and he removed the rust from their power, thus enabling them to challenge falsehood head-on. The noble person of Shāh Waliyyullāh is a great blessing, and the magnitude of such a blessing can only be reckoned with fairness when we take into account the political, social and economic conditions that had been wreaked on that India."[7]

7 Pīr Muḥammad Karam Shāh (1336 AH/1918 CE – 1418 AH/1998 CE), *Qaṣīdah Aṭyab an-Nagham fī Madḥ Sayyid al-'Arab wa'l-'Ajam* ﷺ of Shāh Waliyyullāh al-Muḥaddith ad-Dihlawī (Arabic/Urdu), (Lahore, 1978 CE/1399 AH), p.6, *Introduction*.

Shāh Waliyyullāh was upset and concerned to see the moral degeneration of the Muslim masses and the economic and political instability that had followed the demise of his hero the Emperor Awrangzeb 'Ālamgīr (1027 AH/1618 CE – 1118 AH/1707 CE).[8] Furthermore, the sectarian hostility of various Muslim factions for each other had never been more intense than during that period in history. Shāh Waliyyullāh sought to unify all the Muslim groups under the banner of Islam and revive the Muslim sciences in the footsteps of Muslim scholars, philosophers, thinkers, intellectuals

8 Abu'l-Muẓaffar 'Ālamgīr Muḥiyyuddīn Muḥammad Awrangzeb (1027 AH/1618 CE – 1118 AH/1707 CE), may Allah سبحانه وتعالى have mercy on him, was the sixth Mughal emperor. He was an ardent devotee of Islamic behavioural spirituality (*taṣawwuf*) and a disciple, as well as a caliph, of Khwājah Muḥammad Ma'ṣūm (d. 1079 AH/1668 CE), the son of Aḥmad Sirhindī also known as Mujaddid Alf Thānī (971 AH/1564 CE – 1033 AH/1624 CE), in the Naqshbandī Mujaddidī spiritual order. Awrangzeb 'Ālamgīr ruled over one-quarter (i.e. 150 million subjects) of the world's population for forty-nine years (CE) from 1068 AH/1658 CE till his death in 1118 AH/1707 CE, rendering the state of India the most powerful, politically stable and wealthiest nation under the sun, yet he himself wove prayer caps and wrote copies of the Noble Qur'ān by hand as a means of livelihood. He has been praised by many spiritual masters and saints as 'the Just King' – *Awrang-e-Shāhī* – for example by Sulṭān Bāhū (1037 AH/1628 CE – 1108 AH/1691 CE), and Pīr Muḥammad Karam Shāh (1336 AH/1918 CE – 1418 AH/1998 CE) has written '*may Allāh have mercy on him*' next to his name in the introduction to Shāh Waliyyullāh's *Qaṣīdah Aṭyab an-Nagham fī Madḥ Sayyid al-'Arab wa'l-'Ajam* e. The renowned 'Poet of the East', Dr. Muḥammad Iqbāl (1293 AH/1877 CE – 1356 AH/1938 CE) termed him, albeit with a sorrowful sigh, 'the last arrow in the quiver of Muslim power in India'.

and polymaths such as al-Fārābī,[9] Ibn Sīnā,[10] Imām al-Ghazālī,[11] Ibn Rushd,[12] Imām ash-Shāṭibī,[13] Ibn Khaldūn,[14] Mujaddid Alf

9 He is Abū Naṣr Muḥammad al-Fārābī (also known as Alpharabius) (258 AH/872 CE – 338 AH/950 CE). He was a Muslim scientist and philosopher from Fārāb in the Persian province of Khurāsān. He had interests in cosmology, logic and music and made significant contributions to mathematics, philosophy, music, psychology, education and logic.

10 He is Abū 'Alī al-Ḥusayn ibn 'Abdullāh ibn 'Alī Sīnā (also known as Avicenna) (370 AH/980 CE (Bukhārā) – 428 AH/1037 CE (Hamadān, Iran)). He was a Persian Muslim polymath who is said to have authored almost four hundred and fifty treatises. His magnum opus is *al-Qānūn fī aṭ-Ṭibb* (*The Canon of Medicine*), comprising fourteen volumes, and used as the standard medical text in Europe and the Islamic world up until the eighteenth century CE.

11 He is Abū Ḥāmid Muḥammad ibn Muḥammad al-Ghazālī (also known as Algazel) (449 AH/1058 CE – 504 AH/1111 CE). He was born and died in Tūs, which lies in the Persian region of Khurāsān. Al-Ghazālī was a Muslim scholar of *kalām*, philosopher, and intellectual who sought to purify the Islamic sciences from heresy and reconnect people with the Creator ﷻ in a relationship based on sincerity and intention. He authored many books including his magnum opus, *Iḥyā 'Ulūm ad-Dīn* (Revival of the Islamic Sciences).

12 He is Abu'l-Walīd Muḥammad ibn Aḥmad ibn Rushd (also known as Averroes) (519 AH/1126 CE – 594 AH/1198 CE). He was a Muslim philosopher, polymath, scholar of *kalām*, jurist, logician, psychologist, astronomer, geographer, mathematician and physicist, born in Cordoba, Muslim Andalusia, and died in Marrakech, Morocco.

13 He is Abū Isḥāq Ibrāhīm ibn Mūsā ibn Muḥammad ash-Shāṭibī al-Gharnāṭī (d. 790 AH/1388 CE). Among the many books he authored, his most famous is *al-Muwāfaqāt fī Uṣūl ash-Sharī'ah* (a legal treatise on the principles of Islamic jurisprudence and the objectives of the Sharī'ah). He was a Muslim scholar from Granada (Muslim Spain) who adhered to the Mālikī legal school.

14 He is Abū Zayd 'Abdurraḥmān ibn Muḥammad ibn Khaldūn al-Ḥaḍramī (732 AH/1332 CE – 808 AH/1406 CE). He was a Muslim historian and historiographer from Tūnis, who is famous for his *Muqaddimah (Prolegomenon)*, which is the preface for his voluminous world history known as *Kitāb al-'Ibār (Book of Exemplary Lessons)* or *Tārīkh Ibn Khaldūn*, but has been treated as an independent work since its publication in

Thānī[15] and Jān-e-Jānāṇ.[16] In practice, his approach was meant to be very much Ghazālian, but with added political issues taking a lead role in influencing and redefining that approach. Such issues meant that where one was normally required to be on the defensive, going on the offensive was the real need. Shāh Waliyyullāh had many problems on his hands, and he dealt with them cautiously, prudently and according to opportunity. He needed to revive the moral values among the masses in order to

778 AH/1377 CE. His innovative style and critical and analytical study of history aided him in pioneering two new sciences: sociology and historiography. He is possibly the real father of economics, preceding Adam Smith (1723 CE – 1790 CE) by almost four Gregorian centuries – another contender for the title is Imām Abū Yūsuf Ya'qūb ibn Ibrāhīm al-Anṣārī (113 AH/731 CE – 182 AH/798 CE), a student of Imām Abū Ḥanīfah, who wrote a book on taxation called *Kitāb al-Kharāj* for the 'Abbāsī Caliph Ḥārūn ar-Rashīd (145 AH/763 CE – 193 AH/809 CE), wherein he discusses social development, revenue, capitation, and a comprehensive fiscal policy.

15 He is Imām Rabbānī Shaykh Aḥmad al-Fārūqī as-Sirhindī (971 AH/1564 CE – 1033 AH/1624 CE). Hailing from Sirhind, in what is today the Indian state of Punjāb, he was a Muslim scholar, philosopher, and Ḥanafī jurist who attached himself to the Naqshbandī spiritual order. He is known as Mujaddid Alf Thānī (Reviver of the Second Millennium) for rejuvenating Islam after it had faced many religious and political setbacks, especially during the reign of the Mughal Emperor Akbar (948 AH/1542 CE – 1013 AH /1605 CE). Mujaddid Alf Thānī refused to compromise on Islamic principles, declaring it forbidden to pursue whatever is outside the path shown by the Prophet Muḥammad ﷺ. Of his literary works, *Ithbāt an-Nubuwwah* gained much prominence, as well as his ever-popular *Maktūbāt* (Collected Letters) – a collection of five hundred and thirty-six letters written to Mughal emperors and other contemporaries.

16 He is Mirzā Maẓhar Jān-e-Jānāṇ (also known as Shamsuddīn Ḥabībullāh) (1110 AH/1699 CE – 1195 AH/1781 CE), a famous sufi poet of the Naqshbandī order, but also initiated in the Qādirī, Chishtī and Suhrawardī spiritual orders. He was known by the title *Sunnī-tarāsh* (one who is committed to the Sunnah of the Prophet Muḥammad ﷺ) for his unwavering attachment to and imitation of the Sunnah.

save the Muslim minority in the subcontinent from annihilation. From there he took it to the administrative authorities in order to protect the *dīn* of Islam officially within the national sphere. For this purpose, he set up madrasahs all over Delhi, and the hundreds of students that would graduate from them would extend Shāh Waliyyullāh's vision. This had a profound effect on the climate as a whole; socially, politically and economically. Unfortunately, the full extent of his success and the proof of the truthfulness of his vision were not known until after his demise.

Literary Career

Shāh Waliyyullāh wrote fifty-one works over a period spanning thirty years; twenty-eight of them in Arabic and twenty-three in Persian.

His works fall into six categories:

1. Qur'ān – including his Persian translation of the Noble Qur'ān;
2. Hadith – including his Arabic and Persian commentaries on Imām Mālik's *al-Muwaṭṭa'*;
3. Islamic *Fiqh* – including his history of Islamic *fiqh*;
4. Islamic *Taṣawwuf* – which is reflected in almost all of his works;
5. Islamic *Kalām* and *Ijtihād* – including his magnum opus, *Ḥujjatullāh al-Bālighah*, which deals with both the intellectual and practical aspects of Islam;
6. Issues between People of the Sunnah and the Shī'ah – including the areas of sectarian difference and the aspects where mutual agreement can work for the greater good of all Muslims.

Death

Shāh Waliyyullāh breathed his last at the age of sixty-one hijrī years and four months (fifty-nine solar years and six months) on 29th Muḥarram 1176 AH/20th August 1762 CE at around *ẓuhr*.[17]

17 Pīr Muḥammad Karam Shāh (1336 AH/1918 CE – 1418 AH/1998 CE),

He was buried in the famous *Munhadiyān* graveyard next to his father Shāh 'Abdurraḥīm.

FAMILY

Shāh Waliyyullāh was married twice, and his two wives between them had five sons:

i. Shāh Muḥammad,
ii. Shāh 'Abd al-'Azīz al-Muḥaddith ad-Dihlawī (1159 AH/1746 CE – 1238 AH/1823 CE),
iii. Shāh Rafī' ad-Dīn (1163 AH/1749 CE – 1233 AH/1817 CE),
iv. Shāh 'Abd al-Qādir (1165 AH/1751 CE – 1230 AH/1814 CE), and
v. Shāh 'Abd al-Ghanī.

They had two daughters named Ṣāliḥah and Amat al-'Azīz.

WRITINGS

In his writings, one experiences his earnest focus on the relationship between the creation and the Creator – which is present in all his thinking. The religious and the irreligious, the spiritual and the mundane, the ascetic and the materialist – all are conscious of the Ultimate Reality that is Allah ﷻ, but to assist them in realising this Truth and applying it in their daily lives is the primary duty of the slave, that is Man. *Man* is a generic term referring to mankind. Each human individual must therefore realise the qualities that he or she is to adopt in order to qualify. In brief, Shāh Waliyyullāh emphasises the importance of reconnecting with the Creator.

Shāh Waliyyullāh rejected the philosophical approach of the Greeks in recognising the Divine Being, which was based on mathematical ideas and speculative theories. He also denied the

Qaṣīdah Aṭyab an-Nagham fī Madḥ Sayyid al-'Arab wa'l-'Ajam ﷺ of Shāh Waliyyullāh al-Muḥaddith ad-Dihlawī (Arabic/Urdu), (Lahore, 1978 CE/1399 AH), p.7, *Introduction*.

method of the Hindus, which was based on the corporeality of Divine attributes and of angelic duties.

The political reformism of Shāh Waliyyullāh was based on educational reasoning – that education begets political reform and the lack of it results in stagnation or even retrogression. His thought in this field was a precursor to the various socio-political, educational and academic, intellectual and religious movements that sprang up in the sub-continent after him.

Shāh Waliyyullāh wrote extensively on the subject of Islam, including:

i. The Noble Qur'ān and Qur'ānic Exegesis (*Tafsīr*)

Fatḥ ar-Raḥmān fī Tarjamat al-Qur'ān (a Persian translation of the Noble Qur'ān), *al-Fatḥ al-Khabīr bi Mā Lā Budda min Ḥifẓi-hī fī 'Ilm at-Tafsīr* (an explanation of the intricate and difficult words used in the Noble Qur'ān), *Ta'wīl al-Aḥādīth fī Rumūz Qaṣaṣ al-Anbiyā'* (stories of various prophets of Allah ﷻ mentioned in the Noble Qur'ān in Arabic attempting to elucidate morals, manners and legal rulings from the the Noble Qur'ān through them), *Zahrawayn* (a commentary on Sūrat al-Baqarah and Sūrah Āl 'Imrān), *al-Muqaddimah fī Qawānīn at-Tarjamah* (an Arabic booklet about the author's difficulties when translating the Noble Qur'ān into Persian), *al-Fawz al-Kabīr fī Uṣūl at-Tafsīr* (a treatise on the principles of Qur'ānic hermeneutics).

ii. Prophetic Traditions (*Ḥadīth*)

Al-Musawwā min Aḥādīth al-Muwaṭṭa' (an Arabic commentary on the *ḥadīths* from Imām Mālik's compilation *al-Muwaṭṭa'*), *al-Muṣaffā Sharḥ Muwaṭṭa'* (a Persian commentary on *al-Muwaṭṭa'*), *Sharḥ Tarājim Ba'ḍ Abwāb al-Bukhārī* (an Arabic annotation of the wisdom behind the topic headings adopted by Imām al-Bukhārī in his compilation *al-Jāmi' aṣ-Ṣaḥīḥ*), *Arba'īn* (a collection of forty brief yet comprehensive *ḥadīths*), *al-Faḍl al-Mubīn fi'l-Musalsal min Ḥadīth an-Nabī al-Amīn* (a work in Arabic on *ḥadīths*).

iii. Jurisprudence (*Fiqh*)

Al-Inṣāf fī Bayān Sabab al-Ikhtilāf (a discussion in Arabic of the legal differences between the various schools of Islamic jurisprudence and legal methodology), *al-'Iqd al-Jīd fī Bayān Aḥkām al-Ijtihād wa't-Taqlīd* (an Arabic treatise discussing the various issues surrounding independent decision-making and adherence to juridical schools).

iv. Philosophy

Ḥujjatullāh al-Bālighah (his magnum opus in Arabic covering almost all aspects of human existence, from spirituality to social and political issues and their solutions), *al-Budūr al-Bāzighah* (an exposition in Arabic of Islam in the light of philosophical and rational interpretation), *al-Khayr al-Kathīr* (a short work in Arabic on the fundamentals of Islamic beliefs), *Maktūb-i Madam* (a Persian treatise written to a certain Ismā'īl ibn 'Abdullāh ar-Rūmī dealing with the metaphysical dimensions of existence, synthesising the views of Muḥyuddīn Muḥammad ibn 'Alī ibn Muḥammad ibn 'Arabī (560 AH/1165 CE – 637 AH/1240 CE) and Imām Rabbānī Aḥmad al-Fārūqī as-Sirhindī (971 AH/1564 CE – 1033 AH/1624 CE)), *al-'Aqīdat al-Ḥasanah* (a rational presentation of Islamic beliefs composed in Arabic), *al-Muqaddimah as-Saniyyah fī Intiṣār al-Firqah as-Sunniyyah* (a Persian piece comparing the doctrines of the People of the Sunnah and the Shī'ah).

v. Islamic Behavioural Spirituality (*Taṣawwuf*)

At-Tafhīmāt al-Ilāhiyyah (an Arabic and Persian treatise of spiritual importance in Islam in which the author clearly points out the ills and defects that arise within Muslim societies), *Alṭāf al-Quds* (written in Persian, this work deals with the basic principles of *taṣawwuf*), *Saṭa'āt* (a Persian piece discussing the various dimensions of Divine theophany), *Fuyūḍ al-Ḥaramayn* (an Arabic depiction of the spiritual experiences encountered by the author during his sojourn in the Two Blessed cities of Makkah and Madīnah), *Anfās al-'Ārifīn* (a Persian work mentioning the biological and spiritual ancestors of the author, together with their spiritual attainments), *Bawāriq al-Wilāyah* (a portion of the *Anfās al-'Ārifīn* describing the life and spiritual attainments of his father Shāh 'Abdurraḥīm), *al-Intibāh fī Salāsil Awliyā' Allāh* (a Persian work that details the evolution of various orders of Islamic *taṣawwuf*), *Risālah* (written as a reply to some issues raised with him on Islamic *taṣawwuf*), *Shifā' al-Qulūb* (a Persian treatise on Islamic *taṣawwuf*), *Fatḥ al-Wadūd li Ma'rifat al-Junūd* (an instructional treatise in Arabic on ethics and Islamic behavioural spirituality).

vi. History

Izālat al-Khafā' 'an Khilāfat al-Khulafā' (a treatise in Persian discussing the Caliphates of *al-Khulafā ar-Rāshidūn*), *Qurrat al-'Aynayn fī Tafḍīl ash-Shaykhayn* (written in Persian, it discusses the achievements of the first two *khalīfahs*, Abū Bakr ﵁ and 'Umar ﵁, substantiated by Qur'ānic *āyāt* and *ḥadīths*).

vii. Biography

Al-'Aṭiyyat aṣ-Ṣamadiyyah fī al-Anfās al-Muḥammadiyyah (a short piece in Persian on the biography of Shaykh Muḥammad Phulatī, the author's maternal grandfather), *al-Imdād fī Ma'āthir al-Ajdād* (short biographies in Persian of some of the author's ancestors), *Surūr al-Maḥzūn* (a short biography of the Prophet Muḥammad ﷺ in Persian), *al-Juz' al-Laṭīf fī Tarjamat al-'Abd aḍ-Ḍa'īf* (in Persian, a short autobiography), *al-Irshād ilā Muhimmāt 'Ilm al-Isnād* (it describes in Arabic the scholars of the Ḥijāz who taught Shāh Waliyyullāh).

viii. Poetry

Aṭyab an-Nagham fī Madḥ Sayyid al-'Arab wa'l-'Ajam ﷺ is a collection of odes composed in Arabic eulogising the Prophet Muḥammad ﷺ. This work reflects the poetic abilities of Shāh

Waliyyullāh, and his love for the Prophet ﷺ – a pre-requisite for all Muslims, especially those devoted sincerely to Allah. *Al-Qaṣīdat al-Hamziyyah (fī Madḥ Khayr al-Bariyyah* ﷺ) is an Arabic poem in six parts comprising forty-five couplets in praise of the beloved Messenger Muḥammad ﷺ – the author addresses the Prophet ﷺ in the last three couplets seeking his ﷺ assistance on the Day of Judgement:

رَسُولَ اللّٰهِ يَا خَيْرَ الْبَرَايَا
نَوَالَكَ أَبْتَغِي يَوْمَ الْقَضَاءِ

O Messenger of Allah! O Most Excellent of Allah's creatures!
Only your favours do I desire on the Day of Judgement.

إِذَا مَا حَلَّ خَطْبٌ مُدْلَهِمٌّ
فَأَنْتَ الْحِصْنُ مِنْ كُلِّ الْبَلَاءِ

When any dark and gloomy calamity befalls,
Then you are the fortress [of protection] from every trial.

إِلَيْكَ تَوَجُّهِي وَبِكَ اسْتِنَادِي
وَفِيكَ مَطَامِعِي وَبِكَ ارْتِجَائِي

Only towards you do I direct myself, only on you do I depend,
Only in you are my aspirations and only in you is my hope.[18]

ix. Principles of Islamic Jurisprudence (*Uṣūl al-Fiqh*)

Al-Inṣāf fī Bayān Asbāb al-Ikhtilāf (Arabic).

18 Shaḥ Waliyyullāh al-Muḥaddith ad-Dihlawī, *Qaṣīdat Hamziyyah fī Madḥ Khayr al-Bariyyah* ﷺ.

x. Beliefs (*'Aqīdah*) and its Scholarly Science (*Kalām*)

Ḥusn al-'Aqīdah (in Arabic, the creed of the People of the Sunnah and the Majority Group (*Ahl as-Sunnah wa'l-Jamā'ah*) from the Noble Qur'ān and the Sunnah of the Messenger of Allah ﷺ).

xi. Psychology

Risālah Dānishmandī (a Persian treatise on instructions regarding the methodology of teaching).

Shāh Waliyyullāh also authored works in the fields of grammar, politics and sociology.

All his works are of a reformist nature, reminding man of his responsibility as a steward of Allah on Earth, and Muslims of their responsibility to put the Divine *sharī'ah* into effect on Earth. He strove constantly for a spiritual reawakening that would repair the disconnection, or much weakened link between man and his Creator.

Some people attempt to acquire undue benefit from the fame and popularity of Shāh Waliyyullāh and have authored books containing false beliefs, furthering their own ill agendas and discrediting the true beliefs and doctrine of Islam, then attributing them to Shāh Waliyyullāh in order to win acceptance for them among the masses. Some of those books falsely attributed to Shāh Waliyyullāh are:[19]

1. *Tuḥfat al-Muwaḥḥidīn*: a Persian tract explaining *tawḥīd*
2. *Al-Balāgh al-Mubīn*
3. *Qurrat al-'Aynayn fī Ibṭāl Shahādat al-Ḥusayn*
4. *Al-Jannat al-'Āliyah fī Manāqib al-Mu'āwiyah*

19 Pīr Muḥammad Karam Shāh (1336 AH/1918 CE – 1418 AH/1998 CE), *Qaṣīdah Aṭyab an-Nagham fī Madḥ Sayyid al-'Arab wa'l-'Ajam* e of Shāh Waliyyullāh al-Muḥaddith ad-Dihlawī (Arabic/Urdu), (Lahore, 1978 CE/1399 AH), pp.14-15, *Introduction.*

THIS BOOK

Shāh Waliyyullāh saw man as a manifestation of the will of the Creator,[20] who on the one hand is burdened with duties and liabilities, and on the other hand has rights and enjoys superiority over the rest of creation subject to his deliberate surrender to the will of the Creator and faithful implementation of Divine Law in his life and in the land. This Divine Law is provided to man in the books revealed by Allah ﷻ via the prophets whom He, the Absolute Lawgiver, sent and in the Sunnah that embodies the Message.

The last and final Divine Book revealed by Allah ﷻ to man was on the tongue of His Final and most beloved Messenger Muḥammad ﷺ, the Noble Qur'ān. It is a comprehensive, inalterable, infallible and irreplaceable testament; the Speech of Allah ﷻ covering every aspect of man's existence. It was revealed to the most truthful individual to have set foot on Earth, Muḥammad ﷺ the son of 'Abdullāh, the final Messenger of Allah ﷻ.

Although man is blessed with the gifts of reason and intellect, yet rashness and lack of diligence are never far from him, and so Allah ﷻ provides him with guidance for all his affairs. The Noble Qur'ān is the final instalment of Divine Guidance, and it is revealed in the Arabic language. However, this does not necesssarily render it a great deal easier for Arabs than for non-Arabs to derive everything from it as is intended, nor according to contemporary needs – one of the causes for the differences is the reasoning found in Qur'ānic hermeneutics. The very first students of the Noble Qur'ān were the Noble Companions رضي الله عنهم of the Prophet Muḥammad ﷺ, and even they differed over some of its meanings and interpretations. This only reflects the range of the Qur'ānic knowledge and wisdom that Allah ﷻ has bestowed

20 [21] *"When your Lord said to the angels, 'I am putting a khalif on the earth.'"* (Qur'ān, Sūrat al-Baqarah 2:30)

upon us. However, the interpretations and exegeses of the Noble Qur'ān are uniform in most issues, and the differences between scholars and exegetes are minor and based on subsidiary issues, or they vary in accordance with the topic of the exegesis. Thus, a political Qur'ānic exegesis will differ, possibly in the understanding of the same *āyah*, to a spiritual exegesis, or a scholarly exegesis.

The primary source for interpretation and exegesis of the Noble Qur'ān is the Noble Qur'ān itself. If the scholar finds the clarification of an apparent ambiguity in the Noble Qur'ān, he leaves it at that and acts upon it without any further pursuance of it into any other source. If, however, a solution is not found in the Noble Qur'ān that would provide a clear and logical understanding of the Word of Allah ﷻ, then the scholar seeks assistance from the Sunnah of the Messenger of Allah ﷺ. If the Sunnah turns out to be silent on that issue, the scholar will interpret the *āyah* in the light of the understanding of the Companions رضي الله عنهم or, failing that, by the understanding of those who succeeded the Companions (i.e. the *Tābi'īs*).

As the centuries passed, deviations from the Sunnah crept into all spheres of Islamic teaching and practice. The Noble Qur'ān enjoys divine protection,[21] but Qur'ānic exegesis is not immune from such contamination. Shāh Waliyyullāh al-Muḥaddith ad-Dihlawī, may Allah be merciful to him, was troubled by this until he could tolerate it no longer. He was surprised, and naturally frustrated, that no voice was raised against it and no one did anything about it, and so he decided to take the responsibility upon his own shoulders and tackle the corruption head on.

Al-Fawz al-Kabīr fī Uṣūl at-Tafsīr was written in order to introduce a new dimension to the science of Qur'ānic exegesis. This new dimension was nothing but a modification of centuries' old interpretation, intended to continue expounding the limitless wisdom of the Noble Qur'ān while simultaneously eliminating

21 [22] *"It is We Who have sent down the Reminder and We Who will preserve it."* (Qur'ān, Sūrat al-Ḥijr 15:9)

corrupt elements that contaminate its true meanings. He advocated a direct approach to the Qur'ān and encouraged scholars and exegetes to rely as little as possible on external factors, particularly Judaica (*Isrā'īliyyāt*), in its interpretation. He went a step further and translated the Noble Qur'ān into Persian, the then official language of the Muslims of the subcontinent, in order that the masses could understand the Noble Qur'ān to some extent.

Shāh Waliyyullāh emphasised that the entire Qur'ān was applicable to human thought and experience, and so he accentuated the essential comprehensibility of all of its *āyāt*, including those considered by the exegetes to be *mutashābih* (allegorical), and not merely the five hundred or so that were considered legally important by most scholars.

Shāh Waliyyullāh clarified that the Noble Qur'ān does not address the believers alone, but also the People of the Book (*Ahl al-Kitāb*), hypocrites (*munāfiqūn*) and those who ascribe partners to Allah (*mushrikūn*), i.e. the entire human race.

He also set guidelines for those capable of authoring a Qur'ānic exegesis. It has often been the case that individuals who are unqualified to translate the Noble Qur'ān, let alone interpret its deeper meanings, have failed in their attempts, and the reader has been led to misunderstand the intended meanings of the Lawgiver. The sole reason was their lack of competence. There are many requirements and preconditions for Qur'ānic exegesis. Those interested must know the Arabic language, especially the usages of the Qur'ān, as well as the backdrop to and the causes of the revelation of Qur'ānic *āyāt*. Furthermore, knowledge of grammar, composition, rhetoric, common usage, history, *ḥadīths*, sayings of the Companions, poetry, and prosody are a must for anyone who wants to produce a *tafsīr* of the Speech of Allah ﷻ. Utmost care and attention is not only a requirement of Qur'ānic exegesis but an inescapable *sine qua non*, for the exegete has the solemn duty of disclosing the will of the Creator to people.

This book, *al-Fawz al-Kabīr fī Uṣūl at-Tafsīr*, was originally written in Persian. It has since been translated into Urdu and Arabic. It is comprised of five parts, four of which we have included here. The fifth part is not relevant to the topic of this book, but nevertheless important. Hence we have decided to omit it from this translation. It may be published as a separate volume at a later date, in'shā Allah.

I acquired a couple of Arabic editions and decided to work on an English translation of the same. The task was by no means easy, for the versions varied, and at some points quite significantly. Nevertheless, by the mercy of Allah ﷾, we dealt with technical and some subtler aspects as best as we could, and the task was accomplished, *al-ḥamdu li'llāh.*

For this accomplishment, I extend my heartiest gratitude to Mr. Siddiqui and Dr. Abia Afsar-Siddiqui of Ta-Ha Publishers Ltd. London, for their hard work in the publication and distribution of this book, and to Hajj Abdassamad Clarke for bringing out the best in it in terms of editing and suggestions; what you hold in your hands right now would not have been possible without their assistance and encouragement – may Allah ﷾ bless them with the best of both worlds. *Āmīn.*

Whatever good I have written is from the mercy of Allah ﷾, and whatever is incorrect is a reflection of my own mistakes and misjudgement. I ask Allah ﷾ to accept this humble effort of mine, by the virtue of His Beloved Messenger and our master Muḥammad ﷺ, and that He ﷾ cause it to be a means of forgiveness and blessing to all those involved in its production and publication. We hope this humble offering to the Ummah will be of benefit, both to Muslims and non-Muslims alike.

Ṭāhir Maḥmood Kiānī

إِنَّ ٱلَّذِينَ ءَامَنُوا۟ وَعَمِلُوا۟ ٱلصَّٰلِحَٰتِ

لَهُمْ جَنَّٰتٌ تَجْرِى مِن تَحْتِهَا ٱلْأَنْهَٰرُ

ذَٰلِكَ

ٱلْفَوْزُ ٱلْكَبِيرُ

But those who believe and do right actions
have Gardens with rivers flowing under them.

That is

The Great Victory

Qur'ān, Sūrat al-Burūj 85:11

Shāh Waliyyullāh

Preface

The favours of Allah ﷻ on His weak slave[22] are numerous and innumerable, the greatest of which is the grace granted him to comprehend the meanings of His Wise Book.[23] There are many tremendous blessings of our master, the Messenger of Allah ﷺ to the least of the individuals of his Ummah,[24] the greatest of which is his conveying the Book of his Lord [to the people]. The first generation received the Noble Qur'ān from him ﷺ, and the second generation received it from the first generation, and likewise it continued [through continuous mass-transmission] until it has become part of the good fortunes of this weak slave, who obtained his portion of reciting, understanding and reflecting upon it.

O Allah, shower Your most excellent blessings and choicest benedictions on this Noble Prophet, our Leader, Master and Intercessor and upon his family, his Companions and all the people of knowledge of his Ummah, by Your mercy, O Most Merciful of those who show mercy.

22 The author – Shāh Waliyyullāh Quṭbuddīn Aḥmad ad-Dihlawī – referring to himself. He uses such modes of referring to himself out of humility throughout this book and all his other works and treatises.

23 The Wise Book of Allah ﷻ is the Noble Qur'ān.

24 The author referring to himself.

The needy slave of Allah, Waliyyullāh ibn 'Abdurraḥīm, says, may Allah ﷻ treat them both with His immense gentleness: As Allah ﷻ has disclosed to me a chance to comprehend His Magnificent Book, it occurred to me that I ought to compile some valuable and beneficial points that would benefit people in contemplating the Speech of Allah ﷻ. I hope that the simple understanding of these precepts will open up a broad path for students to understand the meanings of the Book of Allah. Even if they were to spend their lives in studying the books of *tafsīr* or reading them out to the scholars of *tafsīr* – though they are few in this age – they would still not be able to attain these precepts and principles with this degree of precision and harmony. I have named them *al-Fawz al-Kabīr fī Uṣūl at-Tafsīr* (The Great Victory on Qur'ānic Hermeneutics).

My success is only by Allah ﷻ, in Whom I place my trust. He is sufficient for me and the Best Disposer of affairs [for me].[25]

There are five objectives in this treatise:

1. The five sciences that the Noble Qur'ān has identified textually, such that it is as though the Noble Qur'ān was originally revealed for the sake of these five sciences;
2. Aspects of the composition of the Noble Qur'ān that are hidden to the people of this age in order to make them show themselves through the most eloquent of expressions;
3. Description of the intricacies in the composition of the Noble Qur'ān and explanation of its wonderful style;
4. Description of the methodologies of commentary and explanation of the reasons for the differences that occur between the interpretations of the Companions[26] and the

25 This is based on the *āyah* of Qur'ān: "*...and they said, 'Allah is enough for us and the Best of Guardians.'*" Sūrah Āl 'Imrān 3:173.

26 They are the *Ṣaḥābah* (sing. *Ṣaḥābī*): those who accompanied the Prophet

Successors;[27]

5. Explanation of the unusual and rare words mentioned in the Noble Qur'ān (*Gharīb al-Qur'ān*), and the particular circumstances (that give rise to) the revelations that are incumbent on the commentator to memorise,[28] and without which it is forbidden to plunge into *tafsīr.*

Muḥammad ﷺ, accepting Islam as their way of life, and who died as Muslims.

27 They are the *Tābi'ūn* (sing. *Tābi'ī*): those who accompanied the Companions ﷺ and who died as Muslims.

28 This part is beyond the remit of this book, but is nevertheless important and may be translated at a future date, in shā'Allāh.

PART 1

The Five Fundamental Sciences that the Noble Qur'ān Contains

One should know that the meanings which the Qur'ān contains never go beyond the [following] five categories of knowledge:

1. The science of judgements (*aḥkām*): those which are obligatory (*wājib*), recommended (*mandūb*), permitted (*mubāḥ*), detested (*makrūh*) and forbidden (*ḥarām*), whether acts of worship (*'ibadāt*), ordinary transactions (*mu'āmalāt*), domestic management or civil polity. The detailed study of this field is entrusted to the care of the *faqīh* (the jurisprudent).

2. The science of polemic and of refutation of the four deviant groups: the Jews, the Christians, those who associate partners with Allah and the hypocrites. The clarification of this field of science is entrusted to the care of the scholar of rational theology (*mutakallim*).

3. The science of reminding others of the favours of Allah ﷻ by clarifying the creation of the heavens and the earth, and inspiring the slaves of Allah ﷻ with what they need, and making clear the perfect attributes of Allah ﷻ.

4. The science of reminder of the Days of Allah ﷻ. This is the description of the occurrences that Allah ﷻ has caused to take place such as favouring the obedient and punishing criminals.

5. The science of reminding about death and what comes after it,

such as the Rising from the dead, the Gathering, the Reckoning, the Scales, the Garden and the Fire.

Memorisation of the details of these [last] three sciences and connecting the appropriate *ḥadīths* and traditions to them is the function of the remembrancer and admonisher.

The Style of the Noble Qur'ān in Expressing the Five Sciences

These five sciences have been explained according to the first Arabs' method of demonstration and not according to the later scholars' method of demonstration. Hence, unlike textual scholars, Allah ﷻ did not engage in abridgement when mentioning the *āyāt* of judgements (*āyāt al-aḥkām*),[29] and unlike legal theoreticians (*uṣūlī*), He did not revise the principles [removing] unnecessary restrictions.[30] With regards to the *āyāt* relating to polemic (*mukhāṣamah*), Allah ﷻ chose to argue with antagonists regarding beliefs that were widely accepted among them as well as delivering wholesome addresses to them and He chose not to debate them about the intricacy of proofs, contrary to what logicians would do. Allah ﷻ did not Himself choose to advance structurally from topic to topic as is the principle among later litterateurs. In fact, He gathered all that was important to present to the slaves, irrespective of sequence.

29 The divine laws were revealed in a detailed and intelligible manner so that they would be understandable by people of all levels of intelligence. The modern trend in drafting laws is to be brief and comprehensive, but the defect in this is their need for professional interpretation.

30 Modern theoreticians formulate certain restrictions, rules and regulations that govern the subject matter of a science or art or canon of law. Allah ﷻ did not provide such injunctions, and hence the author, Shāh Waliyyullāh, maintains his lack of affiliation with those principles that he deems unnecessary.

Every *Āyah* Does not Need to Have a Cause of Revelation

Most commentators have linked every *āyah* in the Noble Qur'ān relating to polemic and every *āyah* about legal rulings to an event, and they believe that such an event is the cause for that *āyah* being revealed.

The truth is that the underlying purpose of the revelation of the Noble Qur'ān is to instruct the human being, to obliterate false beliefs and to repudiate corrupt actions, because the existence of false beliefs amongst legally responsible persons is the reason for the revelation of the *āyah* relating to polemic, and the existence of corrupt actions and the prevalence of injustices among legally responsible persons is the reason for the revelation of the *āyah* relating to legal judgements. People's lack of alertness and caution in relation to remembrance (*dhikr*) of the favours of Allah ﷻ, the Days of Allah ﷻ, the events of death and of that which follows it are all the reasons for the revelation of the *āyāt* of reminder (*āyāt adh-dhikr*).

As for those specific reasons and stories that [some] commentators have undertaken to explain, they have no significant part in the revelation except for in the case of a few Qur'ānic *āyāt* that refer to some events that took place during or before the lifetime of the Prophet Muḥammad ﷺ. Thus, when the reader reads or listener hears that reference he awaits and anticipates the explanation of that particular event.

Otherwise, it is necessary for us to explain these sciences in such a manner that it does not call for the narration of irrelevant stories.

Chapter 1

The Science of Polemic

The Noble Qur'ān mentions polemical argumentation with the four groups who are astray: the Jews, Christians, those who associate partners with Allah and hypocrites. These polemics take two forms:

1. That He ﷻ mentions the false creed with textual evidence of its falsity, mentioning only His repudiation of it.
2. That He ﷻ mentions their weak ambiguities, and also states their solution by means of demonstrative and rhetorical evidences.

A. Those who Associate Partners with Allah ﷻ

Those who associate partners with Allah used to label themselves '*Ḥanīf*',[31] claiming to follow the way of our master Ibrāhīm ﷺ – whereas a *Ḥanīf* is only someone who follows the Ibrāhīmic way and adopts its rites.

Rites of the Ibrāhīmic Way

The rites of the Ibrāhīmic way include pilgrimage (*ḥajj*) to the House [of Allah ﷻ in Makkah, i.e. the Ka'bah], facing it when praying, performing major ritual purification (*ghusl*) from

31 *Ḥanīf*: by nature upright and inclining to the true path.

major ritual impurity (*janābah*), circumcision, all of the practices of the *fiṭrah*,[32] observing the inviolability of the Sacred Months,[33] honouring the Masjid al-Ḥarām,[34] considering forbidden to oneself women whom one is forbidden to marry because of their connection to one by blood or fosterage, slaughtering [lawfully consumable animals] by *dhabḥ* across the throat [in the case of sheep, goats and cattle] and by *naḥr* in the low point of the neck (*labbah*) [in the case of camels], and slaughtering for the sake of achieving closeness to Allah ﷻ, especially during the days of *ḥajj*.

Its Laws

Its laws include washing for prayer (*wuḍū'*), *ṣalāh*, as well as fasting from the dawning of *fajr* till sunset, spending charitably on orphans and the needy, helping during the ups and downs of the Truth,[35] and joining ties of kinship are amongst the fundamental

32 In addition to circumcision, the practices of the *fiṭrah* also include using the toothstick (*miswāk*), plucking underarm hair, shaving pubic hair, cleaning the excretory organs, shortening the moustache, allowing the beard to grow, rinsing the mouth with water, drawing water into the nostrils, clipping the nails of hands and feet and washing the finger joints.
"There are ten practices of the *fiṭrah*: clipping the moustache, allowing the beard to grow, using the toothstick, drawing water into the nostrils, clipping the nails, washing the finger joints, plucking underarm hair, shaving pubic hair and cleaning one's private parts with water." The narrator said: 'I have forgotten the tenth, but it may have been rinsing the mouth.'" (Muslim, *al-Musnad aṣ-Ṣaḥīḥ*, *aṭ-Ṭahārah*, chapter of *Khiṣāl aṭ-Ṭahārah*, *ḥadīth* 604)

33 The Sacred Months are Dhu'l-Qa'dah (11) and Dhu'l-Ḥijjah (12) and Muḥarram (1), which are consecutive and Rajab (7), which stands alone in the calendar. (See Noble Qur'ān, Sūrat at-Tawbah 9:36; al-Bukhārī, *al-Jāmi' aṣ-Ṣaḥīḥ*, *Kitāb at-Tafsīr*, chapter 8, *ḥadīth* 4662)

34 The Masjid al-Ḥarām is the Sacred Mosque in the city of Makkah that encloses the Ka'bah.

35 These are the natural events and calamities that bring devastation, such as earthquakes, floods and hurricanes. They are termed 'Acts of God' by insurance companies.

legal prescriptions of this way. Commendation of these traits is widespread amongst its adherents [and they would encourage one another in adopting them], but most of those who associate partners with Allah had abandoned them [and turned away from them] to such an extent that these matters became as if nothing in their actual lives.

The prohibition of murder, theft, adultery, usury and expropriation had also been amongst the principles of the Ibrāhīmic way, being denounced by them in general terms. Nevertheless those who associate partners with Allah perpetrate them and follow the self that incites to do evil (*an-nafs al-ammārah bi's-sū'*).[36]

Their Creed

They did believe in the Maker ﷻ, that He is the Creator of the earth and of the lofty heavens, that He is the One Who controls significant [and insignificant] events, that He has the capacity to send messengers to us and to reward creatures according to what they do, that prior to their occurrence He decrees that significant incidents will take place, that the angels are His worshippers who have been brought close to Him and that they are worthy of honour – all of this was a firm belief among them as is evident in their rites. However, for most of those who associate partners with Allah, many ambiguities in respect of these beliefs became mixed up in them because of their thinking [the elements of this creed] improbable and their lack of familiarity with them.

The Deviation of Those who Associate Partners with Allah

Their deviation includes association of partners with Allah, anthropomorphism, alteration of texts, denial of the Hereafter, considering the message of the Prophet ﷺ to be improbable, the spread of ugly traits and injustices among them, innovation of

36 Qur'ān, Sūrah Yūsuf 12:53 and see also Sūrat an-Nāzi'āt 79:40.

false customs and obliteration of the acts of worship.

Clarification of Association of Partners with Allah

Association of partners with Allah is to attribute any of the qualities that are specific to Allah ﷻ to someone other than Him, such as:

- absolute disposal of affairs in the world by His will, as is expressed by His saying, *"Be! And it is!"*;[37]
- intrinsic knowledge (*'ilm dhātī*), which is not acquired through the senses, rational proof, dreams or inspiration (i.e. it is not acquired by material or spiritual means);
- bringing about the healing of a sick person;
- attributing the power to someone to lay a curse or attributing displeasure to him to such an extent that provisions become scarce because of him, or one becomes sick or misfortunate due to that displeasure; or
- attributing mercy to someone to such an extent that provisions become plentiful because of him, one's body becomes healthy and he becomes cheerful due to that mercy.

Those people who associate partners with Allah would not do so in the creation of matter[38] or in the administration of celestial affairs, and they would not attribute to anyone the power to prevent that which Allah ﷻ had decreed.

Their association of partners with Allah lies, however, in specific affairs with reference to certain creatures of Allah ﷻ. They believe that it is just as in the case of a powerful ruler who dispatches emissaries to the far-flung regions of his kingdom, and grants them independence in subsidiary issues until he issues a direct decree about a specific matter; thus the ruler does not himself administer his subjects' affairs nor their subsidiary issues, but rather he delegates that to authorities and leaders from whom

37 Qur'ān, Sūrah Yā-Sīn 36:82.

38 Matter refers to the basic essences (*jawāhir*) that form objects.

he accepts intercession for those who serve them and who seek their mediation. Similarly, [they think] the King [i.e. Allah ﷻ] bestows absolute sovereignty as a robe of divinity to some of His creatures and makes their pleasure and displeasure effective over all other creatures so that they believe it vital to gain proximity to those who are brought near in order to be accepted in the presence of the Absolute Sovereign, and they believe that their intercession on behalf of those who seek to draw near by means of them would be accepted in the execution of affairs. With respect to these matters, [those who associate partners with Allah ﷻ] permit prostration to [those emissaries], slaughtering (animals) to them, swearing oaths by their names, and seeking aid of their absolute power for important matters. They manufacture their images from stone and brass, and make them their direction of worship in order to turn to their spirits, until bit by bit, the ignorant take those specific images as deities, and so avenues of great corruption open up in their creeds.

Description of Anthropomorphism (*Tashbīh*)

Tashbīh refers to the attribution of human characteristics to Allah ﷻ. [Those who associate partners with Allah ﷻ] used to say, "The angels are the daughters of Allah. Allah accepts the intercession of His creatures even if He may not approve of it, just as kings sometimes do from their senior princes."

Since they are unable to comprehend the knowledge of Allah ﷻ and His power of hearing and seeing in a manner that befits His divinity, they treat them as analogous to their own knowledge, hearing and seeing, and hence fall into the [false] belief of anthropomorphism and thus ascribe limitation to Him.

Description of Alteration (*Taḥrīf*)

Descendants of Ismā'īl (Ishmael) ﷺ adhered to the *sharī'ah* of their ancestor Ibrāhīm (Abraham) ﷺ, until the advent of 'Amr ibn Luḥayy,[39] may Allah curse him, who manufactured idols and legislated rites of worship for them. He innovated rites such as releasing into the wild the she-camel that had given birth to five

39 'Amr ibn Luḥayy lived in Makkah just over three centuries prior to the advent of the Prophet Muḥammad ﷺ. It is said that he once went to Syria and, influenced by their manner of worshipping idols, brought an idol, Hubal, back to Makkah, which was made of red agate in the shape of a human with its right hand broken off and replaced with a golden hand. It had seven arrows placed in front of it, which were used for divination. 'Amr placed it in the middle of the Ka'bah and summoned people to worship it. Subsequently, numerous idols, bearing different names, were introduced into the area, including Wadd (or Wudd), Suwā', Yaghūth, Ya'ūq and Nasr. (Qur'ān, Sūrah Nūḥ 71:23)
(Some of those) that had existed in the time of the Prophet Nūḥ (Noah) ﷺ would afterwards become idols for the Arab nation. Wadd was an idol (in the image of an enormous man) of Banū Kalb in Dawmat al-Jandal. Suwā' was an idol (in the image of a woman) of (Banū) Hudhayl. Yaghūth was an idol (in the image of a lion) of (Banū) Murād, and later for Banū Ghuṭayf on a hillside located in Saba'. As for Ya'ūq, it was an idol of Hamdān (in the image of a horse), while Nasr was an idol (in the image of a vulture) of Ḥimyar – for Āl Dhu'l-Kalā'. All are names of prominent figures among the righteous people from (the time of) our master Nūḥ ﷺ. When they died, Shayṭān influenced the people to make sculptures of them and erect them in the places where they used to take their seats. They then named the sculptures with those names and they did (as Shayṭān had inspired them), but they were not yet worshipped. It was not until the time when they were all dead and knowledge began to dim, that the idols were worshipped. (Al-Bukhārī, *al-Jāmi' aṣ-Ṣaḥīḥ, Kitāb Tafsīr al-Qur'ān,* Sūrah Nūḥ (71), chapter 1, *ḥadīth* 4920)
It is reported that the Prophet Muḥammad ﷺ said: "I saw 'Amr ibn Luḥayy al-Khuzā'ī dragging his intestines in Hell. He was the first to introduce the institution of as-Sā'ibah." (Al-Bukhārī, *al-Jāmi' aṣ-Ṣaḥīḥ, Kitāb Tafsīr al-Qur'ān*, chapter 13, *ḥadīth* 4623).

offspring (*baḥīrah*),[40] designating an animal as a *sā'ibah*[41] to be released in the name of an idol and employing a male camel (*ḥām*)[42] as a stud, divining using arrows, and many other rituals. This happened approximately three centuries prior to the advent of the Prophet Muḥammad ﷺ. They used to adhere to the practices of their ancestors,[43] which they took to be irrefutable proofs (*ḥujaj qāṭi'ah*).

Dismissal of the Belief in the Hereafter

Though the previous prophets had explained the doctrine of the Rising from the Dead and the Gathering, their description of it was not detailed or complete – unlike that found in the Noble Qur'ān. Hence most of those who associate partners with Allah lacked awareness of it and were far from comprehending it.

Considering the Message of the Prophet ﷺ Improbable

Even if this group did acknowledge (their belief) in the prophethoods of the Prophet Ibrāhīm ﷺ and of the Prophet Ismā'īl ﷺ, and indeed even that of the Prophet Mūsā (Moses) ﷺ, yet their human characteristics which were veils over their

40 *Baḥīrah*: a she-camel that had given birth to five offspring; if the fifth calf was a male, the she-camel would be slaughtered and only the men would eat of its meat. If the fifth calf was a female, the she-camel's ears would be slit lengthways and it would be set free; it was not yoked, loaded, sheared of its wool or milked. All of its offspring were treated likewise. (Qur'ān, Sūrat al-Mā'idah 5:103; Sūrat al-An'ām 6:139)

41 *Sā'ibah*: a male or female camel, cow or buffalo, sheep or goat, that was released in the name of an idol; it was not yoked, loaded, sheared of its wool nor milked.

42 *Ḥām/Ḥāmī*: a male camel used for the purposes of procreation that would be set free in the name of an idol when it had served its purpose of producing a certain amount of offspring (possibly only female offspring); it was not yoked, loaded, sheared of its wool nor deterred from grazing in pastures or drinking from reservoirs.

43 This was regarded as proof of the veracity of their idol-worship.

perfect prophetic beauty confused them. Similarly, since they were unacquainted with the reality of the divine plan, which is the reason behind the dispatch of the prophets, they considered the Message improbable because of their belief that the one sent (*mursal*)[44] ought to be like the Sender (*Mursil*).[45] So they would raise unheard-of and flimsy doubts such as their saying, "How can the Prophet be in need of food and drink?" or "Why has Allah ﷻ not sent an angel as a messenger?" or "Why is revelation not made [directly] to each person according to his ability?"

THE ONES WHO RESEMBLE THOSE WHO ASSOCIATE PARTNERS WITH ALLAH

If you cannot imagine the state of those who associate partners with Allah, their beliefs and their actions, then just take a look at those who have perverted things in our own time, especially those who live on the fringes of Dar al-Islam.[46] What are their concepts of the condition of being in proximity to Allah ﷻ (*wilāyah*)? Although they do acknowledge the nearness [to Allah] of the *awliyā'* (pl. of *walī*), they deem it impossible for them to exist in this age. So they tend to visit the graves and their thresholds, commit various acts of association of partners with Allah (*shirk*) – how anthropomorphism, perversion and fabrication have become popular among them! We find in accordance with the following sound prophetic tradition (*ḥadīth ṣaḥīḥ*):

$$\text{لَتَتَّبِعُنَّ سُنَنَ مَنْ كَانَ قَبْلَكُمْ}$$

---

44 *Mursal, Rasūl*: one who is sent, i.e. with guidance or a message. He is a messenger, i.e. the Messenger of Allah ﷺ.

45 *Mursil*: the Sender, a name attributed to Allah ﷻ for His sending us the messengers and divine guidance.

46 This may literally refer either to those Muslims who physically reside on or close to either side of the borders of lands under Muslim governance, or it may apply metaphorically to those of weak Muslim faith.

"You will definitely follow the ways
of those who were before you"[47]

that there is no test but that a party of the people of our age will try it out and believe in the like of it, may Allah ﷻ protect us from that. (*Āmīn*)

SUMMARY

Allah ﷻ sent the Master of the Messengers ﷺ among the Arabs by His specific divine grace and mercy, and He ﷻ commanded him to establish the religion of the natural inclination to the truth (*millah ḥanīfiyyah*). He ﷻ debated with them in the Tremendous Qur'ān and reasoned with them polemically using those things they widely accepted that survived from the original religion of the natural inclination to the truth, so as to force them to accept the argument.

Refutation of Association of Partners with Allah

Association of partners with Allah is refuted by:

1. Demanding evidence for what they claim and refuting their

47 The *ḥadīth* is:
حَدَّثَنَا مُحَمَّدُ بْنُ عَبْدِ الْعَزِيزِ حَدَّثَنَا أَبُو عُمَرَ الصَّنْعَانِيُّ - مِنَ الْيَمَنِ - عَنْ زَيْدِ بْنِ أَسْلَمَ عَنْ عَطَاءِ بْنِ يَسَارٍ عَنْ أَبِي سَعِيدٍ الْخُدْرِيِّ عَنِ النَّبِيِّ - صلى الله عليه وسلم - قَالَ: لَتَتْبَعُنَّ سَنَنَ مَنْ كَانَ قَبْلَكُمْ شِبْرًا شِبْرًا وَذِرَاعًا بِذِرَاعٍ ، حَتَّى لَوْ دَخَلُوا جُحْرَ ضَبٍّ تَبِعْتُمُوهُمْ . قُلْنَا: يَا رَسُولَ اللَّهِ الْيَهُودُ وَالنَّصَارَى؟ قَالَ: فَمَنْ؟
The Prophet Muḥammad ﷺ said: "You will surely follow the traits of those before you, handspan by handspan, cubit by cubit, to such extent that if they entered the burrow of a lizard, you would follow them (into it)." Someone asked, "Messenger of Allah, (are they) the Jews and the Christians?" He replied, "Who else!" (A cubit [*dhirā'*] is the distance from the tips of the fingers to the elbow.) (Al-Bukhārī, *al-Jāmī' aṣ-Ṣaḥīḥ*, *Kitāb al-I'tiṣām bi'l-Kitāb wa's-Sunnah*, chapter 14, *ḥadīth* 7320; Also *Kitāb Aḥādīth al-Anbiyā'*, chapter 52, *ḥadīth* 3456; Muslim, *al-Musnad aṣ-Ṣaḥīḥ*, *Kitāb al-'Ilm*, chapter *Ittibā' Sunan al-Yahūd wa'n-Naṣārā*, *ḥadīth* 6781; Also at-Tibrīzī, *Mishkāt al-Maṣābīḥ*, *Kitāb ar-Riqāq*, chapter *Taghayyur an-Nās*, section 1, *ḥadīth* 5361. Also reported by al-Ḥākim in his *al-Mustadrak 'ala'ṣ-Ṣaḥīḥayn* on the authority of Ibn 'Abbās ﵄; as-Suyūṭī, *Jam' al-Jawāmi'*, Vol.6, p.19, ref. 16950)

blind adherence to the traditions of their ancestors;

2. Proving the disparity of those slaves and the Lord ﷻ and clarifying His exclusive right to the utmost reverence, contrary to those slaves;
3. Explaining the consensus of the prophets on this issue, as Allah ﷻ says:

وَمَآ أَرْسَلْنَا مِن قَبْلِكَ مِن رَّسُولٍ إِلَّا نُوحِيٓ إِلَيْهِ أَنَّهُۥ لَآ إِلَٰهَ إِلَّآ أَنَا۠ فَٱعْبُدُونِ

"We sent no Messenger before you without revealing to him: 'There is no god but Me, so worship Me.'"[48]

4. Explaining the ugly nature of idol-worship i.e. that stones fall far below the status of human excellence so how could they attain divine stature? This refutation is directed at those people who believe that idols have an intrinsic right to be worshipped.

Refutation of Anthropomorphism

Anthropomorphism (*Tashbīh*) is refuted by:

1. Demanding evidence for what they claim and refuting their blind adherence to the traditions of their ancestors;
2. Explaining the need for father and son to be of the same species, which is self-evidently missing here;
3. Clarifying the horrible nature of their attributing to Allah ﷻ what they themselves consider to be disliked and blameworthy, as Allah ﷻ says:

أَلِرَبِّكَ ٱلْبَنَاتُ وَلَهُمُ ٱلْبَنُونَ

48 Qur'ān, Sūrat al-Anbiyā' 21:25; see also: Sūrat al-Anbiyā' 21:7; Sūrah Āl 'Imrān 3:184; Sūrat ar-Ra'd 13:43.

"Does your Lord have daughters while they themselves have sons?"[49]

This refutation is directed at those people who are accustomed to accepting popular premises and poetic imaginings – and most of them are of this category of people.

Refutation of Their Alteration [of the Natural Revealed Way]

Their alteration (*taḥrīf*) is refuted by:

1. Explaining that it is not transmitted from the leaders [i.e. imāms][50] of the religion of the natural inclination to the truth;[51]
2. Explaining that all of that is surmise and an innovation of people who were not infallible.

Response to Their Considering their Rising from the Dead and the Gathering Improbable

The answer to their considering the Rising from the Dead and the Gathering improbable is by:

1. Analogy with the revival of the land after its 'death' (after it has become barren), and examples of a similar nature, examining the pivot [of the issue], which is the all- encompassing nature of the Power (of Allah ﷻ), and the possibility of the repetition [of creation];[52]
2. Explaining the agreement of all of the People of the Heavenly Books in informing about it.

Refutation of Those who Deny the Message

Denial of the Message is refuted by:

1. Explaining its existence among the previous Prophets, as

49 Qur'ān, Sūrat aṣ-Ṣāffāt 37:149.

50 Imām: a leader whose example is to be emulated.

51 i.e. from the Messengers and Prophets sent to us by Allah ﷻ, and from the right-acting predecessors, scholars and *awliyā*.

52 i.e. since Allah ﷻ has all-encompassing power, and since it is possible for existence to be brought back again after its cessation, then there is no rational objection to the Rising from the Dead.

Allah ﷻ has said:

وَمَآ أَرْسَلْنَا مِنْ قَبْلِكَ إِلَّا رِجَالًا نُوحِي إِلَيْهِمْ مِنْ أَهْلِ الْقُرَى

"We sent none before you but men inspired with revelation from among the people of the cities."[53]

And He ﷻ said:

وَيَقُولُ ٱلَّذِينَ كَفَرُوا۟ لَسْتَ مُرْسَلًا ۚ قُلْ كَفَىٰ بِٱللَّهِ شَهِيدًۢا
بَيْنِى وَبَيْنَكُمْ وَمَنْ عِندَهُۥ عِلْمُ ٱلْكِتَٰبِ

"Those who disbelieve say, 'You are not a Messenger.' Say: 'Allah is a sufficient witness between you and me, and anyone else who has knowledge of the Book.'

2. Refuting their incredulity by making clear that messengership here is an expression denoting revelation. Allah ﷻ says:

قُلْ إِنَّمَآ أَنَا بَشَرٌ مِثْلُكُمْ يُوحَىٰ إِلَيَّ

"Say: 'I am only a human being like yourselves who has received revelation.'"[54]

Then revelation is explained as not being one of those things that are impossible, as Allah ﷻ says:

وَمَا كَانَ لِبَشَرٍ أَنْ يُكَلِّمَهُ اللَّهُ إِلَّا وَحْيًا أَوْ مِنْ وَرَآءِ حِجَابٍ أَوْ
يُرْسِلَ رَسُولًا فَيُوحِيَ بِإِذْنِهِ مَا يَشَآءُ إِنَّهُ عَلِيٌّ حَكِيمٌ

"It does not befit Allah to address any human being

53 Qur'ān, Sūrah Yūsuf 12:109; see also Sūrat an-Naḥl 16:43; Sūrat al-Anbiyā 21:7.

54 Qur'ān, Sūrat al-Kahf 18:110.

except by inspiration, or from behind a veil, or He sends a messenger who then reveals by His permission whatever He wills. He is indeed Most High, All-Wise."[55]

3. By explaining that:
   a. the non-appearance of the [specific] miracles that they insist upon;
   b. the fact that Allah ﷻ does not agree with them regarding their choice of a particular person to be a messenger; and
   c. Allah ﷻ does not send angels as messengers;
   d. He does not make revelation to each single individual;

   are all for a general benefit, which their knowledge falls short of grasping.

Because most of the people to whom Allah ﷻ sent the Messenger ﷺ were those who associated partners with Allah, these topics were expressed in many *sūrahs* of the Noble Qur'ān in various modes with profound emphasis. Allah ﷻ did not shy away from repeating and reiterating these topics. Of course, this is how the address of the Absolutely Wise ought to be to these ignoramuses; the argument with these fools is worthy of this serious emphasis:

ذَٰلِكَ تَقْدِيرُ ٱلْعَزِيزِ ٱلْعَلِيمِ

"That is what the Almighty, the All-Knowing has ordained."[56]

B. The Jews

The Jews used to believe in the Torah (*Tawrāh*). Their error includes:

- Alteration (*taḥrīf*) of the judgements in the Tawrāh, whether alteration of the actual words (*taḥrīf lafẓī*)[57] or alteration of the

55 Qur'ān, Sūrat ash-Shūrā 42:51.

56 Qur'ān, Sūrat al-An'am 6:96.

57 *Taḥrīf lafẓī:* alteration of the literal wording.

meaning (*taḥrīf ma'nawī*);[58]

- Concealing *āyāt* of the Tawrāh;
- Adding into it what is not a part of it, lyingly on their part;
- Falling short in the application of its judgements;
- Extremely partisan support for their own religion;
- Denial of the message of our Prophet ﷺ, and insolence towards him and slander – indeed, towards Allah ﷻ too;
- Their being afflicted with miserliness, greed and other such discreditable qualities.

Clarification of [the Nature of] Alteration

This needy person[59] verified that the alteration of the actual words was more in the translation of the Tawrāh and the like of it and not in the original [text] of the Tawrāh itself – this is [also] the verdict of Ibn 'Abbās ؓ.[60]

Alteration of the meaning (*taḥrīf ma'nawī*) was by means of invalid interpretation (*ta'wīl fāsid*) done by arbitrarily applying an inappropriate meaning to an *āyah* and thus deviating from the true course.

Illustrations of the Alteration of Meaning

1. Allah ﷻ clarified the differences between deviant adherents of the *dīn* and denying disbelievers in all religious communities. He threatened disbelievers with perpetuity in Hell-Fire and in painful torment, whereas He has granted that it is conceivable for deviant [believers] to come out of Hell-Fire by virtue of the intercession of the prophets. He ﷻ declared that in every religion, in the name of every person who adheres to that

58 *Taḥrīf ma'nawī:* alteration of the meaning.

59 The author refers to himself.

60 He is 'Abdullāh ibn 'Abbās ؓ (5 AH/618 CE – 68 AH/687 CE), a paternal cousin of the Prophet Muḥammad ﷺ; an expert in Qur'ānic *tafsīr* and a reliable *ḥadīth* transmitter; he is said to have transmitted 1,660 *ḥadīths* from the Prophet Muḥammad ﷺ.

religion and so He confirmed that for the Jews and the Hebrews in the Tawrāh, the Christians in the Injīl[61] and the Muslims in the Noble Qur'ān. Hence, the basis of this ruling is:

a. belief in Allah ﷻ and the Last Day;
b. belief in the prophet who was sent to them;
c. obedience to him;
d. acting according to the laws of their religion;
e. abstaining from the proscriptions of that faith except for singling out one of the sects in particular.

However, the Jews claimed that whoever is a Jew or a Hebrew is one of the people of the Garden, and that the intercession of the prophets would save him from punishment, and that he would only dwell in the Fire for a few days, even if he did not have the above-mentioned basis and his belief in Allah ﷻ was not sound or he had no portion of belief in the Hereafter or in the message of the prophet who had been sent to them. This is pure error and absolute ignorance. The Tremendous Qur'ān had unveiled this specious argument in the most complete manner, since it is a guardian of the previously revealed scriptures which clarifies the subjects that are problematic in them, for He ﷻ says:

بَلَىٰ مَنْ كَسَبَ سَيِّئَةً وَأَحَاطَتْ بِهِ خَطِيئَتُهُ
فَأُولَٰئِكَ أَصْحَابُ النَّارِ هُمْ فِيهَا خَالِدُونَ

"No indeed! Those who accumulate bad actions
and are surrounded by their mistakes,
such people are the Companions of the Fire,
remaining in it timelessly, for ever."[62]

2. Allah ﷻ explained the rulings of each *millah* (religious community) clearly in accordance with the requirements of its

61 Qur'ān, Sūrat al-Baqarah 2:80; Sūrah Āl 'Imrān 3:24.
62 Qur'ān, Sūrat al-Baqarah 2:81.

age. When legislating, He took into consideration the good customs and habits of the people, and so He stressed the command that they were to be adopted and He emphatically called for belief in them and their practice, for the truth is limited to them, meaning that the truth is confined within [those *millahs*] during that particular age and hence, the perpetuity of that *millah* is relative not actual, i.e. until the advent of another prophet and until his message is unveiled. However, the Jews took that to mean the impossibility of the abrogation of Judaism, whereas the actual meaning of the counsel to hold on tight to it referred to *īmān*[63] in Allah and holding to right action; there was no special significance attached to that religion *per se*, but the Jews believed in the special significance [of the Jewish religion] and they believed that Ya'qūb (Jacob) ﷺ had counselled his sons to adhere to Judaism forever.

3. Allah ﷻ honoured the prophets as well as those who followed them in *iḥsān*[64] in every *millah* by describing them as those who are brought near (*muqarrab*) and beloved (*maḥbūb*) and He ﷻ described those who rejected the *millah* as objects of anger (*maghḍūb*). In this regard, He used a phrase that was applicable to all peoples. Thus, it is not surprising if He used the word 'sons' in lieu of the word 'beloved ones', but the Jews thought that this particular honour revolves around the names 'Jew', 'Hebrew' and 'Isrā'īlī' not realising that it revolves around nothing but the characteristics of submissive obedience, humility and traversing the [path of] the truth that Allah ﷻ has revealed to the prophets and nothing else.

63 *Īmān* is both belief, trust and affirmation.

64 *Iḥsān* is literally to make something excellent or beautiful. It is defined as being that you worship Allah as if you see Him, for if you do not see Him, He sees you. It is generally a term for good behaviour, especially doing good to others.

Many such false interpretations that they embraced [in this way] had become fixed in their minds, and they received and inherited them from their forefathers and ancestors, and so the Noble Qur'ān completely refuted these specious arguments.

Clarification of [Their] Concealing *Āyāt*

The Jews would conceal some judgements and *āyāt* in order to protect a noble standing or to seek high rank, so that people's beliefs in them would not diminish and so that they would not be blamed for omitting to practise those *āyāt*. For example:

1. The law regarding stoning adulterers is explicitly mentioned in the Torah (*Tawrāh)* but they omitted it based on the consensus of their rabbis to do that, and they replaced it with flogging and darkening the face. They concealed those *āyāt* out of fear of disgrace.
2. There are *āyāt* in the Torah prophesying the advent of a prophet from the descendants of Hājar (Hagar) and Ismā'īl ﷺ, which refer to a nation whose appearance and fame would occur in the land of Ḥijāz[65] due to which the mountains of 'Arafah would reverberate [to the sound of] the *talbiyah,*[66] and that people from all lands and regions would visit that place. This exists in the Torah till this very day but the Jews would

65 The Ḥijāz province stretches from central to the northern tip of the western Arabian Peninsula, separating the Najd province from the Red Sea. The cities of Makkah – where Hājar and Ismā'īl, peace be upon them, are buried and which is the birthplace of the Prophet Muḥammad ﷺ – and Madīnah – where he ﷺ is buried – are in Ḥijāz.

66 *Talbiyah*: the *ḥajj* chant proclaimed by all pilgrims in and around the city of Makkah when performing the rites:

لَبَّيْكَ اللَّهُمَّ لَبَّيْكَ لَبَّيْكَ لَا شَرِيكَ لَكَ لَبَّيْكَ، إِنَّ الْحَمْدَ وَالنِّعْمَةَ لَكَ وَالْمُلْكَ لَا شَرِيكَ لَكَ

"*Labbayk'Allāhumma labbayk, labbayka lā sharika laka, labbayk, inna'l-ḥamda wa'n-ni'mata laka wa'l-mulk, lā sharīka lak*" – "Here I am, at Your service, O Allah, here I am at Your service. Here I am at your service, You have no partner, here I am at Your service. All praise and all bounty is Yours, and the Kingdom. You have no partner."

interpret it merely to inform about the presence of that nation, and that there was no command to follow it. They would repeat this phrase:

مَلْحَمَةٌ كُتِبَتْ عَلَيْنَا

– *malḥamah kutibat ʿalaynā* –
"an epic war that has been enjoined upon us."

Since this weak interpretation is unheard-of and no one regards it as sound, they advised one another to keep it a secret and not permit any of the public or the élite to reveal it, as Allah ﷻ cites them as saying:

قَالُوٓاْ أَتُحَدِّثُونَهُم بِمَا فَتَحَ ٱللَّهُ عَلَيْكُمْ لِيُحَآجُّوكُم بِهِۦ عِندَ رَبِّكُمْ ۚ أَفَلَا تَعْقِلُونَ

"They say, 'Why do you speak to them about what Allah has disclosed to you, so they can use it as an argument against you before your Lord? Will you not use your intellect?'"[67]

How ignorant of them! Is it possible to interpret this favour bestowed on Hājar and Ismāʿīl ﷺ with such emphasis and the mention of this nation [of Muslims] as having such merit as simply informing of this religion without urging or encouraging to adopt this *dīn*?

سُبْحَٰنَكَ هَٰذَا بُهْتَٰنٌ عَظِيمٌ

"Glory be to You! This is a terrible slander!"[68]

67 Qur'ān, Sūrat al-Baqarah 2:76.
68 Qur'ān, Sūrat an-Nūr 24:16.

Clarification of [Their] Fabrication (*Iftirā'*)

As for fabrication, its causes are:

1. Their priests and monks delving deeply into matters and becoming fanatical;
2. Juristic preference (*istiḥsān*), i.e. the deduction of some legal judgements based upon the sense of matters of general interest in them, but without a text from the Lawgiver (i.e. Allah ﷻ);
3. Promotion of unsubstantiated deductions; their proponents attached them to the original[69] claiming the consensus of their ancestors to be irrefutable evidence. So, they did not possess any documentary evidence to disprove the prophethood of 'Īsā (Jesus) ﷺ save for the sayings of their ancestors. They behaved in the same way regarding many rulings.

The Reasons Behind their Carelessness and Commission of Proscribed Actions

As for the Jews' carelessness when implementing the rulings of the Torah (*Tawrāh)*, as well as their perpetrating [acts of] miserliness and greed, evidently they are the logical consequences of the self that incites [to do evil] (*an-nafs al-ammārah*), which overwhelms all people, save for those whom Allah ﷻ chooses to save. He ﷻ says:

إِنَّ ٱلنَّفْسَ لَأَمَّارَةٌۢ بِٱلسُّوٓءِ إِلَّا مَا رَحِمَ رَبِّىٓ

"The self indeed commands to evil acts –
except for those my Lord has mercy on."[70]

However, this ignoble behaviour had taken on another colour with the People of the Book (*Ahl al-Kitāb*); they undertook to

69 The original here refers to the divine texts and heavenly laws given to any particular religion revealed by Allah ﷻ.

70 Qur'ān, Sūrah Yūsuf 12:53.

validate it with a false interpretation, which they would make public, tinged with the colourings of the *dīn*.[71]

Reasons for [Their] Considering the Message of our Master Muḥammad ﷺ Improbable

With regards to their considering the message of our master Muḥammad ﷺ improbable, its reasons [include]:

1. The differences in the customary behaviour of the prophets and their circumstances in terms of the large or small number of their marriages;
2. The differences in their laws;
3. The differences in the Sunnah (i.e. custom) of Allah ﷻ in dealing with them;[72]
4. [Allah] sending the Prophet Muḥammad ﷺ from the descendants of Ismāʿīl ﷺ (*Banū Ismāʿīl*)[73] after most of the prophets had been from Banī Isrā'īl;[74]
5. There are many other examples of a similar nature.

71 *Dīn:* 'life-transaction' derives from a root related to *dayn* – 'debt' and signifies the transaction between the indebted slave and his Lord. It comprises Islam, *Īmān* and *Iḥsān*, whose three sciences are *fiqh*, *'aqīdah* and *taṣawwuf*. *Fiqh* covers both acts of worship and ordinary transactions such as marriage and divorce, buying, selling and renting.

72 This inconsistency was in accordance with the nature of the variance in the epochs, cultures and messages, and so one must not misconstrue it as unfairness between them.

73 Banū Ismāʿīl, or the Ishmaelites, trace their lineage back to the Prophet Ismāʿīl (Ishmael) ﷺ, the elder son of Ibrāhīm (Abraham) ﷺ.

74 Banī Isrā'īl, or the Israelites, trace their lineage back to the Prophet Yaʿqūb (Jacob) ﷺ, and then to Isḥāq (Isaac) ﷺ the younger son of Ibrāhīm ﷺ. Bear in mind the differences between the three terms: first, Banī Isrā'īl, second, the Jews – members of Judah, one of the twelve tribes of Banī Isrā'īl – and third, the Hebrews – an ethnolinguistic term for the historical speakers of the Hebrew language. All three terms are often used synonymously.

Prophethood and Its Method of Reforming People

The source of this issue is that prophethood is established principally in order to reform people's selves, to refine their worship and to bring balance in their customs, not to bring the principles of virtue and vice into being. Each people have their own customs in acts of worship, domestic management and civil politics. When prophethood appears among them, these customs are not eliminated in one stroke nor are new traditions imposed on them. Rather, it distinguishes between those customs, so that those that are right actions conforming to the good pleasure of Allah ﷻ, it allows them to continue and safeguards them, whereas those that are contrary to the principle [of the revelation and the *sharī'ah*], contrary to the good pleasure of Allah, exalted is He, it alters and puts in order.

Similarly, the reminder of the Favours of Allah ﷻ and the Days of Allah ﷻ will be according to the manner that was well known and familiar to them. This is the reason for the differences in the *sharī'ahs* of the prophets, may blessings and peace be upon them.

Differences in Sharī'ahs are Similar to Differences in Doctors' Prescriptions

When one diagnoses the illnesses of two different patients, he prescribes medicine and nutrition of a cold temperament for one of them, and medicine and nutrition of a hot temperament for the other. The doctor's aim when treating them both is the same, and that is only to rectify their condition and remove harmful toxins. He thus prescribes varying medication and nutrition that are suitable for the patients. Similarly, he may adopt different forms of treatment in different seasons that are suitable for those particular seasons.

In a similar fashion, whenever the Real Doctor[75] – majestic is

75 Allah ﷻ.

He – wants to treat those who suffer psychological [and spiritual] illnesses, by reinforcing their angelic faculty and by removing the corruption that has happened to them, the treatment varies according to the peoples of each epoch, the difference in their customs, their well-known traditions and their sanctioned ways.

Those Like the Jews

If you want to observe those [among the Muslims] who are like the Jews, then just take a look at evil *'ulamā'* (scholars) who seek the world; they are dead set on [blindly] following their ancestors , they deviate from the texts of the Book and the Sunnah, while they support their arguments with the way one particular scholar delves deeply and his fanaticism, or with his [personal] juristic preference (*istiḥsān*), which leads them to diverge from the statement of the infallible Lawgiver;[76] they present fabricated *ḥadīths* and invalid interpretations as the model to follow. Look! It is as if they themselves are those Jews!

C. The Christians

The Doctrine of Trinity and its Refutation

With regards to the Christians, they believe in 'Īsā (Jesus) ﷺ but their deviation lies in their claim that Allah ﷻ has three branches that are different from one perspective but united from another, which they call 'the Three Persons':[77]

1. The Father, corresponding to the source of the world (i.e. the First Principle);
2. The Son, corresponding to the first emanation, which is a universal meaning encompassing all existent beings;
3. The Holy Spirit, which corresponds to bare intellect.

76 Allah ﷻ.
77 Also 'The Three Hypostases'.

They believed that the Son person clothed itself in the spirit of ʻĪsā ﷺ, i.e. just as Jibrīl (Gabriel) ﷺ may appear in the form of man. Similarly, 'the Son' appeared in the spirit of ʻĪsā ﷺ so that ʻĪsā ﷺ was a 'god', a 'son of a god' and also a human at the same time, and both human and divine rulings are applied together to him. In affirming this creed, they hold to some texts of the Gospel[78] that use the word 'son' for ʻĪsā ﷺ,[79] and similarly they sought evidence from the *āyāt* [of the Gospel] wherein ʻĪsā ﷺ appears to attribute some divine acts to himself.[80]

First Problematic Issue [Those Texts in the Gospel that Refer to ʻĪsā ﷺ as 'The Son']

The response to the first problematic issue, based on the supposition that the texts of the Gospel are sound and without alteration, then the word 'son' was used in the sense of 'beloved', 'near one' and 'chosen one', as many pieces of contextual evidence in the Gospel indicate.

Second Problematic Issue [Those Texts in the Gospel in Which ʻĪsā ﷺ Appears to Attribute Some Divine Acts to Himself]

1. The first response to this problematic issue is that his ascription [of a divine act to himself] is by way of citation, just as the emissary of a king may say, "We conquered such-and-

78 The Injīl is the Arabic name of the revelation granted to ʻĪsā ﷺ. It is confusing to translate it as 'Gospel' since the Gospels that we have, both those in the New Testament and apocryphal ones, are all the authorship of historical people narrating something of his life and containing within them quotations from what may well be the original Injīl, but written in Greek and then translated into other languages. However, here the author, may Allah be merciful to him, is referring to the texts that we do have, which are only those of the Gospels and not the original Injīl, even though he uses the word Injīl. Ed.

79 The Bible, Mark 13:32, Luke 23:46, etc.

80 The Bible, Matthew 8:1-3. Also, Qur'ān, Sūrah Āl ʻImrān 3:49-51.

such a country, and we invaded such-and-such a fortress", the reality being that this refers to the king. As for the emissary, he is only a mouthpiece.

2. The second response to this problematic issue is that it is likewise a possibility that the divine revelation (*waḥy*) could have been imprinted on the tablet of his heart directly from the upper spiritual realm and not via Jibrīl ﷺ appearing to him in the form of a man in order to transmit the [divine] speech to him, and hence, [on account of this imprint] statements would emanate from him ﷺ that would tend to refer those actions to himself, whereas the reality is not hidden [that they were from Allah ﷻ].

In short, Allah ﷻ rejected this false school of thought and clarified that 'Īsā ﷺ is the slave of Allah ﷻ, and His purified spirit that He breathed into the womb of Maryam (Mary) the Truthful (*Ṣiddīqah*), and that He, exalted is He, supported him with the Holy Spirit and surrounded him with His special concern.

Even if we take the position,[81] for instance, that Allah had appeared in a spiritual garb that was of the spirit species and had then donned humanness, nevertheless, after thorough investigation and careful scrutiny, the word 'union' does not necessarily follow from this meaning unless we are not overparticular. The expressions nearest to this meaning are that it is formative (*taqwīm*) and the like. Exalted is Allah with a great exaltedness above what the wrongdoers say.[82]

81 Shāh Waliyyullāh does not admit this premise, but he adopts it for the sake of argument to show that the Christian conclusion of divine union with a human being does not follow. Ed.

82 Christians conceptualise the union of Allah ﷻ and 'Īsā ﷺ in what they say, which is that Allah ﷻ dressed in the image of 'Īsā ﷺ and so He was 'unified' with him. Even if we suppose that Allah ﷻ initially assumed a spiritual form and then as a spirit He appeared in the human form of 'Īsā ﷺ, we will not use the word 'union (*ittiḥād*)' for that, because Allah ﷻ has not become 'one' with him; He became in the form of spirit whereas

سُبۡحَٰنَهُۥ وَتَعَٰلَىٰ عَمَّا يَقُولُونَ عُلُوّٗا كَبِيرٗا

"Glorified is He, and high and exalted above what they say."[83]

Those Like the Christians

If you want to observe those [among the Muslims] who are like this party, then just take a look at the descendants of the shaykhs (i.e. of the erudite scholars) and *awliyā'*[84] and what they believe about their forefathers and to what extent they reach with [those beliefs]!

وَسَيَعۡلَمُ ٱلَّذِينَ ظَلَمُوٓاْ أَيَّ مُنقَلَبٖ يَنقَلِبُونَ

"Those who do wrong will soon know
the kind of reversal they will receive!"[85]

The Doctrine of the Crucifixion of 'Īsā ﷺ and its Refutation

Moreover, the Christians insistently assert that 'Īsā ﷺ was killed whereas the reality is contrary to that. In actual fact when the matter was made to seem confusing to them, they thought he had been raised to the heavens having been killed, and they have continued to transmit this false myth from generation to generation. Allah ﷻ has lifted the veil from the reality of the matter in the Tremendous Qur'ān saying:

وَمَا قَتَلُوهُ وَمَا صَلَبُوهُ وَلَٰكِن شُبِّهَ لَهُمۡۚ

"They did not kill him and they did not crucify him

'Īsā ﷺ was in the form of flesh – a spirit can never become 'one' with flesh, but it is formative (*taqwīm*) and puts it in order (*ta'dīl*). However, Allah ﷻ is the Creator and He does not resemble the creation.

83 Qur'ān, Sūrat al-Isrā' 17:43.

84 *Awliyā'* are those who are close to Allah. By the Qur'ānic definition, they are the *mu'minūn*. Ed.

85 Qur'ān, Sūrat ash-Shu'arā' 26:227.

but it was made to seem so to them."[86]

As for the saying of 'Īsā ﷺ that has been mentioned in the Gospel with reference to this,[87] it makes us aware of the impudence of the Jews and their plans to kill him, but Allah ﷻ saved him from this mode of death.

As for what the Disciples said [regarding the crucifixion of 'Īsā ﷺ], that arose from the confusion and their unawareness of his having been raised [to the heavens], something which their hearing and their minds were not prepared for.

Their Alteration of the Prophecy of the Paraclete

The deviation [of the Christians] also includes their claim that the promised Paraclete is 'Īsā ﷺ himself, who visited his Disciples after his crucifixion and instructed them to abide by the Gospel. They say that 'Īsā ﷺ told them that there would be many false claimants to prophethood, 'but you must accept the one who mentions my name, but if he does not then do not [accept him].'

The Noble Qur'ān testifies to the fact that the one foretold by 'Īsā ﷺ was our Prophet [Muḥammad] ﷺ and not the spiritual form of 'Īsā ﷺ, because it is stated clearly in the Gospel, "The Paraclete will abide with you for a long time, teach you knowledge and purify the people."[88] This meaning did not appear in anyone other than our Prophet Muḥammad ﷺ. With regards to the mention of 'Īsā ﷺ and affirmation of him, it means that he (i.e. the true prophet) would testify to his prophethood,[89] and it does

86 Qur'ān, Sūrat an-Nisā' 4:157.

87 The Bible, Matthew 26:45.

88 The Bible, John 4:16-17, 14:15-17, 14:26, 15:26, 16:7-8; Acts 1:5, 1:8, 2:4, 2:38, Matthew 3:10-12 and Luke 3:9-17. The Bible is replete with direct or indirect references to the Final Prophet of Allah, namely Muḥammad ﷺ, such as Song of Songs [of Solomon] 15:16, Deuteronomy 18:15-19, 33:1-2, Isaiah 41:1-17, etc.

89 The following are some of the *āyāt* of the Qur'ān that mention 'Īsā (Jesus) ﷺ: 2:87, 2:135-141, 2:252-253, 3:42-64, 3:55, 3:81-85, 4:155-159,

not mean that he would take him as a lord or believe that he is the son of God.

D. The Hypocrites

Hypocrisy in Creed and Hypocrisy in Action

There are two kinds of hypocrite:

1. Those who declare, "*Ashhadu a'l-lā ilāha illa-llāhu, wa ashhadu anna Muḥammadan rasūlu-llāh* – I witness that there is no god but Allah, and I witness that Muḥammad ﷺ is the Messenger of Allah" with their mouths while their hearts are absolutely at ease with disbelief; they conceal utter rejection and denial within themselves. Allah ﷻ says about them:

إِنَّ ٱلْمُنَـٰفِقِينَ فِى ٱلدَّرْكِ ٱلْأَسْفَلِ مِنَ ٱلنَّارِ

"The hypocrites are in the lowest level of the Fire."[90]

2. The other kind are those who enter Islam but are weak in it.
   a. Some of them follow the customs of their community; if their community becomes firmly established in *īmān*, so do they, and if their community returns to disbelief, so do they.
   b. There are some whose hearts incline towards the pursuit of material desires to such an extent that no capacity for the love of Allah ﷻ and of His Messenger ﷺ remains in them.
   c. There are some whose hearts are governed by material greed, envy, hatred for each other, and suchlike repugnant qualities, so that there remains no space in their hearts for the sweetness of devotion and intimate discourse [with Allah] nor for the blessings of the acts of worship.
   d. Some are so engrossed in worldly affairs and in seeking a

4:163-165, 4:171, 5:17-18, 5:46-47, 5:72, 5:116, 6:83-90, 9:30-31, 19:27-39, 19:16-40, 19:88-95, 21:91-93, 23:50, 33:7-8, 42:14, 43:57-65, 43:81-82, 61:6 and 61:14.

90 Qur'ān, Sūrat an-Nisā' 4:145.

livelihood that they have no time to be concerned about the Hereafter or to ponder it or reflect on it.

e. There are some to whose minds weak suspicions and feeble doubts about the message of our Prophet Muḥammad ﷺ occur, although they do not reach the extent of removing the yoke of Islam from their necks and shaking it off entirely. The reason for their doubt is the fact that our Prophet Muḥammad ﷺ exhibited ordinary human qualities, as well as the *millah* of Islam appearing in the form of the control of kings throughout the lands, and so forth.

f. Some of them had such love for [their] tribes and close families that it made them exert themselves strenuously to assist, strengthen and help that, even if that meant showing enmity towards the Muslims. Thus they weakened Islam and caused it harm in the event of any dispute.

This [latter] type of hypocrisy is in actions and qualities of character. The former type of hypocrisy cannot be discovered after our master Muḥammad ﷺ, because it pertains to matters that are invisible,[91] and it is not possible [for us] to know what is in the hidden depths of people's hearts. The second type of hypocrisy is very common, especially in our times, and to this the noble *ḥadīth* refers:

"There are four characteristics which when found in anyone, then he is a complete hypocrite: when he is trusted he is treacherous, when he speaks he lies, when he makes a contract he does not keep it and when he argues he goes to excess. If anyone has even one of them, he will continue to have the

91 The Prophet Muḥammad ﷺ may have exposed hypocrites and also divulged other kinds of unseen knowledge (*'ilm al-ghayb*) because he is a prophet, i.e. نَبِيّ – *nabī*; "...who acquaints or informs mankind, or who is acquainted or informed, respecting God and things unseen." (Lane, Edward William, *Arabic-English Lexicon,* London: Williams and Norgate, 1863. p.2753)

characteristic of a hypocrite until he leaves it."[92]

"The hypocrite is concerned for his own stomach, whereas the believer is concerned for his horse."[93]

There are many other similar *ḥadīths*.

The Objective Behind Mentioning the Hypocrites in the Noble Qur'ān

Allah ﷻ unveiled the flaws and actions of the hypocrites in the Noble Qur'ān and mentioned many aspects of both groups [of hypocrites] in order that the Ummah may beware of them.

Examples of the Hypocrites

If you want to observe examples of the hypocrites, then just go to the rulers' assemblies, and look at their associates and close companions who prefer the pleasure of their leaders over that of

92 This *ḥadīth* is mentioned by most of the authentic books of *ḥadīth*. Also: "*There are three characteristics which if they are found in anyone, he is a complete hypocrite: i. when he speaks, he lies; ii. when he is entrusted with something, he breaks the trust; and iii. when he makes a promise, he does not keep it. If anyone has even one of them, he continues to have the characteristic of a hypocrite until he leaves it.*" (An-Nasā'ī, *as-Sunan*, *al-Īmān wa Sharā'i'i-hī*, chapter *'Alāmāt al-Munāfiq*, *ḥadīth* 5026) Also: "There are four characteristics which if found in anyone, then he is a complete hypocrite, and if he has (only) one of these characteristics, he has one characteristic of hypocrisy until he leaves it: when he speaks, he lies; when he makes a promise, he does not keep it; when he swears a pledge, he breaks it, and when he argues, he insults." (Al-Bukhārī, *al-Jāmi' aṣ-Ṣaḥīḥ*, *Kitāb al-Īmān*, chapter *'Alāmāt al-Munāfiq*, *ḥadīth* 34; also *ḥadīth* 2327) Also: "There are four characteristics which if found in anyone, then he is a complete hypocrite: when he speaks, he lies; when he swears a pledge, he breaks it; when he is entrusted with something, he does not fulfil the trust and when he argues, he insults." (Al-Bukhārī, *al-Jāmi' aṣ-Ṣaḥīḥ*, *Kitāb al-Jizyah wa'l-Mawāda'ah*, chapter *Ithm Man 'Āhada Thumma Ghadara*, *ḥadīth* 3178)

93 We have been unable to source this *ḥadīth*. Ed.

Allah ﷻ. There is no difference, in the author's view, between those hypocrites who having heard the speech of the Messenger of Allah ﷺ directly, became hypocrites, and those who were born in this age who, after having known the legal injunctions of the Sharī'ah with certainty and conviction, acted against it and deviated from it.

There is also a group of rationalists to whose minds many doubts and suspicions occurred, and they became oblivious of the Final Abode;[94] they too are a kind of hypocrite.

The Noble Qur'ān is the Book for All Times

In every case, when you read the Noble Qur'ān you ought not to think that the polemic is addressed to a people who have since become extinct, but rather there is no test and trial[95] that has existed in the past except that an example of it exists even today as is narrated in the noble *ḥadīth*:

لَتَتَّبِعُنَّ سُنَنَ مَنْ كَانَ قَبْلَكُمْ

"You will surely follow the traits of those before you."[96]

The objective of the Noble Qur'ān is to explain the universality of these corruptive matters and not the particularity [or intricate details] of events.

This is the explanation of the creeds of the deviant sects that it has been possible for me to produce in this treatise, as well as their refutation. I think this amount is sufficient to understand the meanings of the *āyāt* relating to polemic (*āyāt al-jadal*), *in shā'Allāh* ﷻ.

94 This is the Hereafter, the final abode of all people; Paradise for the good and Hell for the evil.

95 This refers to the tests and trials of those who strive to cause harm to Islam and the Muslims, externally as well as from within.

96 See note 47.

Chapter 2:

The Remainder of the Five Sciences

Clarifying the Reminder of the Favours of Allah ﷻ

One ought to know that [the purpose of] the revelation of the Noble Qur'ān is to reform human beings, be they Arabs or non-Arabs, city-dwellers or country-dwellers. Hence, divine wisdom necessitates that people not be addressed when reminding them of the favours of Allah ﷻ in ways that they cannot fathom or their intellects cannot comprehend, or going excessively into detail and explanation. [The Noble Qur'ān] presents its discourse regarding the names and attributes of Allah ﷻ in a way in which it is possible to understand and to grasp with the comprehension and intellect that most individuals have originally been created with, without any need for the practice of divine philosophy or scholastic theology (*'ilm al-kalām*).

Affirmation of the Divine Essence and Explanation of the Attributes

Allah ﷻ affirmed the Essence of the Originator in a general manner since knowledge of Him is already inherent in the nature of man, and you will not find any group in the liveable climates and the regions of a temperate nature who would deny that.

Affirmation of the Divine Attributes by means of careful

consideration and investigation of the facts is impossible for each individual human being. If they do not discover His attributes, exalted is He, totally they will never attain knowledge of *rubūbiyyah* (the divine Lordship of Allah ﷻ), which is the most beneficial factor of all in civilising the inner self. Thus, it is a part of the wisdom of Allah ﷻ that He chooses some of the sound human attributes which people recognise [as good] and which they praise amongst themselves and which correspond to fine concealed meanings, the majestic nature of whose loftiness human intellects cannot penetrate, and He ﷻ uses them. He ﷻ makes the fundamental declaration لَيْسَ كَمِثْلِهِ شَيْءٌ – *"Nothing is like Him"*[97] – an antidote for the irremediable illness of compound ignorance, and forbids us from using human qualities that stir unbridled illusions [to grow] into false beliefs [regarding Allah ﷻ], such as attributing a child [to Him] or [attributing to Him] crying and impatience.

The Attributes of Allah ﷻ are Textual (*Tawqīfiyyah*)[98]

If you take a deeper look into the issue of the Divine Attributes, it will become obvious to you that pursuing the line of the human sciences which are not acquired, and distinguishing the qualities that it is conceivable to attribute to Allah ﷻ – in which no imbalances or defects occur – from those attributes whose affirmation leads to false illusions, is a very fine matter that is extremely dangerous, whose depths the vast majority of people do not know. Thus, this [category of] knowledge is undoubtedly textual; exploring it freely and without qualification is forbidden.

The Favours of Allah ﷻ and the Signs of His Power

Allah ﷻ has chosen [to mention] those favours and signs of

97 Qur'ān, Sūrat ash-Shūrā 42:11.

98 تَوْقِيفِيَّة is the adjective from تَوْقِيف which means 'the text of the Lawgiver connected to some matters'. (*Al-Wasīṭ*)

His that would be equally easy for all to understand, be they city-dwellers or country-dwellers, Arabs or non-Arabs. Hence, He did not mention the spiritual favours specific to *'ulamā'* and *awliyā'*,[99] and He did not inform us of blessings and privileges specific to kings. He only mentioned those that ought to have been mentioned, such as the creation of the heavens and the earth, how He showers rain from the clouds, how He brings forth springs from the earth for us, producing fruits, grains and flowers with [that] water, how He gave the inspiration for various indispensable skills and crafts, and created the ability to practise and pursue them.

In many places, He has warned of the differences in people's attitudes when calamities strike and when they are removed, by explaining the more common psychological illnesses.[100]

Celebrating the Days of Allah

With regards to the Days of Allah ﷻ – i.e. events that He caused to happen such as His bestowing blessings upon His obedient slaves and punishing offenders – He chose those that had already come to their attention and which they had heard of in a summary form, such as the stories of the people of Nūḥ (Noah) ﷺ,[101] 'Ād[102] and Thamūd,[103] which the Arabs had received from

99 These specific favours include joy at the unveiling of beneficial points of knowledge, the happiness at the solution of difficulties, the sweetness of *'ibādah* (worship), expansion upon seeing divine lights, and the stations of proximity to Allah ﷻ.

100 People's attitudes change in times of sorrow and joy, wealth and poverty, and so Allah ﷻ mentioned some of the more common psychological illnesses that afflict people:

إِنَّ ٱلْإِنسَـٰنَ خُلِقَ هَلُوعًا، إِذَا مَسَّهُ ٱلشَّرُّ جَزُوعًا، وَإِذَا مَسَّهُ ٱلْخَيْرُ مَنُوعًا

"Truly man was created headstrong – desperate when bad things happen, begrudging when good things come." (Qur'ān, Sūrat al-Ma'ārij 70:19-21)

101 Qur'ān, Sūrat al-Isrā' 17:3; Sūrat aṣ-Ṣāffāt 7:75-79; Sūrah Āl 'Imrān 3:33.

102 See the story of the Prophet Hūd ﷺ in the Qur'ān, e.g. Sūrat al-A'rāf 7:65.

103 See the story of the Prophet Ṣāliḥ ﷺ in Qur'ān, e.g. Sūrat al-A'rāf 7:73.

their forefathers, and the stories of Ibrāhīm 🕊 and the prophets of Banī Isrā'īl, peace be upon them, that they were accustomed to hearing because of the long intermixing of Arabs and Jews. He did not mention those unusual stories that the Arabs were not familiar with nor the episodes of reward and punishment of the Persians and the Indians.[104]

MENTIONING THE PURPOSES OF STORIES

Allah 🕊 extracted a group of the famous stories that would be useful for reminder and exhortation, but He did not narrate the stories in their entirety with every particular detail. The reason behind this is that when people hear a unique and strange story, or when a story is mentioned to them with all its details and particulars, their interest inclines towards the story itself and they miss the fundamental objective of that story, which is the reminder.

An illustration of that is what one of the gnostics (*'ārifūn*) once said, "Since people have [enthusiastically] memorised and safeguarded the rules of elocution (*tajwīd*) [when reciting the Noble Qur'ān], they have become devoid of humility when reciting it, and when the commentators began to delve into remote analyses, the [genuine] science of Qur'ānic commentary (*tafsīr*) became so rare as to be non-existent."

Stories that are Oft-Repeated in the Noble Qur'ān

Of those [stories] that are oft-repeated in the Noble Qur'ān, there are:

• The creation of Ādam 🕊 from clay, the prostration of the angels to him, the arrogant refusal of Shayṭān [to prostrate], his [consequently] being rendered accursed and his striving to

---

104 The stories of the gains and the losses of the Persians and of the Indians include their warriors and heroes, such as Rustum, and the great epic, the *Mahābhārata*.

lead humanity astray;

- The stories of the confrontations of Nūḥ عليه السلام, Hūd (Heber) عليه السلام, Ṣāliḥ[105] عليه السلام, Ibrāhīm عليه السلام, Lūṭ (Lot) عليه السلام and Shu'ayb (Jethro) عليه السلام with their respective nations regarding *tawḥīd*,[106] their enjoining what is good and forbidding what is bad, the refusal of [these] nations to embrace *īmān* and their offering flimsy doubts as evidence, which the prophets rebutted, those nations' being afflicted with Divine punishment, and the appearance of the help of Allah ﷻ for the prophets and their followers;
- The stories of [the encounter of] Mūsā عليه السلام with Pharaoh (Fir'awn) and his circle, and [his encounters] with foolish people among Banī Isrā'īl and their superciliousness towards him, Allah's punishment of those wretched people and the successive manifestations of Allah's aid to rescue him عليه السلام;
- The stories of Dāwūd (David) عليه السلام and Sulaymān (Solomon) عليه السلام, their caliphates, and their signs and miracles;
- The stories of the trials and tests of Ayyūb (Job) عليه السلام and Yūnus (Jonah) عليه السلام, and the manifestation of mercy for them;
- The story of the supplication of Zakariyyā (Zachariah) عليه السلام and Allah's ﷻ answering it;
- The wonderful stories of 'Īsā (Jesus) عليه السلام, from his birth without a father to his speaking in the cradle, to the manifestation of miracles at his hands.

These stories have been mentioned in the Noble Qur'ān in various succinct ways in accordance with the requirements of each chapter.

105 The Prophet Ṣāliḥ عليه السلام has been equated with the Biblical Shelah – something that is often disputed.

106 *Tawḥīd*, literally 'unification' or 'making one', encompasses both the sense that there is only one God 'monotheism' and the sense that Allah, exalted is He, is One in His Essence, Attributes and Actions. These are the senses in *'ilm al-kalām*, but existentially it refers to a person's lived experience that everything comes from Allah alone. Ed.

Stories Mentioned in the Noble Qur'ān Only Once or Twice

As for those stories that are not repeated in the Noble Qur'ān, or that are only mentioned in one or two places, they are:
- The story of Idrīs (Enoch) 🕊 and his being raised to a lofty place;
- The story of Ibrāhīm's 🕊 argument with Nimrūdh (Nimrod), Ibrāhīm's 🕊 witnessing life being given to the dead birds and the story of his sacrificing his only son (Ismāʿīl 🕊);
- The story of Yūsuf (Joseph) 🕊;
- The story of the birth of Mūsā 🕊, his being cast into the sea, his killing the Copt, his setting off towards Madyan (Midian)[107], his becoming married there, and his seeing the fire on the tree and hearing speech from it;
- The story of [the Israelites] slaughtering the cow;
- The story of Mūsā 🕊 meeting with our master Khaḍir (Khiḍr) 🕊[108];

---

107 Madyan (Midian) is believed to be the region that lies to the east of the Sinai Peninsula, on the eastern shore of the Gulf of ʿAqabah (Aqaba), in northwestern Saudi Arabia. Qur'ān mentions Madyan in Sūrat al-Aʿrāf 7:85; Sūrat at-Tawbah 9:70; Sūrah Hūd 11:84; Sūrah Ṭā-Hā 20:40; Sūrat al-Ḥajj 22:44; Sūrat al-Qaṣaṣ 28:22, 23 and 45; and Sūrat al-ʿAnkabūt 29:36. Our master Shuʿayb 🕊 was sent to guide the inhabitants of Madyan, who rejected him and were consequently destroyed by an epic earthquake.

108 Khaḍir (means green): his real name is Balyā ibn Malkān. His title is Khaḍir (or Khiḍr) because wherever he would settle, that place would become green (al-Baghawī, Abū Muḥammad al-Ḥusayn ibn Masʿūd ibn Muḥammad, al-Farrāʾ (436 AH/1044 CE – 516 AH/1122 CE), *Tafsīr al-Baghawī (Maʿālim at-Tanzīl)*, in the margin of *Tafsīr al-Khāzin (Lubāb at-Taʾwīl fī Maʿānī at-Tanzīl)* by al-Khāzin, ʿAlāʾuddīn ʿAlī ibn Muḥammad ibn Ibrāhīm al-Baghdādī (678 AH/1278 CE – 741 AH/1341 CE) 4 volumes, Beirut, 1399 AH/1979 CE, Vol. 3, Part 4, commentary on Sūrat al-Kahf (18:60)). The Prophet Muḥammad 🕊 is reported to have said, "He is called al-Khaḍir (the Green One) because he sat on some white furs that turned shimmering green under him." (Al-Bukhārī, *al-Jāmiʿ*

- The story of Ṭālūt (Saul) 🕮 and Jālūt (Goliath);[109]
- The story of Bilqīs;[110,111]
- The story of Dhu'l-Qarnayn;[112,113]
- The story of the Companions of the Cave (Aṣḥab al-Kahf);[114]
- The story of the two men who disputed with one another;[115]

as-Ṣaḥīḥ, Kitāb Aḥādīth al-Anbiyā', chapter 27, ḥadīth 3402) It is also pronounced Khiḍar but he is more famous as Khiḍr (in Urdu it is Khizar). He has sometimes been identified with St. George. His story is told in Qur'ān, Sūrat al-Kahf 18:65-82.

109   Qur'ān, Sūrat al-Baqarah 2:246-251.

110   Bilqīs was the Queen of Saba' (Sheba). A sun-worshipper, her kingdom either lay in the eastern region of Africa (modern day Ethiopia and Eritrea) or the southern area of the Arabian Peninsula (modern day Yemen and Oman); the latter being the more probable of the two. She was invited to visit the crystal palace of the Prophet Sulaymān 🕮, said to have been in al-Quds (Jerusalem), which she accepted, and where, after his invitation to Islam (da'wah), she became Muslim. (Qur'ān, Sūrat an-Naml 27:22-44)

111   Qur'ān, Sūrat an-Naml 27:23-24.

112   Dhu'l-Qarnayn (He of the Two Horns/Two Generations/Two Centuries/Two Ages) built a barrier to thwart the attacks of Ya'jūj (Gog) and Ma'jūj (Magog) at the request of their victims. It has been claimed by some that Dhu'l-Qarnayn was the title of Alexander III of Macedon (356 BC – 323 BC), otherwise known as Alexander the Great, which may be ill-founded, and it is possible that the claim of Cyrus II of Persia (576 BC – 530 BC), otherwise known as Cyrus the Great, is more correct. (Pīr Muḥammad Karam Shāh (1336 AH/1918 CE – 1418 AH/1998 CE), Ziyā al-Qur'ān (Urdu), 5 Volumes (Lahore, 1978 CE/1399 AH), Vol. 3, pp.46-49, Commentary on Sūrat al-Kahf 18:83, note 105)

113   Qur'ān, Sūrat al-Kahf 18:83-98.

114   The Christian tradition refers to the Seven Sleepers of Ephesus who are often identified with the Qur'ānic story. Unlike the Qur'ānic version, they are not accompanied by a dog. The Qur'ān does not give their exact number but states that people said they were three, five or seven, with the addition of a dog. The exact location of the Cave where they reposed is itself a matter for debate, and may either be in Ephesus (Turkey), or in 'Ammān (Jordan). See Qur'ān, Sūrat al-Kahf 18:9-26.

115   Qur'ān, Sūrat al-Kahf 18:32-44.

- The story of the men and the garden;[116]
- The story of the three envoys whom ʿĪsā ﷺ sent in order to invite people to the *dīn;*[117]
- The story of the believer whom the disbelievers martyred;
- The story of the people of the Elephant.[118,119]

The objective behind recounting these stories in the Noble Qur'ān is not to raise awareness of the stories *per se*, but rather the fundamental purpose is to move the mind of the reader and the listener on to understanding the ugliness of associating partners with Allah and of acts of disobedience, and [to make them aware of] the punishment of Allah ﷻ for those evils, as well as the joy of the believers at the help of Allah ﷻ and His support, and His grace and favours towards His sincere slaves.

The Reminder of Death and What is After It

Allah ﷻ has described death and what follows it: the condition of a human at death and his helplessness at that particular moment, his being shown the Garden and the Fire after his death, the appearance of the angels of torment before him, and the signs of the Last Hour (*as-Sāʿah*), which include:

- The descent of ʿĪsā ﷺ;[120]

116 Qur'ān, Sūrat al-Qalam 68:17-32.

117 Qur'ān, Sūrah Yā-Sīn 36:13-27.

118 Abrahah, the Christian ruler of an Abyssinian principality in Yemen, marched upon the Kaʿbah intending to destroy it, with an army and many elephants. The elephants stopped outside of Makkah and refused to advance, and the entire army was destroyed by flocks of birds bombarding them from the air with small stones of baked clay. This event took place in the same year but before the birth of the Prophet Muḥammad ﷺ. (Pīr Muḥammad Karam Shāh (1336 AH/1918 CE – 1418 AH/1998 CE), *Ziyā al-Qur'ān* (Urdu), 5 volumes (Lahore, 1978 CE/1399 AH), Vol. 5, p.664, *Introduction to Sūrat al-Fīl* (105))

119 Qur'ān, Sūrat al-Fīl 105:1-5.

120 Qur'ān, Sūrat az-Zukhruf 43:61.

- The emergence of the Dajjāl;[121]
- The emergence of the Beast of the Earth (ḍābbat al-arḍ);[122]
- The emergence of Ya'jūj and Ma'jūj (Gog and Magog);[123,124]
- The blowing of the [first] Trumpet for the swooning;[125]
- The blowing of the [second] Trumpet for the Rising from the Dead;[126]
- The Rising from the Dead and the Gathering;[127,128]

121 *Al-Masīḥ ad-Dajjāl* (The Lying Messiah) will appear near the end of time posing to be the promised Messiah (*Masīḥ*, i.e. 'Īsā 靉). In Christian and Jewish eschatology, he is often identified with the Antichrist and Armilus respectively. As an envoy of Shayṭān, he will lead people to moral and spiritual corruption, wars and destruction. Numerous sound *ḥadīths* have been transmitted about him, such as in al-Bukhārī, *al-Jāmi' aṣ-Ṣaḥīḥ*, *Kitāb al-Fitan*, chapters 26-27; reports are also narrated by Muslim, Abū Dāwūd, at-Tirmidhī, an-Nasā'ī, Ibn Mājah and at-Tibrīzī, and others.

122 Qur'ān, Sūrat an-Naml 27:82.

123 Ya'jūj and Ma'jūj were two savage peoples whom Dhu'l-Qarnayn pushed behind a barrier, locking them behind it in order to contain their attacks. Islamic eschatology suggests their return prior to the Last Day. The intepretation of their true identity has differed with various proponents throughout the ages, with names such as the Scythians, the Romans, the Goths, the Huns, the Saracens, the Khazars, the Mongols, Eastern European Jews, the Illuminati, the Freemasons (i.e. Bohemian Grove, Skull and Bones, and other secret societies), Caucasians, the USSR and the USA coming to the fore. Amusingly, some have even claimed that Ya'jūj and Ma'jūj are not even of this world – that they may be aliens, and that Dhu'l-Qarnayn may have built a cosmic field around 'our world' in order to repel their attacks. Disregarding the many spurious interpretations, there is still no certainty regarding the true identity or whereabouts of Ya'jūj and Ma'jūj. What is certain, however, is that they will appear, heralding the Final Hour.

124 Qur'ān, Sūrat al- Kahf 18:94; Sūrat al-Anbiyā' 21:96.

125 Qur'ān, Sūrat al-Ḥāqqah 69:13-17.

126 Qur'ān, Sūrat al-An'ām 6:73; Sūrat az-Zumar 39:68; the Bible, 1 Corinthians 15:52.

127 The Jews, Christians, Zoroastrians and Muslims all believe in the rising after death.

128 Qur'ān, Sūrah Qāf 50:44.

- The Interrogation and the Answering;[129]
- The Scales;[130]
- Receiving the record of one's deeds in either the right or the left hand;[131]
- The entry of the believers into the Garden;[132]
- The entry of the disbelievers into the Fire;[133]
- The inmates of the Fire – both followers and those they followed – accusing, repudiating and cursing one another;[134]
- The believers being singled out to see Allah ﷻ;[135]
- Various kinds of punishment such as chains[136], [fetters[137],] shackles[138], scalding water (*ḥamīm*)[139], the suppurating pus discharged from the wounds of the inmates of the Fire (*ghassāq*)[140] and the [tree of] *Zaqqūm*[141];
- Various kinds of blessings such as *houris* (*ḥūr*)[142], palaces[143],

129 Qur'ān, Sūrat al-Anbiyā' 21:1; Sūrat al-Ghāshiyah 88:25-26; Sūrah Āl 'Imrān 3:30.

130 Qur'ān, Sūrat ar-Raḥmān 55:7-9; Sūrat al-Anbiyā' 21:47.

131 Qur'ān, Sūrat al-Isrā' 17:71; Sūrat al-Ḥāqqah 69:19 and 25; Sūrat al-Inshiqāq 84:7.

132 Qur'ān, Sūrat al-Isrā' 17:19; Sūrat al-Furqān 25:15; Sūrah Muḥammad 47:15.

133 Qur'ān, Sūrah Āl 'Imrān 3:12; Sūrat al-Anfāl 8:36; Sūrat al-Mulk 67:6.

134 Qur'ān, Sūrat al-Baqarah 2:166-167; Sūrat al-A'rāf 7:38; Sūrat al-'Ankabūt 29:25; Sūrat al-Aḥzāb 33:67-68; Sūrat ash-Shu'ārā 26:99.

135 Qur'ān, Sūrat al-Qiyāmah 75:23.

136 Qur'ān, Sūrah Ghāfir 40:71.

137 Qur'ān, Sūrah Ghāfir 40:71.

138 Qur'ān, Sūrat al-Insān 76:4.

139 Qur'ān, Sūrat an-Naba' 78:25; Sūrat aṣ-Ṣāffāt 37:67; Sūrat al-Wāqi'ah 56:42.

140 Qur'ān, Sūrat an-Naba' 78:25; Sūrat ad-Dukhān 44:48.

141 Qur'ān, Sūrat ad-Dukhān 44:43-46; Sūrat aṣ-Ṣāffāt 37:62-66; Sūrat al-Wāqi'ah 56:51-53.

142 Qur'ān, Sūrat ad-Dukhān 44:54; Sūrat aṭ-Ṭūr 52:20; Sūrat ar-Raḥmān 55:72.

143 Qur'ān, Sūrat al-Furqān 25:10.

rivers[144], delicious food and fine clothing;

- The association of the inhabitants of the Garden with one another will be gracious, delightful and joyous for the hearts.[145]

He ﷻ spread these issues throughout the Noble Qur'ān, both in summary and in detail, observing particular methods.

The Science of Rulings (*Aḥkām*)

The general principle in the discussion on the rulings is that our master, the Messenger of Allah ﷺ was sent with the primordial Ibrāhīmic way and hence it was necessary to continue the laws of that way. No change took place in any of its fundamental issues save to make its unqualified decrees specific and additions to the appointed times and limits [for them].

When Allah ﷻ wanted to purify the Arabs through our Prophet ﷺ, and then [purify] all the groups by means of the Arabs, it was necessary to take the substance of his ﷺ *sharī'ah* from the rules[146] and customs[147] of the Arabs.

If one was to take a look at the entire catalogue of the rulings of the primordial way, observe the rules and customs of the Arabs, and then ponder over the *sharī'ah* of the Prophet Muḥammad ﷺ, which arrived to reform and refine those habits and customs, you will learn that every ruling has a cause, and you will understand that there is benefit in every command and every prohibition, but to detail this would be too lengthy [and so we have refrained from discussing them].

The Role of Islamic Legislation in Reforming the Corrupted Primordial Way

A great slackness had found its way into worship, such as in purification (*ṭahārah*), prayers (*ṣalāh*), fasting (*ṣawm*), *zakāh*,

144 Qur'ān, Sūrah Āl 'Imrān 3:136.
145 Qur'ān, Sūrah Yā Sīn 36:55.
146 Those that were based on the primordial Ibrāhīmic way.
147 Customs contrary to *tawḥīd* and socio-political well-being were discarded.

pilgrimage (*ḥajj*), and remembrance (*dhikr*), due to carelessness in establishing them, people's disagreements about them because of ignorance of the larger part of them, and their infiltration by distortions from the Era of Ignorance, and so the Tremendous Qur'ān completely did away with that deficiency and rectified and corrected them until they stood straight.

As for domestic management, inimical and excessive practices had entered it, and likewise civil and political laws were corrupted, and so the Tremendous Qur'ān composed principles for them, prescribed their limits, and made mention of the major wrong actions as well as many of the minor so that the Ummah would be on guard against them.

It mentions the issues pertaining to *ṣalāh* in a summary manner, in which it employs the words '*iqāmat aṣ-ṣalāh* (establishment of prayer)', then the Messenger of Allah ﷺ described it in detail with the call to prayer (*adhān*), construction of masjids, the gathering (*jamā'ah*) and timings [of the *ṣalāh*]. In similar fashion, *zakāh* issues were mentioned in brief [in the Qur'ān] and then the Messenger of Allah ﷺ explained them in detail. Fasting was mentioned in Sūrat al-Baqarah (2) in which He also mentions *ḥajj* issues, and also in Sūrat al-Ḥajj (22). Jihād issues have been mentioned in Sūrat al-Baqarah (2), Sūrat al-Anfāl (8), and in many other places; *hadd* (limits)[148] issues have been mentioned in Sūrat al-Mā'idah (5) and Sūrat an-Nūr (24); inheritance issues in Sūrat an-Nisā' (4); and He ﷻ explained marital and divorce issues in Sūrat al-Baqarah (2), Sūrat an-Nisā' (4), Sūrat aṭ-Ṭalāq (65), and in many other *sūrahs*.

Allusions Needing Explanation

Once you understand this type whose benefit encompasses the entire Ummah, know that there is another type:

148 A *ḥadd* is both a 'limit' and the punishment for contravention of the limit. Ed.

1. Those which the Prophet Muḥammad ﷺ was asked about, to which he responded;
2. A specific event wherein the believers offered their lives and their properties generously, and the hypocrites held back, followed their passions, and hence Allah ﷻ praised the believers and denounced and threatened the hypocrites;[149] or
3. An event took place, such as vanquishing the enemy and repelling their mischief, which Allah ﷻ had granted as favour to the believers and then reminded them of that blessing; or
4. Circumstances were such that the need arose for warning, reprimand, allusion, indication, order or prohibition, and so Allah ﷻ provided an appropriate revelation.

With reference to this type, it is incumbent for the commentator to narrate these stories in their entirety.

Instances

Allusions have been made to the events of:

- The campaign of Badr in Sūrat al-Anfāl;[150]
- The campaign of Uḥud in Sūrah Āl 'Imrān;[151]
- The campaign of the Trench (*Khandaq*) in Sūrat al-Aḥzāb;[152]
- The treaty of Ḥudaybiyyah in Sūrat al-Fatḥ;[153]
- The campaign of Banū Naḍīr in Sūrat al-Ḥashr (59);
- Exhortation towards and urging on the Opening (*Fatḥ*)[154] of Makkah [to Islam] and the campaign of Tabūk are in Sūrat

149 This took place in the Battle of Tabūk; many *āyāt* of Sūrat at-Tawbah (9) were revealed in this regard.
150 Qur'ān, Sūrat al-Anfāl 8:7.
151 Qur'ān, Sūrah Āl 'Imrān 3:152.
152 Qur'ān, Sūrat al-Aḥzāb 33:9-22.
153 Qur'ān, Sūrat al-Fatḥ 48:18.
154 *Fatḥ* does not mean 'conquest' but 'opening' i.e. the Opening to Islam. Ed.

al-Barā'ah.[155,156]

Allusions have also been made to:

- The Farewell Pilgrimage (*Ḥajjat al-Wadā'*) in Sūrat al-Mā'idah;[157]
- The story of the marriage of Zaynab in Sūrat al-Aḥzāb;[158]
- [His own] prohibition [to himself ﷺ] of the concubine in Sūrat at-Taḥrīm;[159]
- The slander [against Sayyidah 'Ā'ishah] in Sūrat an-Nūr;[160]
- There is mention of the delegation of the jinn hearing the Prophet's ﷺ recitation of the Noble Qur'ān in Sūrat al-Jinn[161] and Sūrat al-Aḥqāf[162];
- The story of *Masjid aḍ-Ḍirār* (the Mosque of Mischief) is mentioned in Sūrat al-Barā'ah;[163]
- The Night Journey (*Isrā'*) is indicated at the beginning of Sūrah Banī Isrā'īl.[164,165]

This category of noble Qur'ānic *āyāt* is actually comprised under those that remind of the Days of Allah ﷻ, but since the understanding of their allusions is dependant on listening to the original story, they have thus been differentiated from the others.

155 Sūrat al-Barā'ah (9) is also known as Sūrat at-Tawbah.
156 Qur'ān, Sūrat at-Tawbah 9:29, 42-49, and 81.
157 Qur'ān, Sūrat al-Mā'idah 5:67.
158 Qur'ān, Sūrat al-Aḥzāb 33:39.
159 Qur'ān, Sūrat at-Taḥrīm 66:3.
160 Qur'ān, Sūrat an-Nūr 24:11.
161 Qur'ān, Sūrat al-Jinn 72:1.
162 Qur'ān, Sūrat al-Aḥqāf 46:29-32.
163 Qur'ān, Sūrat al-Barā'ah (at-Tawbah) 9:9.
164 Qur'ān, Sūrat al-Isrā' 17:1.
165 Sūrah Banī Isrā'īl (17) is also known as Sūrat al-Isrā'.

PART 2

The Kinds of Meaning Hidden from the People of this Age in the Composition of the Qur'ān, and the Removal of their Concealed Nature by the Clearest of Explanations

One should know that the Noble Qur'ān was revealed in the pure clear Arabic language that clarifies things. The Arabs understand the meanings expressed by the Noble Qur'ān because of their inborn disposition which they had been created upon, as Allah ﷻ says:

وَٱلْكِتَٰبِ ٱلْمُبِينِ

"By the Book which makes things clear."[166]

He also says:

إِنَّآ أَنزَلْنَٰهُ قُرْءَٰنًا عَرَبِيًّا لَّعَلَّكُمْ تَعْقِلُونَ

"We have sent it down as an Arabic Qur'ān so that hopefully you will use your intellect."[167]

and:

كِتَٰبٌ أُحْكِمَتْ ءَايَٰتُهُۥ ثُمَّ فُصِّلَتْ مِن لَّدُنْ حَكِيمٍ خَبِيرٍ

"A Book whose āyāt are perfectly constructed, and then demarcated, coming directly from One Who is All-Wise, All-Aware."[168]

It is pleasing to the Wise Lawgiver that one does not plunge deeply into the following:

166 Qur'ān, Sūrat az-Zukhruf 43:2.
167 Qur'ān, Sūrah Yūsuf 12:2.
168 Qur'ān, Sūrah Hūd 11:1.

- the allegorical (*mutashābih*) *āyāt* in the Noble Qur'ān;
- making an image of the real meanings (*ḥaqā'iq*) of the Divine Attributes;
- the demonstrative pronoun;
- exploring the Qur'ānic stories in detail;
- and the likes of that.

This is why [the Companions 🙏] would rarely ask him 🙏 about these topics, and hence the paucity of such narrations transmitted to us.

When, however, that generation had passed and non-Arabs entered [the *dīn*], this primordial language was abandoned and it became difficult to understand what was meant in some places. There thus was a need to study language and its grammar. Queries and responses to them in this regard began to emerge amongst people, and books on Qur'ānic *tafsīr* were composed. Thus, it has become necessary for us to mention the difficult areas in a summary fashion and illustrate them with suitable examples in order for the commentator not to need further explanation when exploring them or be forced to go to extremes in uncovering them and explaining them.

REASONS BEHIND THE DIFFICULTY IN UNDERSTANDING THE INTENDED MEANINGS OF SPEECH

The reasons for not grasping the intended meaning of an expression are sometimes:

- The use of a rare word. It is solved by transmitting the meaning of the expression from the Companions 🙏, their Successors and all those who are acquainted with its meaning.
- Inability to differentiate between abrogating (*nāsikh*) and abrogated (*mansūkh*) [*āyāt*].
- Being oblivious of the causes of the revelations (*asbāb an-nuzūl*).

- The omission of the first noun of a genitive construction[169] (*muḍāf*) or the qualified noun[170] (*mawṣūf*), etc.
- The substitution of one thing for another, or a preposition for another, or a noun for another, or a verb for another, or mentioning a plural in place of the singular or vice versa.
- Changing from addressing the second person to the third person.
- Advancing that which ought to be deferred [in the word order], and vice versa.
- The dispersal of pronouns.
- Multiplicity of meanings for a single expression.
- Repetition and exaggeration.
- Brevity and concision.
- Use of indirect expressions, allusions, allegories and intellectual metaphors.

Our noble brothers ought to familiarise themselves with the truth of these matters, as well as some of the illustrations of them, prior to embarking on any discussion. They ought to content themselves with indications and symbolic (references) in places that require more detail.

169 e.g. in *bayt ar-rajuli* – the man's house – *bayt* is the *muḍāf* and *ar-rajuli* is the *muḍāf ilayhi*. Ed.

170 e.g. in *al-ḥayāt ad-dunyā* – literally 'the lower life' – the word *al-ḥayāt* – life – is the noun which is qualified by the adjective *ad-dunyā*. Ed.

Chapter 1

Unusual Expressions of the Qur'ān
(*Gharīb al-Qur'ān*)

In explaining the unusual expressions of the Noble Qur'ān (*gharīb al-Qur'ān*),[171] the most excellent explanation is that of our master 'Abdullāh ibn 'Abbās ⬡ that has reached us by *ṣaḥīḥ* transmission[172] via Ibn Abī Talḥah,[173] which Imām al-Bukhārī[174] relied upon in his *ṣaḥīḥ* collection of *ḥadīths*,[175] and then after that

---

171 Known as *Gharīb al-Qur'ān* (pl.: *Gharā'ib al-Qur'ān*), it denotes a word used in the Qur'ān but rarely used in the Arabic language; its science is said to have a distinct and meritorious status.

172 *Ṣaḥīḥ* – 'authentic' – transmissions are those which are narrated through an unbroken chain of people of unquestionable integrity and capacity for memorisation. Ed.

173 He is 'Alī ibn Abī Talḥah (d. 143 AH/760 CE). He was born in Arabia but spent most of his life in Ḥums (modern day Syria).

174 He is Abū 'Abdullāh Muḥammad ibn Ismā'īl ibn Ibrāhīm ibn al-Mughīrah al-Bukhārī (194 AH/809 CE – 256 AH/870 CE), a famous scholar, with expertise in *ḥadīth* and its sciences. He heard *ḥadīths* from over a thousand people and knew over 700,000 *ḥadīths*. He compiled the famous and ever-popular *al-Jāmi' aṣ-Ṣaḥīḥ* (or *Ṣaḥīḥ al-Bukhārī*) – see following note.

175 It is *al-Jāmi' al-Musnad aṣ-Ṣaḥīḥ al-Mukhtaṣar min Umūr Rasūl Allāhi wa Sunani-hi wa Ayyāmi-hi* (The Collection of Connected Chains of

the transmission of aḍ-Ḍaḥḥāk[176] from Ibn 'Abbās 🕮 as well as the compilation of the responses of Ibn 'Abbās 🕮 to the questions posed to him by Nāfi' ibn al-Azraq.[177,178] Imām as-Suyūṭī[179] has mentioned all three modes in his book *al-Itqān fī 'Ulūm al-Qur'ān*.[180]

Then there is that which al-Bukhārī transmitted from the imams of *tafsīr*. Then there is what all the other commentators have transmitted from the Companions 🕮, the Successors and those who came after them[181] in explanation of the unusual expressions of the Qur'ān.

I think it appropriate to collect a reliable and useful compilation regarding the unusual expressions mentioned in the Noble Qur'ān, together with the occasions of their revelation, in Part Five of this

Authentic Hadiths Abridged from Matters Pertaining to the Messenger of Allah, His Practices and His Times), i.e. *Ṣaḥīḥ al-Bukhārī* (referred to in this book as *al-Jāmi' aṣ-Ṣaḥīḥ*), regarded by many as the most authentic collection of Prophetic traditions (*ḥadīths*).

176 He is aḍ-Ḍaḥḥāk ibn Muzāḥim al-Hilālī at-Tābi'ī (the Successor) (d. 105 AH/723 CE). He narrated *ḥadīths* from 'Abdullāh ibn 'Umar, Abū Hurayrah and Anas ibn Mālik among others.

177 He is Nāfi' ibn al-Azraq al-Ḥarūrī (also known as Abū Rāshid al-Ḥarūrī), one of the leaders of the *Khawārij* (Seceders). He was killed in 65 AH/685 CE.

178 The issues raised by Nāfi' ibn al-Azraq with Ibn 'Abbās 🕮 with respect to the Qur'ān are said to amount to sixty in total.

179 He is Abu'l-Faḍl 'Abd ar-Raḥmān ibn Abī Bakr Jalāl ad-Dīn as-Suyūṭī (848 AH/1445 CE – 911 AH/1505 CE), a famous scholar of the classical period of Islam, authoring many scholarly works and having a lofty status in juristic decision-making (*ijtihād*). He compiled many valuable works, including *al-Itqān fī 'Ulūm al-Qur'ān* (The Perfection of the Qur'ānic Sciences), *Tadrīb ar-Rāwī* on *ḥadīth* terminology, *Tārīkh al-Khulafā'* (History of the Khalīfahs) – he co-authored *Tafsīr al-Jalālayn* (on *tafsīr* of the Qur'ān) by completing the work of his own shaykh Jalāl ad-Dīn al-Maḥallī (d. 864 AH/1459 CE).

180 It is *al-Itqān fī 'Ulūm al-Qur'ān* (The Perfection of the Qur'ānic Sciences).

181 Those who came after the Successors (*Tābi'īs*) are known as the *Tābi'ū at-Tābi'īn* (Successors of the Successors).

book, and to make that part an independent treatise[182] so that anyone wishing to add it to this treatise may do so or they may study it separately, for *'people have different approaches to that which they love'*.

The Early Generations Would Often Explain an Expression by its Most Obvious Meaning

One ought to bear in mind here that the Companions and Successors ﷺ would often present the *tafsīr* of a word according to its most obvious meaning. The later commentators would sometimes follow that old form of *tafsīr* when adhering to its linguistic expression and when investigating its place of use.

In this treatise, we aim to cite the commentaries of the earlier generations of Muslims. The place for criticism and discussion is elsewhere,

"for every station has its expression
and every point has its domain."

182 It is entitled *Fatḥ al-Khabīr bi Mā Lā Budda min Ḥifẓi-hī fī 'Ilm at-Tafsīr* (The Aid in Knowing What Must Necessarily be Memorised Regarding the Science of *Tafsīr*).

Chapter 2

Abrogating (*Nāsikh*) and Abrogated (*Mansūkh*) *Āyāt*

Recognition of the abrogating and the abrogated *āyāt* of the Noble Qur'ān is such an arduous task in the science of *tafsīr* that many discussions and numerous disagreements have taken place in it. The most significant reason for these difficulties is the different terminologies of the early and the later scholars.

The Meaning of Abrogation for the Early Generations

In this regard, research into the statements of the Companions and the Successors tells us that they used the word '*naskh* (abrogation)' in the literal sense: "the removal of one thing by another", and not in the sense used by the theoreticians of commentary; they termed *naskh* "the replacement of some of the characteristics of a particular *āyah* by another *āyah*" whether that was:

- by explaining [that it was] the coming to an end of the period of practice;
- by directing discussion from its most likely meaning to a less likely meaning;
- by explaining the fact that the restriction is conventional;
- or because of the particularisation of a general text;

- by explaining the difference between the text and what was treated literally as analogous to it;
- the removal of customs from the *jāhiliyyah;*
- the removal of the laws of a previous *sharī'ah.*

Number of Abrogated *Āyāt*

According to Earlier Scholars

According to these scholars, *naskh* was a large category as was the scope for intellect and the possibilities for differences of opinion. Thus, the number of abrogated *āyāt* amounted to five hundred in their view. A little more consideration, however, leads one to discover that they are countless. But as for the *āyāt* that are considered abrogated according to the definition of later scholars they do not amount to more than a few, especially when seen in the light of the explanation that we have adopted.

According to Later Scholars

Shaykh Jalāl ad-Dīn as-Suyūṭī, having studied the views of some scholars regarding what we have mentioned above, has presented an appropriately detailed explanation about them in his book *al-Itqān* and then he enumerated the abrogated *āyāt* according to the views of later scholars in accordance with the view of Shaykh [Abū Bakr] Ibn al-'Arabī,[183] who counted them as approximately twenty *āyāt*. However, with regards to most of those twenty *āyāt*, this needy man (*faqīr*) has a further difference of opinion. So we will take [Imām Jalāl ad-Dīn as-Suyūṭī's] sayings with our observations on them:

183 He is Abū Bakr Muḥammad ibn 'Abdullāh al-Ma'āfirī (468 AH/1076 CE – 543 AH/1148 CE), the famous Andalusian jurist of the Mālikī school. Amongst other works, he authored the popular legal Qur'ānic *tafsīr, Aḥkām al-Qur'ān.*

Sūrat al-Baqarah (2)

1. His ﷻ words:

كُتِبَ عَلَيْكُمْ إِذَا حَضَرَ أَحَدَكُمُ ٱلْمَوْتُ

"It is prescribed for you,
when death approaches one of you"[184]

are abrogated, some say by the *āyah* of inheritance,[185] while others have said that they are abrogated by the *ḥadīth*:

لَا وَصِيَّةَ لِوَارِثٍ

"There is no bequest for an heir [since he has an obligatory fixed share]."[186]

Some have said that the Qur'ānic *āyah* is abrogated through scholarly consensus (*ijmā'*) as cited by Ibn al-'Arabī. I say that, on the contrary, this *āyah* is abrogated by the *āyah*:

يُوصِيكُمُ ٱللَّهُ فِىٓ أَوْلَٰدِكُمْ

"Allah instructs you regarding your children"[187]

As for the *ḥadīth*: لَا وَصِيَّةَ لِوَارِثٍ – "There is no bequest for an heir [since he has an obligatory fixed share]" – it only explains this abrogation.

2. It is said that the Qur'ānic *āyah*:

184 Qur'ān, Sūrat al-Baqarah 2:180.
185 Qur'ān, Sūrat an-Nisā' 4:11-12.
186 Al-Bukhārī, *al-Jāmi' aṣ-Ṣaḥīḥ*, *Kitāb al-Waṣāyā*, chapter 6, *ḥadīth* 2747; Abū Dāwūd, *as-Sunan*, *Kitāb al-Waṣāyā,* chapter *Mā Jā'a fi'l-Waṣiyyati li'l-Wārith*, *ḥadīth* 2870; also reported by at-Tirmidhī, *al-Jāmi' al-Kabīr*, *Kitāb al-Waṣāyā*, chapter *Mā Jā'a Lā Waṣiyyata li-Wārith*; *ḥadīth* 2120; etc.
187 Qur'ān, Sūrat an-Nisā' 4:11.

وَعَلَى ٱلَّذِينَ يُطِيقُونَهُۥ فِدْيَةٌ

"For those who are able to fast [but with difficulty], their fidyah"[188] is abrogated by the *āyah:*

فَمَن شَهِدَ مِنكُمُ ٱلشَّهْرَ فَلْيَصُمْهُ

"Any of you who are resident for the month should fast it."[189]

It is also said that this *āyah* is a decisive (*muḥkam*) *āyah*, and that the word لَا – "not" – is omitted but implicitly understood within it (i.e. "*For those who are [not] able to fast...*"). I say that there is another reason, and that is that the former *āyah*:

وَعَلَى ٱلَّذِينَ يُطِيقُونَ الطَّعَامَ فِدْيَةٌ

meaning that 'those people who are capable of feeding others, they are liable to provide the ransom, which is feeding a needy person' and so He ﷻ used the pronoun before mentioning [the noun] because it takes precedence in rank and He ﷻ put the pronoun here in the masculine gender because the ransom is referring to the food.[190] The food here indicates the *ṣadaqat al-fiṭr* (incumbent *ṣadaqah* paid on 'Īd al-Fiṭr). In this *āyah*, Allah ﷻ has mentioned *ṣadaqat al-fiṭr* after the command to fast [in the month of Ramaḍān] just as He gave the command to proclaim His greatness on the day of 'Īd [in the *āyah*: وَلِتُكَبِّرُوا۟ ٱللَّهَ عَلَىٰ مَا هَدَىٰكُمْ "*and proclaim Allah's greatness for the guidance He has given*

188 Qur'ān, Sūrat al-Baqarah 2:184.

189 Qur'ān, Sūrat al-Baqarah 2:185.

190 The word فِدْيَةٌ (ransom) is in the feminine gender whereas the word الطَّعَام (food) is masculine; its pronoun ought to be similar to it in gender, number, state, etc. and hence the use of the masculine pronoun هُ – which refers to a masculine noun, its antecedent.

you"[191] after the portion of the *āyah*: فَمَن شَهِدَ مِنكُمُ ٱلشَّهْرَ فَلْيَصُمْهُ *"Any of you who are resident for the month should fast it."*[192]].

3. His ﷻ words ﷻ:

أُحِلَّ لَكُمْ لَيْلَةَ ٱلصِّيَامِ ٱلرَّفَثُ إِلَىٰ نِسَآئِكُمْ

"On the night of the fast it is lawful for you to have sexual relations with your wives"[193]

have abrogated the *āyah*:

يَـٰٓأَيُّهَا ٱلَّذِينَ ءَامَنُوا۟ كُتِبَ عَلَيْكُمُ ٱلصِّيَامُ كَمَا كُتِبَ عَلَى ٱلَّذِينَ مِن قَبْلِكُمْ

"You who believe! fasting is prescribed for you, as it was prescribed for those before you"[194]

which ought necessarily to require conformity with the [practice of] previous nations for whom eating, drinking and conjugal relationships were forbidden at night after sleeping. Ibn al-'Arabī states this, and he has also mentioned that the former *āyah* abrogates the proscription of conjugal relationships which had previously been Sunnah. I say that the words:

كَمَا كُتِبَ

"As it was prescribed"

is striking a simile about the obligation of fasting and so there is no abrogation here. This is because it only changes their practice

191 Qur'ān, Sūrat al-Baqarah 2:185.
192 Qur'ān, Sūrat al-Baqarah 2:185.
193 Qur'ān, Sūrat al-Baqarah 2:187.
194 Qur'ān, Sūrat al-Baqarah 2:183.

prior to the promulgation of the *sharī'ah*. We find no evidence that the Prophet ﷺ had ever made that [abstinence from sexual relations at night during the fast] *sharī'ah* for them. If we accept that, then that was only by the Sunnah [and not Divine command].

4. His ﷻ words:

يَسْـَٔلُونَكَ عَنِ ٱلشَّهْرِ ٱلْحَرَامِ قِتَالٍ فِيهِ

"They will ask you about the Sacred Month and fighting in it"[195] are abrogated by the *āyah*:

وَقَـٰتِلُوا۟ ٱلْمُشْرِكِينَ كَآفَّةً كَمَا يُقَـٰتِلُونَكُمْ كَآفَّةً

"However, fight the idolators totally just as they fight you totally."[196]

The relevant narration regarding this abrogation is mentioned by Ibn Jarīr[197] on the authority of 'Aṭā' ibn Maysarah.[198]

I say that this *āyah* does not refer to the prohibition of fighting but rather to its permissibility, and it presents the reason but shows the obstacle. Thus, this *āyah* means 'though fighting a war during the Sacred Months is extremely serious, nevertheless, the mischief [of disbelief (*kufr*) and association of partners with Allah (*shirk*)] is worse, and hence, consequently it is permitted'. This meaning is evident from the context itself as it is not hidden.

195 Qur'ān, Sūrat al-Baqarah 2:217.

196 Qur'ān, Sūrat at-Tawbah 9:36.

197 He is Abū Ja'far Muḥammad ibn Jarīr aṭ-Ṭabarī (224 AH/838 CE – 310 AH/922 CE). He was one of the earliest historians and commentators of the Qur'ān. He authored *Tārīkh ar-Rusul wa'l-Mulūk* (The History of the Messengers and Kings) *also known as Tārīkh aṭ-Ṭabarī* in history, *Jāmi' al-Bayān fī Ta'wīl al-Qur'ān* (The Comprehensive Exposition in the Interpretation of the Qur'ān) in Qur'ānic *tafsīr*, and *Tahdhīb al-Āthār* (Collection of Reports) – a book of traditions that remained incomplete.

198 'Aṭā' ibn al-Maysarah (d. 134 AH/751 CE) was one of the Successors.

5. His ﷻ words:

وَالَّذِينَ يُتَوَفَّوْنَ مِنكُمْ وَيَذَرُونَ أَزْوَاجًا وَصِيَّةً لِّأَزْوَاجِهِم مَّتَاعًا إِلَى الْحَوْلِ

"Those of you who die leaving wives behind should make a bequest to their wives of maintenance for a year"[199]

are abrogated by the *āyah:*

أَرْبَعَةَ أَشْهُرٍ وَعَشْرًا

"four months and ten [nights]"[200]

and the abrogation of the bequest is by [the *āyāt* relating to] inheritance.

According to one group (of scholars), the command of '*suknā* – lodging (i.e. for the husband to make provision for his widow's lodging)' stands whereas another group believes it to be abrogated by the *ḥadīth* '*lā suknā* – there is no [obligation to provide] lodging...'[201]

I say that, as he said, this *āyah*, according to the majority of scholars, is abrogated. It is also possible to say that it is permitted or recommended for the dying person to make such a bequest, but the wife is not obliged to remain in that which he bequeathes;[202] this is the position of Ibn 'Abbās ؓ, and this orientation is the

199 Qur'ān, Sūrat al-Baqarah 2:240.

200 Qur'ān, Sūrat al-Baqarah 2:234.

201 Al-Bukhārī, *al-Jāmi' aṣ-Ṣaḥīḥ*, *Kitāb Tafsīr al-Qur'ān*, chapter 41, *ḥadīth* 4531.

202 It is important for the moribund husband to bequeath one year's maintenance money as well as shelter, but it is not necessary for the widow to remain in her deceased husband's house for up to that period of time. She only ought to remain therein for a maximum of four months and ten days. Thus, according to this interpretation, no *āyah* is abrogated.

apparent meaning of the *āyah*.

6. His ﷻ words:

وَإِن تُبْدُوا۟ مَا فِىٓ أَنفُسِكُمْ أَوْ تُخْفُوهُ يُحَاسِبْكُم بِهِ ٱللَّهُ ۖ

"Whether you divulge what is in yourselves or keep it hidden, Allah will still call you to account for it"[203]

are abrogated by the *āyah*:

لَا يُكَلِّفُ ٱللَّهُ نَفْسًا إِلَّا وُسْعَهَا

"Allah does not impose on any self any more than it can stand."[204]

I say that the latter *āyah* particularises the former; the former tells us that the intended [meaning] is "what is in yourselves of sincerity and hypocrisy" and not the inner dialogues of the self that no one has control over. That is because legal responsibility has been imposed only in areas of human capacity.

Sūrah Āl 'Imrān (3)

7. It is said that His ﷻ words:

ٱتَّقُوا۟ ٱللَّهَ حَقَّ تُقَاتِهِۦ

"(O you who believe) have taqwā[205] *of Allah with the taqwā due to Him"*[206]

are abrogated by the *āyah*:

203 Qur'ān, Sūrat al-Baqarah 2:284.

204 Qur'ān, Sūrat al-Baqarah 2:286.

205 *Taqwā* derives from *wiqāyah* – 'protection' and 'safeguarding'. It comprises avoidance of acts of disobedience and fulfilment of the acts of obedience, and contains the sense of fear of Allah.

206 Qur'ān, Sūrah Āl 'Imrān 3:102.

فَٱتَّقُواْ ٱللَّهَ مَا ٱسْتَطَعْتُمْ

"So have taqwā of Allah, as much as you are able to"[207]

or that it is not abrogated at all, but rather, it is a decisive (*muḥkam*) *āyah*. Apart from this one, there is no other *āyah* in Sūrah Āl 'Imrān about which abrogation may soundly be claimed.

I say that حَقَّ تُقَاتِهِۦ – *'with the taqwā due to Him'* – is with respect to association of partners with Allah and disbelief and those things that are related to one's creed, whereas مَا ٱسْتَطَعْتُمْ – *'as much as you are able to'* – refers to actions, i.e. one who cannot perform *wuḍū'* ought to perform *tayammum* (dry substitute ablution), and if he is unable to stand and pray he may pray seated. This is evident from the continuation of the *āyah*, which is:

وَلَا تَمُوتُنَّ إِلَّا وَأَنتُم مُّسْلِمُونَ

"and do not die except as Muslims."[208]

Sūrat an-Nisā' (4)

8. His ﷻ words:

وَٱلَّذِينَ عَقَدَتْ أَيْمَٰنُكُمْ فَـَٔاتُوهُمْ نَصِيبَهُمْ

"If you have a bond with people, give them their share"[209]

are abrogated by the *āyah*:

وَأُوْلُواْ ٱلْأَرْحَامِ بَعْضُهُمْ أَوْلَىٰ بِبَعْضٍ

"But blood relations are closer to one another"[210]

207 Qur'ān, Sūrat at-Taghābun 64:16.
208 Qur'ān, Sūrah Āl 'Imrān 3:102.
209 Qur'ān, Sūrat an-Nisā' 4:33.
210 Qur'ān, Sūrat al-Anfāl 8:75.

I say that the obvious meaning of this *āyah* is that 'inheritance is for the legal heirs (*mawālī*)[211] and good treatment and joining ties are for clients through contract (*mawlā al-muwālāh*)'.[212] Therefore, there is no abrogation here.

9. It is said that His ﷻ words:

$$\text{وَإِذَا حَضَرَ ٱلْقِسْمَةَ أُوْلُواْ ٱلْقُرْبَىٰ وَٱلْيَتَٰمَىٰ وَٱلْمَسَٰكِينُ فَٱرْزُقُوهُم مِّنْهُ وَقُولُواْ لَهُمْ قَوْلاً مَّعْرُوفاً}$$

"If other relatives or orphans or poor people attend the sharing-out, provide for them out of it, and speak to them correctly and courteously"[213]

are abrogated, and it is also said that they are not abrogated but the people are too relaxed in practising it.

I say: Ibn 'Abbās ؓ said, "This *āyah* is decisive (*muḥkam*) and the command is in the sense of it being recommended." This is the most obvious verdict on it.

10. His ﷻ words:

$$\text{وَٱلَّٰتِى يَأْتِينَ ٱلْفَٰحِشَةَ مِن نِّسَآئِكُمْ}$$

"If any of your women commit fornication"[214]
are abrogated by the *āyah* from [Sūrat] an-Nūr.[215]

---

211 *Mawālī* sing. *mawlā*: here refers to the close relatives who are legal heirs. Ed.
212 *Mawlā al-muwālāh* is the client who enters Islam at the hands of another man. The latter inherits from him and his tribe or kin pay any compensatory payments for injury he inflicts on a third party or homicide. This was common in the early days of Islam. Ed.
213 Qur'ān, Sūrat an-Nisā' 4:8.
214 Qur'ān, Sūrat an-Nisā' 4:15.
215 *"A woman and a man who commit fornication: flog both of them with one hundred lashes..."* Qur'ān, Sūrat an-Nūr 24:2.

I say that there is no abrogation here. On the contrary, it was deferred to a later time,[216] and when the time arrived the Prophet Muḥammad ﷺ explained the promised procedure.[217] Hence, there is no abrogation here.

Sūrat al-Mā'idah (5)

11. His ﷻ words:

وَلَا ٱلشَّهْرَ ٱلْحَرَامَ

"[do not profane the sacred rites of Allah] or the sacred months"[218] are abrogated by the granting of permission to fight during them.

I say that we do not find an abrogating [*āyah*] in the Qur'ān for it nor in the authentic Sunnah. However, it means that 'the fighting in armed conflicts that is generally *ḥarām* is even more abhorrent during the sacred month' as the Prophet ﷺ said during the [Farewell] *khuṭbah*, 'Your lives and your properties are sacred

216 *"...until death releases them or Allah ordains another procedure for their case."* Qur'ān, Sūrat an-Nisā' 4:15.

217 'Ubādah ibn aṣ-Ṣāmit ﷺ narrated that the Prophet ﷺ said: "Take from me! take from me! Allah has laid down a procedure for them (women): for a virgin (who commits fornication) with a bachelor there are one hundred lashes and banishment for a year, whereas for the married woman (who commits adultery) with a married man there are one hundred lashes (for them both) plus stoning." (Muslim, *al-Musnad aṣ-Ṣaḥīḥ*, *Kitāb al-Ḥudūd*, chapter of *Ḥadd az-Zinā*, *ḥadīth* 4414; also at-Tabrīzī, *Mishkāt al-Maṣābīḥ*, *Kitāb al-Ḥudūd*, chapter of *Taghayyur an-Nās*, *ḥadīth* 3558)

Bikr is here translated as 'virgin' in the case of a woman and 'bachelor' in the case of a man. In both cases it denotes someone who has not consummated a marriage. *Thayyib* is here translated as 'married woman' and 'married man' but denotes someone who is or has consummated a marriage whether or not they are still married. The judgement applies equally to men and women, but here refers only to women because it is the 'procedure' that was promised in the *āyah* *"...or [until] Allah ordains another procedure for their case."* Qur'ān, Sūrat an-Nisā' 4:15

218 Qur'ān, Sūrat al-Mā'idah 5:2.

to one another like the sanctity of this day of yours in this month of yours in this city of yours'.[219]

12. His ﷻ words:

فَإِن جَآءُوكَ فَٱحۡكُم بَيۡنَهُمۡ أَوۡ أَعۡرِضۡ عَنۡهُمۡ

"If they come to you, you can either judge between them or turn away from them"[220]

are abrogated by the *āyah*:

وَأَنِ ٱحۡكُم بَيۡنَهُم بِمَآ أَنزَلَ ٱللَّهُ

"Judge between them by what Allah has sent down"[221]

I say that this *āyah* means that 'if you were yourself to decide then do it in accordance with the law that Allah ﷻ has revealed, and do not follow their desires'. In brief, both choices are permitted to us:

i. if we want, we may allow the *dhimmīs* (non-Muslims living under Islamic governance) to raise legal disputes to their own leaders so that those leaders may decide according to their own [religious] laws;
ii. if we want, we may decide their legal disputes according to what Allah ﷻ revealed to us.

13. His ﷻ words:

أَوۡ ءَاخَرَانِ مِنۡ غَيۡرِكُمۡ

"or two men who are strangers to you"[222]

are abrogated by the *āyah*:

219 Al-Bukhārī, *al-Jāmiʿ aṣ-Ṣaḥīḥ*, *Kitāb al-Ḥajj*, chapter 133, *ḥadīth* 1741.
220 Qur'ān, Sūrat al-Mā'idah 5:42.
221 Qur'ān, Sūrat al-Mā'idah 5:49.
222 Qur'ān, Sūrat al-Mā'idah 5:106.

وَأَشْهِدُوا۟ ذَوَىْ عَدْلٍ مِّنكُمْ

"Call two upright men from among yourselves as witnesses."[223]

Imām Aḥmad[224] passed judgement in accordance with the apparent meaning of this *āyah* but according to the other Imāms this *āyah* means أَوْ ءَاخَرَانِ مِنْ غَيْرِ أَقَارِبِكُمْ – 'or two others who are not your relatives,' but who are from the rest of the Muslims.

Sūrat al-Anfāl (8)

14. His ﷻ words:

إِن يَكُن مِّنكُمْ عِشْرُونَ صَٰبِرُونَ يَغْلِبُوا۟ مِا۟ئَتَيْنِ

"If there are twenty of you who are steadfast, they will overcome two hundred"[225]

are abrogated by the *āyah* that follows it: [الْـَٔنَ خَفَّفَ ٱللَّهُ عَنكُمْ وَعَلِمَ أَنَّ فِيكُمْ ضَعْفًا فَإِن يَكُن مِّنكُم مِّاْئَةٌ صَابِرَةٌ يَغْلِبُوا مِاْئَتَيْنِ *"Now Allah has made it lighter on you, knowing there is weakness in you. If there are a hundred of you who are steadfast, they will overcome two hundred."*][226]

I say that it is, as is said, abrogated.

Sūrat al-Barā'ah (9)[227]

15. His ﷻ words:

ٱنفِرُوا۟ خِفَافًا وَثِقَالًا

223 Qur'ān, Sūrat aṭ-Ṭalāq 65:2.

224 He is Aḥmad ibn Muḥammad ibn Ḥanbal Abū 'Abdullāh ash-Shaybānī (164 AH/780 CE – 241 AH/855 CE). He was a scholar, a jurist, a theologian and a *ḥadīth* expert, and the founder of the Ḥanbalī school of law.

225 Qur'ān, Sūrat al-Anfāl 8:65.

226 Qur'ān, Sūrat al-Anfāl 8:66.

227 Sūrat al-Barā'ah is also known as Sūrat at-Tawbah.

"Go out to fight, lightly-armed or heavily-armed"[228]

are abrogated by the *āyāt* of legal excuse (from fighting), which are His ﷻ words:

لَّيْسَ عَلَى ٱلضُّعَفَآءِ...

"Nothing is held against the weak..."[229]

and:

لَّيْسَ عَلَى ٱلْأَعْمَىٰ حَرَجٌ...

"There is no constraint on the blind...."[230]

I say that 'خِفَافٌ (lightly-armed)' refers to the tools of military use (such as) mounts, men for service, and sufficient funds to provide for one. 'ثِقَالٌ (heavily-armed)' means with many servants and mounts, and thus there is no abrogation here, or we could say that abrogation is not specifically intended.

Sūrat an-Nūr (24)

16. His ﷻ words:

ٱلزَّانِى لَا يَنكِحُ إِلَّا زَانِيَةً

"A man who has fornicated may only marry a woman who has fornicated"[231]

are abrogated by the *āyah*:

وَأَنكِحُوا۟ ٱلْأَيَـٰمَىٰ مِنكُمْ...

228 Qur'ān, Sūrat al-Barā'ah 9:41.
229 Qur'ān, Sūrat al-Barā'ah 9:91-92.
230 Qur'ān, Sūrat al-Fatḥ 48:17.
231 Qur'ān, Sūrat an-Nūr 24:3.

"Marry off those among you who are unmarried"[232]

I say that Imām Aḥmad ibn Ḥanbal has applied the literal meaning of this *āyah*. Other scholars give it the following meaning: 'the one who commits major wrong actions is only equal in legal status to a fornicatress',[233] or 'it is not *recommended* for one to choose a fornicatress'.

In the *āyah*, the words حُرِّمَ ذَٰلِكَ عَلَى ٱلْمُؤْمِنِينَ – *"Doing such a thing is unlawful for the believers"* – indicate unlawful sexual intercourse (*zinā*) and association of partners with Allah, and so therefore abrogation does not apply. Moreover, the *āyah* وَأَنكِحُوا۟ ٱلْأَيَـٰمَىٰ – *"marry off those among you who are unmarried"* – is general (*'āmm*) and does not abrogate something that is specific (*khāṣṣ*).

17. His ﷻ words:

لِيَسْتَـْٔذِنكُمُ ٱلَّذِينَ مَلَكَتْ أَيْمَـٰنُكُمْ وَٱلَّذِينَ لَمْ يَبْلُغُوا۟ ٱلْحُلُمَ

"Those you own as slaves and those of you who have not yet reached puberty should ask your permission to enter"[234]

are said to be abrogated, and are also said not to be abrogated but people have taken a relaxed attitude in practising them.

I say that according to Ibn 'Abbās ﷺ they are not abrogated, and that is the most reliable verdict.

Sūrat al-Aḥzāb (33)

18. His ﷻ words:

لَّا يَحِلُّ لَكَ ٱلنِّسَآءُ مِنۢ بَعْدُ

"After that no other women are ḥalāl for you"[235]

232 Qur'ān, Sūrat an-Nūr 24:32.
233 Consideration of the compatibility of the couple in terms of social and economic status is a factor in marriage according to Ḥanafī *fiqh*. Ed.
234 Qur'ān, Sūrat an-Nūr 24:58.
235 Qur'ān, Sūrat al-Aḥzāb 33:52.

are abrogated by the *āyah*:

إِنَّآ أَحۡلَلۡنَا لَكَ أَزۡوَٰجَكَ

"We have made ḥalāl for you: your wives"[236]

I say that it is possible for the abrogating *āyah* to appear in recitation prior to the *āyah* that is abrogated, and this is the more obvious explanation to me (i.e. that they are abrogated).

Sūrat al-Mujādilah (58)

19. His ﷻ words:

يَٰٓأَيُّهَا ٱلَّذِينَ ءَامَنُوٓاْ إِذَا نَٰجَيۡتُمُ ٱلرَّسُولَ
فَقَدِّمُواْ بَيۡنَ يَدَيۡ نَجۡوَىٰكُمۡ صَدَقَةٗ

"You who believe! when you consult the Messenger privately, precede your private consultation by giving ṣadaqah"[237]

are abrogated by the *āyah* that follows it, i.e.:

ءَأَشۡفَقۡتُمۡ أَن تُقَدِّمُواْ بَيۡنَ يَدَيۡ نَجۡوَىٰكُمۡ صَدَقَٰتٖۚ
فَإِذۡ لَمۡ تَفۡعَلُواْ وَتَابَ ٱللَّهُ عَلَيۡكُمۡ...

"Are you afraid to give gifts of ṣadaqah before your private consultation? If you do not and Allah turns to you (in forgiveness)"[238]

I agree, this is [abrogated] as is said.

Sūrat al-Mumtaḥanah (60)

20. His ﷻ words:

236 Qur'ān, Sūrat al-Aḥzāb 33:50.
237 Qur'ān, Sūrat al-Mujādilah 58:12.
238 Qur'ān, Sūrat al-Mujādilah 58:13.

فَـَٔاتُواْ ٱلَّذِينَ ذَهَبَتْ أَزْوَٰجُهُم مِّثْلَ مَآ أَنفَقُواْ

"So repay to those whose wives have gone the dowry they paid out"[239]

are said to be:

i. abrogated by the *Āyah* of the Sword (*Āyat aṣ-Ṣayf*);[240]
ii. abrogated by the *Āyah* of Booty (*Āyat al-Ghanīmah*);[241]
iii. decisive (*muḥkam*) [i.e. not abrogated].

I say that it is more evident that this *āyah* is decisive (*muḥkam*), but this relates specifically to the time of having a peace treaty with the disbelievers and at times when they have military superiority.

Sūrat al-Muzzammil (73)

21. His ﷻ words:

قُمِ ٱلَّيْلَ إِلَّا قَلِيلاً

"Stay up at night, except a little"[242]

are abrogated by the last *āyah* of the same *sūrah*,[243] which are in turn abrogated by the prescription of the five daily prayers.[244]

I say that the claim of those *āyāt* being abrogated by the five daily prayers is unfounded. In fact, the beginning of the *sūrah*

239 Qur'ān, Sūrat al-Mumtaḥanah 60:11.

240 وَقَـٰتِلُواْ ٱلْمُشْرِكِينَ كَآفَّةً كَمَا يُقَـٰتِلُونَكُمْ كَآفَّةً – *"And fight the idolators totally just as they fight you totally."* Qur'ān, Sūrat at-Tawbah 9:36

241 وَٱعْلَمُوٓاْ أَنَّمَا غَنِمْتُم مِّن شَىْءٍ فَأَنَّ لِلَّهِ خُمُسَهُۥ وَلِلرَّسُولِ وَلِذِى ٱلْقُرْبَىٰ وَٱلْيَتَـٰمَىٰ وَٱلْمَسَـٰكِينِ وَٱبْنِ ٱلسَّبِيلِ – *"Know that when you take any booty a fifth of it belongs to Allah, and to the Messenger, and to close relatives, orphans, the very poor and travellers…"* Qur'ān, Sūrat al-Anfāl 8:41

242 Qur'ān, Sūrat al-Muzzammil 73:2.

243 فَٱقْرَءُواْ مَا تَيَسَّرَ مِنَ ٱلْقُرْءَانِ – *"Recite as much of the Qur'an as is easy for you."* Qur'ān, Sūrat al-Muzzammil 73:20

244 The five prayers are ordered by His ﷻ words at the very end of this last *āyah*: وَأَقِيمُواْ ٱلصَّلَوٰةَ وَءَاتُواْ ٱلزَّكَوٰةَ – *"And establish the ṣalāh and pay zakāh."* Qur'ān, Sūrat al-Muzzammil 73:20

emphasises the recommendation to pray at night, and the latter part abrogated the emphasis but retained the recommendation.

Jalāl ad-Dīn as-Suyūṭī said, in agreement with Ibn al-'Arabī:

> "These twenty-one *āyāt* are abrogated, with some differences of opinion about some of them. Claims about the abrogation of other *āyāt* are not sound. The correct view regarding the *āyāt* relating to seeking permission to enter (see no. 17)[245] and distribution of inheritance shares (see no. 9)[246] is that they are applicable and are not abrogated. This leaves us with nineteen abrogated *āyāt*. According to my research, abrogation is only necessary in five *āyāt*.[247]

245 Qur'ān, Sūrat an-Nūr 24:58.

246 Qur'ān, Sūrat an-Nisā' 4:8.

247 From the aforementioned twenty-one *āyāt*, the five that Shāh Waliyyullāh, may Allah be merciful to him, agrees to being abrogated are: 1. Sūrat al-Baqarah 2:180, 5. Sūrat al-Baqarah 2:240, 14. Sūrat al-Anfāl 8:65, 18. Sūrat al-Aḥzāb 33:52, and 19. Sūrat al-Mujādilah 58:12.

Chapter 3

The Circumstances of Revelation (*Asbāb an-Nuzūl*)

Another extremely difficult issue of Qur'ānic *tafsīr* is knowledge of the circumstances of particular revelations. The reason for its difficulty is the variation of technical terminologies between the earlier and the later scholars.

Meaning of the Expression 'It was Revealed About Such-and-Such' in the First Generations

What is apparent from reading the words of the Companions and the Successors carefully is that they did not employ the expression 'نَزَلَتْ فِي كَذَا – this *āyah* was revealed with regards to such-and-such' simply to explain an event that happened in [the Prophet Muḥammad's ﷺ] time and which was the cause for the revelation of an *āyah*, but rather:

1. They would sometimes say 'نَزَلَتْ فِي كَذَا – this *āyah* was revealed with regards to such-and-such' about something which an *āyah* confirmed that happened during his ﷺ era or even happened after him ﷺ and so they would say 'نَزَلَتْ فِي كَذَا – it was revealed about such-and-such'. In such a case, it is not necessary that all of the restrictions mentioned in the *āyah* are applicable, but rather it is enough to apply the principle judgement.

2. They may sometimes clarify questions which the Messenger of Allah ﷺ was asked, or something that took place during the era of the Prophet ﷺ, and he ﷺ would derive a judgement from the *āyah*, which he would recite to them in that connection and so they would say 'نَزَلَتْ فِي كَذَا – this *āyah* was revealed with regards to such-and-such', or 'فَأَنْزَلَ اللهُ تَعَالَى قَوْلَ كَذَا – and so Allah ﷻ revealed such-and-such a statement of His', or only 'فَنَزَلَتْ كَذَا – so it was revealed'. It is as if it were an allusion to his ﷺ deducing that ruling from the *āyah*, and its being cast into his blessed mind at that moment is also a kind of revelation and inspiration in his mind (*rūʿ*). It is why the use of the words 'فَأُنْزِلَتْ – and so it was revealed' are permitted in this respect. And even if someone expressed that as repetition of the revelation of a particular relevant *āyah* he would have permission for that.

The Narrations of Hadith Scholars That Have no Connection to the Circumstances of Revelation

Hadith scholars (*muḥaddithūn*) mention many things in reference to Qur'ānic *āyāt* that in reality are not of the category of the circumstances of revelation, such as:

- the Companions رضي الله عنهم would cite *āyāt* or use them as illustrations in their exchange of views; or
- his ﷺ recitation of an *āyah* as evidence in his noble speech;
- the narration of a *ḥadīth* that agrees with a Qur'ānic *āyah* in its main purpose; or
- which specifies the location of the revelation; or
- which specifies names [or nouns] mentioned in the *āyah* allusively; or
- which explains the method for the articulation of a particular word in the Noble Qur'ān; or
- which explains the virtues of Qur'ānic *sūrahs* and *āyāt*; or
- which explains the way that he ﷺ complied with one of the

commands of the Noble Qur'ān.

None of the above are, in reality, circumstances that occasioned the revelation of Qur'ānic *āyāt*, and hence, it is not a precondition that the commentator is required to know them all comprehensively.

The Precondition for the Commentator in the Area of the Circumstances of Revelation

In order for one to provide a *tafsīr* of the Noble Qur'ān, it is only stipulated for him to be acquainted with two things:

1. those stories to which the *āyāt* allude – for it is not easy to understand the indication of those *āyāt* without background knowledge;
2. those stories that particularise the general case and similar aspects in which the outward meaning of the *āyah* points towards something else – because it is impossible to know the true objective of the *āyāt* without them.

Stories of the Prophets Narrated by the People of the Book

At this point, it is essential to understand that the stories of the previous prophets are not mentioned so much in *ḥadīths*, so that the commentators of the Noble Qur'ān have taken all of their lengthy stories from the scholars of the People of the Book (*Ahl al-Kitāb*)[248] except for that which Allah willed. It has been narrated in *Ṣaḥīḥ al-Bukhārī* as an elevated (*marfū'*) report [attributed to the Prophet ﷺ]:[249] لَا تُصَدِّقُوا أَهْلَ الْكِتَابِ وَلَا تُكَذِّبُوهُمْ – "Neither confirm the

248 The People of the Book (*Ahl al-Kitāb*) are those who believe in the revelation of at least one of the books revealed by Allah ﷻ, as well as in a prophet sent by Allah ﷻ. Generally, they include Christians, Jews and Sabians.

249 An elevated report or *ḥadīth marfū'*, is a report that is ascribed to the Prophet Muḥammad ﷺ with an *isnād* (chain of narration) connecting back to him.

People of the Book nor deny them."[250]

Another Meaning of Their Saying 'It was Revealed About Such-and-such'

It is also important to know that the Companions and Successors would narrate insignificant stories to explain the various schools of those who associate partners with Allah and the Jews and their uncouth customs, in order that their beliefs and traditions would be clear. They would say 'نَزَلَت الآيَةُ فِي كَذَا – the *āyah* was revealed with regards to such-and-such', by which they intended to mean that 'such an *āyah* was revealed with regards to stories of this nature' whether it was those particular events or different events similar to them or close to them, intending to show that form not those stories in particular, but rather mentioning them because these were accurate forms of these universal matters. For that reason their sayings would appear to differ in many places, each one drawing the words to his own side. In fact, their purpose was one. Abū ad-Dardā' ﷺ[251] indicated this very point when he said, "No person can ever be a *faqīh*[252] until he has the capacity to draw

250 Al-Bukhārī, *al-Jāmi' aṣ-Ṣaḥīḥ, Kitāb Tafsīr al-Qur'ān*, chapter *Qūlū Āmannā Bi'llāhi* (Qur'ān, 2:136), *ḥadīth* 4485, 7362 and 7542. The *ḥadīth* has a number of different possibilities in translation: "Neither believe the People of the Book nor disbelieve them" and "Neither say that the People of the Book are telling the truth nor say that they are lying."

251 He is Abū ad-Dardā' 'Uwaymir ibn Mālik ibn Zayd ibn Qays al-Khazrajī al-Anṣārī ﷺ (d. 32 AH/652 CE). He became Muslim on the day of Badr. Among the Companions, he was known for his legal knowledge and *zuhd* (doing-without). He moved to Damascus where he passed away and where his tomb lies.

252 The *faqīh* is someone who has *fiqh*, literally 'understanding' of the *dīn*. This comprises understanding whether a matter is obligatory, recommended, permissible, disapproved or forbidden. The *fuqahā'* of the different madhhabs agree on these but sometimes use slightly different terms and add other sub-divisions. Ed.

multiple interpretations from a single *āyah* [of the Noble Qur'ān]."[253]

The Form of a Story Which has no Story

According to this method two scenarios are often mentioned in the Tremendous Qur'ān:

1. the scenario of joy, that describes some of the characteristics of felicity [in the *ākhirah (Hereafter)*], and
2. the scenario of grief, that describes some of the characteristics of wretchedness [in the *ākhirah*].

The purpose of that is to explain the judgements on those particular attributes and actions, not to show a specific person, as He ﷻ said:

وَوَصَّيْنَا ٱلْإِنسَٰنَ بِوَٰلِدَيْهِ إِحْسَٰنًا ۖ
حَمَلَتْهُ أُمُّهُۥ كُرْهًا وَوَضَعَتْهُ كُرْهًا

"We have instructed man to be good to his parents. His mother bore him with difficulty and with difficulty gave birth to him."[254]

Then, Allah ﷻ mentions two scenarios of felicity and

253 Imām Aḥmad ibn Ḥanbal narrates:
قَالَ أَبُو الدَّرْدَاءِ رَضِيَ اللَّهُ عَنْهُ : إِنَّكَ لَا تَفْقَهُ كُلَّ الْفِقْهِ حَتَّى تَرَى لِلْقُرْآنِ وُجُوهًا، وَإِنَّكَ لَا تَفْقَهُ كُلَّ الْفِقْهِ حَتَّى تَمْقُتَ النَّاسَ فِي جَنْبِ اللَّهِ، ثُمَّ تَرْجِعَ إِلَى نَفْسِكَ فَتَكُونَ لَهَا أَشَدَّ مَقْتًا مِنْكَ لِلنَّاسِ
Abū ad-Dardā' said, "You will never know *fiqh* entirely until you see different aspects of the Qur'ān. You will never know *fiqh* entirely until you hate people for the sake of Allah, and then you turn to your self and it is more hateful to you than people." (Aḥmad, *Kitāb az-Zuhd*)
Ma'mar ibn Rāshid narrates:
عَنْ أَبِي الدَّرْدَاءِ، قَالَ: لَا تَفْقَهُ كُلَّ الْفِقْهِ حَتَّى تَرَى لِلْقُرْآنِ وُجُوهًا كَثِيرَةً، وَلَنْ تَفْقَهَ كُلَّ الْفِقْهِ حَتَّى تَمْقُتَ النَّاسَ فِي ذَاتِ اللَّهِ، ثُمَّ تُقْبِلَ عَلَى نَفْسِكَ فَتَكُونَ لَهَا أَشَدَّ مَقْتًا مِنْ مَقْتِكَ النَّاسَ
Abū ad-Dardā' said, "You will never know *fiqh* entirely until you see many different aspects of the Qur'ān, and you will never know *fiqh* entirely until you hate people for the sake of Allah, and then you turn to your self and it is more hateful to you than people." (Ma'mar ibn Rāshid, *al-Jāmi'*)

254 Qur'ān, Sūrat al-Aḥqāf 46:15.

wretchedness [in the subsequent *āyāt*].[255]

Similar to this are His ﷻ words:

وَإِذَا قِيلَ لَهُم مَّاذَآ أَنزَلَ رَبُّكُمْ ۙ قَالُوٓا۟ أَسَـٰطِيرُ ٱلْأَوَّلِينَ

"When they are asked, 'What has your Lord sent down?' they say, 'Myths and legends of previous peoples.'"[256]

And His ﷻ words:

وَقِيلَ لِلَّذِينَ ٱتَّقَوْا۟ مَاذَآ أَنزَلَ رَبُّكُمْ ۚ قَالُوا۟ خَيْرًا

"When those who have taqwā of Allah are asked, 'What has your Lord sent down?' their reply is, 'Good!'"[257]

The following *āyāt* ought also to be interpreted in this way:

ضَرَبَ ٱللَّهُ مَثَلًا قَرْيَةً كَانَتْ ءَامِنَةً مُّطْمَئِنَّةً

"Allah makes an example of a city which was safe and at peace"[258] and His ﷻ words:

هُوَ ٱلَّذِى خَلَقَكُم مِّن نَّفْسٍ وَٰحِدَةٍ وَجَعَلَ مِنْهَا زَوْجَهَا
لِيَسْكُنَ إِلَيْهَا ۖ فَلَمَّا تَغَشَّىٰهَا

"It is He who created you from a single self and made from him his spouse so that he might find repose in her. Then when he covered her"[259] and His ﷻ words:

255 Qur'ān, Sūrat al-Aḥqāf 46:16-17.
256 Qur'ān, Sūrat an-Naḥl 16:24.
257 Qur'ān, Sūrat an-Naḥl 16:30.
258 Qur'ān, Sūrat an-Naḥl 16:112.
259 Qur'ān, Sūrat al-A'rāf 7:189.

قَدْ أَفْلَحَ الْمُؤْمِنُونَ، الَّذِينَ هُمْ فِي صَلَاتِهِمْ خَاشِعُونَ

"It is the believers who are successful:
those who are humble in their prayer"[260]

and His ﷻ words:

وَلَا تُطِعْ كُلَّ حَلَّافٍ مَهِينٍ

"But do not obey any vile swearer of oaths."[261]

It is not necessary in these for such characteristics specifically to be found abundantly in any individual, just as it is not necessary that the following *āyah*:

مَّثَلُ ٱلَّذِينَ يُنفِقُونَ أَمْوَٰلَهُمْ فِى سَبِيلِ ٱللَّهِ كَمَثَلِ حَبَّةٍ أَنۢبَتَتْ سَبْعَ سَنَابِلَ فِي كُلِّ سُنۢبُلَةٍ مِّاْئَةُ حَبَّةٍ

"The metaphor of those who spend their wealth in the Way of Allah
is that of a grain which produces seven ears;
in every ear there are a hundred grains"[262]

denotes the existence of any real seed of that nature, for the objective here is to conjure up an image of the multiplication of reward and nothing else. If any scenario was found that accorded with that, in all or most of its characteristics, it would have been understood to be in the sense of 'لُزُومُ مَا لَا يَلْزِمُ – adherence to that which is unnecessary'.[263]

260 Qur'ān, Sūrat al-Mu'minūn 23:1-2.
261 Qur'ān, Sūrat al-Qalam 68:10.
262 Qur'ān, Sūrat al-Baqarah 2:261.
263 In Arabic poetry, each verse ends on the same letter. لُزُومُ مَا لَا يَلْزِمُ in the context of poetry would consist of an extra rhyme in addition to the rhyme at the end of the line that strictly speaking did not have to be there. In these passages, there is no need for specific concrete instances

Sometimes They Would Assume a Question and Answer in *Tafsīr*

Sometimes, in the Qur'ān a doubt of obvious origin or a query that is easily understood is answered in order to elucidate a preceding statement, not because someone asked that question in particular or because that specific doubt occurred. Often, in determining that topic the Companions ﷺ would assume a query and would explain things in the form of question and answer. If one was to investigate more fully, then the statement (i.e. relevant *āyah* of the Noble Qur'ān) is single and carefully ordered and is not interpretable as being revealed one after another all at one time in a carefully structured manner, its particulars not being interpreted according to any principle.

They May Mean Being Brought Forward or Put Back in Rank not in Succession

The Companions ﷺ may also mention bringing something forward and putting it back, referring to bringing something forward and putting it back in rank not in sequence, as Ibn 'Umar[264] ﷺ said in reference to the *āyah*:

وَالَّذِينَ يَكْنِزُونَ الذَّهَبَ وَالْفِضَّةَ

"As for those who hoard up gold and silver"[265]

"This *āyah* was revealed prior to (the obligation to pay) *zakāh*. Then, after it was revealed, Allah ﷻ rendered it (*zakāh*) a purification of wealth." We know that Sūrat al-Barā'ah (9)[266] was

corresponding to the examples given, but if there are, it is an example of the *āyāt* adhering to what they do not need to adhere to, i.e. a concrete example. Ed.

264 He is 'Abdullāh ibn 'Umar ibn al-Khaṭṭāb ﷺ (9 BH/614 CE – 74 AH/693 CE), the Companion of the Prophet ﷺ and a major narrator of *ḥadīths*.

265 Qur'ān, Sūrat at-Tawbah 9:34.

266 This is also known as Sūrat at-Tawbah. It is the ninth *sūrah* of the

the last *sūrah* to be revealed,[267] and this *āyah* is a part of those

Qur'ān.

267 Abū Isḥāq said that he heard al-Barā' ibn 'Āzib 🙵 saying, "The last
     āyah revealed (in Qur'ān) is that pertaining to *kalālah* (someone who
     dies leaving no ancestors or descendants), and the last *sūrah* revealed is
     Sūrat al-Barā'ah (*i.e. at-Tawbah*). (Muslim, *al-Musnad aṣ-Ṣaḥīḥ, Kitāb al-
     Farā'iḍ, ḥadīth* 4153; al-Bukhārī, *al-Jāmi' aṣ-Ṣaḥīḥ, Kitāb Tafsīr al-Qur'ān,
     ḥadīth* 4654)
     Az-Zarkashī (745 AH/1344 CE – 794 AH/1391 CE) writes: There is a
     difference of opinion with regards to the last portion of Qur'ān to be
     revealed. According to Ibn 'Abbās 🙵 it was Sūrat an-Naṣr (110); according
     to 'Ā'ishah it was Sūrat al-Mā'idah (5), and it has also been said that it
     was Sūrat al-Baqarah 2:281. Sudayy said that the last to be revealed was
     Sūrat at-Tawbah 9:129. In *Ṣaḥīḥ al-Bukhārī*, the *Kitāb Tafsīr al-Qur'ān*,
     chapter *Sūrat al-Barā'ah, ḥadīth* 4654, according to the *ḥadīth* reported by
     al-Barā' ibn 'Āzib 🙵, the last *āyah* to be revealed was Sūrat an-Nisā' 4:176,
     and the last *sūrah* to be revealed was Sūrat al-Barā'ah (at-Tawbah) (9).
     Another narration tells us that the last *sūrah* to be revealed was the
     completing portion of Sūrat al-Barā'ah (9) and the last *āyah* to be revealed
     was the last *āyah* of Sūrat an-Nisā' (4).
     It has been reported in *Mustadrak al-Ḥākim* on the authority of Ubayy
     ibn Ka'b 🙵 who said, "The last *āyah* to be revealed during the era of the
     Messenger of Allah 🙵 was... (then he recited the last two *āyāt* of Sūrat
     al-Barā'ah (9).)."
     In his *Musnad*, Imām Aḥmad ibn Ḥanbal reports something similar.
     Some even said that Imām al-Bukhārī reported that the last *āyah* to be
     revealed was that of *ribā* (usury).
     Imām Muslim reported that the last full *sūrah* to be revealed was Sūrat
     an-Naṣr (110).
     In *al-Intiṣār*, al-Qāḍī Abū Bakr ibn al-'Arabī (468 AH/1076 CE – 543
     AH/1148 CE) said, "None of these statements have been elevated to the
     Prophet 🙵. It is possible that each respective narrator has resorted to
     deductive reasoning or an inclination of the mind. It is not something
     that is of the obligations of religion... . It is also possible that each one
     of these narrators has only conveyed the last statement they heard from
     the Messenger of Allah 🙵 the day he passed away, or a few moments
     before he became terminally ill, and someone else may have heard
     something after him, the former not knowing of it from the latter due
     to the distance between them, and the Qur'ānic revelation coming after

that were last revealed, whereas the obligation to pay *zakāh* was made many years prior to that. Nevertheless, Ibn 'Umar ⬥ meant to say that as far as the rank is concerned, the summary has priority in rank to the elaboration.

TWO PRECONDITIONS FOR THE COMMENTATOR

In short, the preconditions for a commentator [of the Noble Qur'ān] are no more than these two:

1. Knowledge of the military expeditions etc. whose particulars are indicated in *āyāt* [of the Noble Qur'ān], for as long as one has [insufficient] knowledge of these stories it is impossible to understand the reality of [those *āyāt*];

2. Knowledge of the benefits of certain restrictions and similarly the reasons behind the strictness in certain places, the knowledge of which depends on the circumstances of revelation.

This last topic [of the preconditions for commentary] in reality belongs to the arts of resolving apparent contradictions (*fann at-tawjīh*). The meaning of *tawjīh* is 'to explain the intent of speech'. The upshot of this word (i.e. the definition of *tawjīh*) is that there may be an apparent ambiguity in an *āyah* either due to the improbability of the scenario that is the sense of the *āyah* or the mutual contradiction of two *āyāt*, and the beginner finds it difficult to understand the sense of the given *āyah* in his mind, or he finds it difficult to understand the benefit of a restriction. When the commentator resolves these difficulties, it is called '*tawjīh*'.

For example:

> his departure (from the Prophet ﷺ). There also remains the possibility that the last *āyāt* that the Messenger of Allah ﷺ recited may have been revealed together with other *āyāt*, and he ﷺ may have given the orders for them to be written down after the writing down of those *āyāt* that were revealed at the end, which caused the narrator to believe them to be the last revealed, respectively. (Az-Zarkashī, *al-Burhān fī 'Ulūm al-Qur'ān*, 4 volumes, Vol. 1, pp.209-210)

1. As in the *āyah*:

يَا أُخْتَ هَارُونَ

"Sister of Hārūn (Aaron)"[268]

they asked how it could be possible for Hārūn ﷺ to be the brother of Maryam عليها السلام when there was a huge time gap[269] between Mūsā ﷺ and 'Īsā ﷺ. The questioner had assumed that this Hārūn was Hārūn the very brother of Mūsā ﷺ. He ﷺ responded by saying that Banī Isrā'īl (Israelites) would take the names of their right-acting predecessors.[270]

2. They asked how people would walk on their faces on the Day of Judgement, to which he ﷺ replied:

إِنَّ الَّذِي أَمْشَاهُ فِي الدُّنْيَا عَلَى رِجْلَيْهِ لَقَادِرٌ أَنْ يُمْشِيَهُ عَلَى وَجْهِهِ

"He Who made him walk on his feet in this world is definitely able to make him crawl upon his face (on the Day of Rising)."[271]

3. They asked Ibn 'Abbās ﷺ about reconciling the following two *āyāt*:

فَإِذَا نُفِخَ فِي ٱلصُّورِ فَلَآ أَنسَابَ بَيْنَهُمْ يَوْمَئِذٍ وَلَا يَتَسَآءَلُونَ

268 Qur'ān, Sūrah Maryam 19:28.

269 Between the 'Imrān – father of Mūsā ﷺ and the 'Imrān – father of Maryam, was a gap of 1,800 years. (Aṣ-Ṣāwī, *Ḥāshiyat aṣ-Ṣāwī 'alā Tafsīr al-Jalālayn*, 4 volumes, Vol.1, p.138, Introduction to Sūrah Āl 'Imrān (3))

270 At-Tirmidhī, *al-Jāmi' al-Kabīr*, *Tafsīr al-Qur'ān 'an Rasūl Allāh* ﷺ, chapter *Min Sūrah Maryam*, *ḥadīth* 3155.

271 Al-Bukhārī, *al-Jāmi' aṣ-Ṣaḥīḥ*, *Kitāb Tafsīr al-Qur'ān*, *ḥadīth* 4760; *Kitāb ar-Riqāq*, *ḥadīth* 6523; Muslim, *al-Musnad aṣ-Ṣaḥīḥ*, *Kitāb Ṣifāt al-Munāfiqīn*, *ḥadīth* 7087.

"Then when the Trumpet is blown, that Day there will be no family ties between them; they will not be able to question one another"[272] and:

وَأَقْبَلَ بَعْضُهُمْ عَلَىٰ بَعْضٍ يَتَسَآءَلُونَ

"They will confront each other, questioning one another."[273]

He ﷺ replied that they will not question each other (i.e. in reference to the former *āyah*) on the Day of *Ḥashr* (the Gathering),[274] but will question each other (i.e. the latter *āyah*) after their admittance into the Garden.

4. They asked 'Ā'ishah saying, "If *sa'y* (the rite of hastening) between Ṣafā and Marwah [in the city of Makkah] is incumbent (*wājib*) why does Allah, exalted is He, say:

فَلَا جُنَاحَ عَلَيْهِ أَن يَطَّوَّفَ بِهِمَا

"[one] incurs no wrong in going back and forth between them"[275]?

She replied that some people had avoided it and abstained from it and for that reason Allah, exalted is He, had said, *"[one] incurs no wrong."*[276]

5. 'Umar [ibn al-Khaṭṭāb][277] ؓ once asked the Prophet

272 Qur'ān, Sūrat al-Mu'minūn 23:101.
273 Qur'ān, Sūrat aṣ-Ṣāffāt 37:27.
274 The gathering of mankind on the Day of Judgement.
275 Qur'ān, Sūrat al-Baqarah 2:158.
276 It had become a pagan custom to walk between the two mountains, Ṣafā and Marwah, and the advent of Islam caused the Muslims to avoid that ritual in apprehension of a wrong action being committed, until the revelation of this *āyah*. (Ibn al-'Arabī (468 AH/1076 CE – 543 AH/1148 CE), *Aḥkām al-Qur'ān, 4 volumes, Beirut, 1424 AH / 2003 CE, Vol.1, p.69, commentary on Sūrat al-Baqarah* (*2:158*))
277 He is 'Umar ibn al-Khaṭṭāb ibn Nufayl ؓ (38 BH / 586 CE – 23 AH / 644 CE), the second *khalīfah* after the Prophet ﷺ. He is known as al-

Muḥammad ﷺ the meanings of the restriction إِنْ خِفْتُمْ – *"if you fear."*[278] He ﷺ replied:

صَدَقَةٌ تَصَدَّقَ اللَّهُ بِهَا عَلَيْكُمْ فَاقْبَلُوا صَدَقَتَهُ

"It is a *ṣadaqah* that Allah ﷻ has bestowed upon you, so accept His *ṣadaqah*"[279]

i.e. the generous are not constricted in their generosity, and likewise, Allah ﷻ has not stated this restriction in order to impose a constriction, but rather it is conventional.[280]

There are many similar examples of explaining the intent of speech but our aim is only to draw attention to its intended meaning.

I think it would be apt to mention in Part Five[281] that which al-Bukhārī, at-Tirmidhī[282] and al-Ḥākim[283] have reported in

Fārūq (the one who discriminated between truth and falsehood).

278 In the *āyah*: وَإِذَا ضَرَبْتُمْ فِي الْأَرْضِ فَلَيْسَ عَلَيْكُمْ جُنَاحٌ أَنْ تَقْصُرُوا مِنَ الصَّلَاةِ إِنْ خِفْتُمْ أَنْ يَفْتِنَكُمُ الَّذِينَ كَفَرُوا – *"When you are travelling in the land, there is nothing wrong in your shortening your prayer if you fear that those who disbelieve may harass you."* (Qur'ān, Sūrat an-Nisā' 4:101)

279 Muslim, *al-Musnad aṣ-Ṣaḥīḥ*, *Kitāb Ṣalāt al-Musāfirīn*, *ḥadīth* 1573.

280 It is a restriction linguistically but not in reality. Ed.

281 Part Five is not included in this translation. It is *al-Fatḥ al-Khabīr bi Mā Lā Budda min Ḥifẓi-hī fī 'Ilm at-Tafsīr* (an explanation of the intricate and difficult words used in the Noble Qur'ān).

282 He is Abū 'Īsā Muḥammad ibn 'Īsā ibn Sawrah ibn Mūsā ibn aḍ-Ḍaḥḥāk as-Sulamī at-Tirmidhī (209 AH/824 CE – 279 AH/892 CE). He compiled the famous *ḥadīth* collection *al-Jāmi' al-Kabīr*, also known as *Sunan at-Tirmidhī*, which is one of the six major and most authentic compilations of prophetic traditions.

283 He is Abū 'Abdullāh Muḥammad ibn 'Abdullāh al-Ḥākim an-Nīshābūrī (321 AH/933 CE – 403 AH/1012 CE). He authored many books, of which the most notable is his *ḥadīth* compilation *al-Mustadrak 'ala'ṣ-Ṣaḥīḥayn* (in the year 393 AH/1002 CE). Of his students, the most well-known is Abū Bakr Aḥmad ibn Ḥusayn ibn 'Alī ibn Mūsā al-Khosrojerdī al-

their [collections in the chapters of] Qur'ānic *tafsīr* about the circumstances of the revelation and elucidation of the meanings for problematic passages using narrations with sound chains leading back to the Companions ﷺ or to the Messenger of Allah ﷺ along with revision of that material and abridgement. This will benefit us in two ways:

1. Being able to produce this amount of narrations is unavoidable for the commentator, just as memorisation of the amount we have presented in explanation of rare [or unusual] words in the Qur'ān (*Gharā'ib al-Qur'ān*) is unavoidable;
2. So that it may be understood that most of that which is narrated of the causes behind revelations has nothing to do with understanding the meanings of the noble *āyāt* except for the few stories mentioned in the aforementioned three Qur'ānic commentaries[284] which are the most authentic according to *ḥadīth* experts.

The over-enthusiasm of Muḥammad ibn Isḥāq,[285] al-Wāqidī[286] and al-Kalbī[287] and what they have mentioned in presenting a story behind every Qur'ānic *āyah*, *ḥadīth* experts deem most of

Bayhaqī (384 AH/994 CE – 458 AH/1066 CE).

284 Though the collections of al-Bukhārī, at-Tirmidhī and al-Ḥākim are of *ḥadīths*, those *ḥadīths* are the primary source of Qur'ānic *tafsīr*, and hence the author has referred to them as commentaries in their own right.

285 He is Muḥammad ibn Isḥāq ibn Yasār ibn Khiyār (84 AH/704 CE – 153 AH/770 CE). He was a Muslim historian and a hagiographer. He wrote a biography of the Prophet Muḥammad ﷺ entitled *Sīrat Rasūl Allāh – Biography of the Messenger of Allāh* ﷺ.

286 He is Abū 'Abdullāh Muḥammad ibn 'Umar ibn Wāqid al-Aslamī (130 AH/748 CE – 207 AH/822 CE). He was a Muslim historian who wrote *Kitāb at-Tārīkh wa'l-Maghāzī – Book of History and Campaigns.*

287 He is Abu'l-Mundhir Hishām ibn Muḥammad ibn as-Sā'ib ibn Bishr al-Kalbī (118 AH/737 CE – 204 AH/819 CE). He was a Muslim historian and is said to have authored one hundred and forty works, which include *Kitāb al-Aṣnām – The Book of Idols*. According to some, the name 'al-Kalbī – of the tribe of Kalb' refers to Abu'l-Mundhir's father.

them to be inauthentic and there are shortcomings in their chains of narration. It is a blatant mistake to make that a condition of Qur'ānic *tafsīr*. Whoever thinks that reflection on the Book of Allah is dependent on having fully memorised all of them has missed his share of the Book of Allah.

وَمَا تَوْفِيقِي إِلَّا بِاللَّهِ عَلَيْهِ تَوَكَّلْتُ وَهُوَ رَبُّ الْعَرْشِ الْعَظِيمِ

"My success is with Allah alone. I have put my trust in Him and He is the Lord of the Tremendous Throne."

Chapter 4

Remaining Aspects of this Subject

Elements that lead to Obscurity

1. Omission of some parts or particles of speech;
2. Exchanging one thing for another;
3. Bringing forward that which should rightfully be delayed and vice versa;
4. The use of allegories (*mutashābihāt*), allusions (*ta'rīḍāt*) and indirect expressions (*kināyāt*) – especially in presenting the intended meaning in a sensory form such as would ordinarily be one of the inherent qualities of that meaning, and the use of allusive metaphor (*isti'ārah makniyyah*[288]) and conceptual metaphor (*majāz 'aqlī*[289]).

Let us present some brief illustrations of the above-mentioned points in order to provide some further insight.

288 *Isti'ārah makniyyah*: allusive metaphor where the object of comparison (*mushabbah bihī*) is dropped and is alluded to by one of its necessary qualities.

289 *Majāz 'aqlī*: conceptual metaphor, or cognitive metaphor, refers to the understanding of one idea, or conceptual domain, in terms of another, for example, understanding quantity in terms of directionality (e.g. prices are rising). (Wikipedia: http://en.wikipedia.org/wiki/Metaphors_We_Live_By, accessed 2/7/2012)

1. Omission (*Ḥadhf*)

There are many types of omission, for example, the omission of the first or governing noun of a genitive construction (مُضَافٌ *muḍāf*),[290] the omission of the noun qualified by an adjective (مَوْصُوفٌ *mawṣūf*) and the omission of the related item (مُتَعَلَّق *muta'allaq*).

Examples of Omission

i. The first or governing noun of a genitive construction (*muḍāf*): وَلَكِنَّ الْبِرَّ مَنْ آمَنَ – *"Rather, true devoutness is whoever believes"*[291] i.e. وَلَكِنَّ الْبِرَّ بِرُّ مَنْ آمَنَ – *"Rather, true devoutness is the **devoutness** of whoever believes."*[292]

ii. The noun qualified by an adjective (*mawṣūf*): وَآتَيْنَا ثَمُودَ النَّاقَةَ مُبْصِرَةً [Literally] *"We gave Thamud the she-camel seeing"* [293] i.e. آيَةً مُبْصِرَةً *"a visible **Sign**."* Evidently this does not mean that the she-camel could see and was not blind.[294]

iii. The first or governing noun of a genitive construction (*muḍāf*): وَأُشْرِبُوا فِي قُلُوبِهِمُ الْعِجْلَ – *"They were made to drink the Calf into their hearts"*[295] i.e. حُبَّ الْعِجْلِ – *"**love** of the calf."*

iv. The first or governing noun of a genitive construction (*muḍāf*): أَقَتَلْتَ نَفْسًا زَكِيَّةً بِغَيْرِ نَفْسٍ – *"Have you killed a boy who has done no wrong, without it being for someone else?"*[296] i.e. بِغَيْرِ قَتْلِ

290 In the expression 'بَيْتُ الرَّجُلِ – the man's house', the first term *bayt* is the مُضَافٌ i.e. the first noun which governs in the genitive construction and the second noun *ar-rajuli* is the مُضَافٌ إِلَيْهِ i.e. the second term which is governed.

291 Qur'ān, Sūrat al-Baqarah 2:177.

292 The word بِرٌّ is used here as the subject of the sentence and the noun (*ism*) of لَكِنَّ, and مَنْ آمَنَ is its predicate, but it is interpreted that its predicate is the omitted word بِرٌّ which is the first term in genitive construction whose second term is مَنْ آمَنَ.

293 Qur'ān, Sūrat al-Isrā' 17:59.

294 The word مُبْصِرَةً means 'one that sees' and also 'manifest' – in this context, the word آيَةً is understood although omitted.

295 Qur'ān, Sūrat al-Baqarah 2:93.

296 Qur'ān, Sūrat al-Kahf 18:74.

نَفْس – *"without it being **for killing** someone else."*

v. Relative pronoun: مَن فِي ٱلسَّمَٰوَٰتِ وَٱلْأَرْضِ – *"Whoever is in the heavens and the earth,"*[297] i.e. مَن فِي ٱلسَّمَٰوَٰتِ وَمَن فِي ٱلْأَرْضِ – *"Whoever is in the heavens and **whoever is in** the earth,"* i.e. not a single entity that is in [both] the heavens and the earth.[298]

vi. The first or governing noun of a genitive construction (*muḍāf*): ضِعْفَ الْحَيَاةِ وَضِعْفَ الْمَمَاتِ – *"a double of life and a double of death,"*[299] i.e. ضِعْفَ عَذَابِ الْحَيَاةِ وَضِعْفَ عَذَابِ الْمَمَاتِ – *"a double **punishment** in life and a double **punishment** in death."*

vii. The first or governing noun of a genitive construction (*muḍāf*): وَاسْأَلِ الْقَرْيَةَ – *"Ask questions of the town,"*[300] i.e. وَاسْأَلْ أَهْلَ الْقَرْيَةِ – *"Ask questions of **the people of** the town."*

viii. بَدَّلُوا نِعْمَتَ اللَّهِ كُفْرًا – *"They exchanged Allah's blessing for ingratitude,"*[301] i.e. فَعَلُوا مَكَانَ شُكْرِ نِعْمَتِ اللَّهِ كُفْرًا – *"They exchanged **in place of gratitude for** Allah's blessings ingratitude."*

ix. The noun qualified by an adjective: يَهْدِي لِلَّتِي هِيَ أَقْوَمُ - *"Guides to the most upright,"*[302] i.e. يَهْدِي لِلْخَصْلَةِ الَّتِي هِيَ أَقْوَمُ – *"Guides to the **quality which is** most upright."*

x. The noun qualified by an adjective: بِالَّتِي هِيَ أَحْسَنُ – *"With that which is kindest,"*[303] i.e. بِالْخَصْلَةِ الَّتِي هِيَ أَحْسَنُ – *"With the **quality that is** kindest."*

xi. The noun qualified by an adjective: سَبَقَتْ لَهُمْ مِنَّا الْحُسْنَى – *"Those for whom the best from Us was pre-ordained,"*[304] i.e. سَبَقَتْ لَهُمْ مِنَّا الْكَلِمَةُ الْحُسْنَى أَوْ الْعِدَةُ الْحُسْنَى – *"Those for whom the best **word** or **the best promise** from Us was pre-ordained."*

297 Qur'ān, Sūrat ar-Ra'd 13:15.
298 This *āyah* refers to those created beings who worship Allah irrespective of whether they are in the heavens or in the earth.
299 Qur'ān, Sūrat al-Isrā' 17:75.
300 Qur'ān, Sūrah Yūsuf 12:82.
301 Qur'ān, Sūrah Ibrāhīm 14:28.
302 Qur'ān, Sūrat al-Isrā' 17:19.
303 Qur'ān, Sūrat an-Naḥl 16:125.
304 Qur'ān, Sūrat al-Anbiyā' 21:101.

xii. The first or governing noun of a genitive construction: عَلَى مُلْكِ سُلَيْمَانَ – *"In the kingdom of Sulaymān,"*[305] i.e. عَلَى عَهْدِ مُلْكِ سُلَيْمَانَ – *"At the **time of the** kingdom of Sulaymān."*

xiii. The first or governing noun of a genitive construction: وَعَدتَّنَا عَلَى رُسُلِكَ – *"Through Your Messengers,"*[306] i.e. عَلَى أَلْسِنَةِ رُسُلِكَ – *"Through **the tongues of** Your Messengers."*

xiv. A noun: إِنَّا أَنزَلْنَاهُ فِي لَيْلَةِ الْقَدْرِ – *"Truly We sent it down on the Night of Power,"*[307] i.e. إِنَّا أَنْزَلْنَا الْقُرْآنَ – *"Truly We sent **the Qur'ān** down"* even if it had not previously been mentioned.

xv. A noun: حَتَّى تَوَارَتْ بِالْحِجَابِ – *"Until it disappeared behind the veil,"*[308] i.e. حَتَّى تَوَارَتِ الشَّمْسُ بِالْحِجَابِ – *"Until **the sun** disappeared behind the veil* (i.e. it set)."

xvi. A noun: وَمَا يُلَقَّاهَا – *"And none will obtain it,"*[309] i.e. وَمَا يُلَقَّا خَصْلَةَ الصَّبْرِ – *"And none will obtain **the quality of patience**."*

xvii. Relative Pronoun: وَعَبَدَ الطَّاغُوتَ if pronounced in the accusative case (*naṣb*) – *"And who worshipped false gods,"* i.e. جَعَلَ مِنْهُمْ مَنْ عَبَدَ الطَّاغُوتَ – *"And He made some of them **those** who worshipped false gods."*[310]

xviii. Genitive Preposition (*ḥarf al-jarr*): فَجَعَلَهُ نَسَبًا وَصِهْرًا – *"Then made him relations by blood and marriage,"*[311] i.e. فَجَعَلَ لَهُ نَسَبًا وَصِهْرًا – *"Then made **for him**."*[312]

xix. Genitive Preposition (*ḥarf al-jarr*): وَاخْتَارَ مُوسَى قَوْمَهُ – *"And Mūsā chose his people,"*[313] i.e. وَاخْتَارَ مُوسَى مِنْ قَوْمِهِ – *"And Mūsā ﷺ chose*

305 Qur'ān, Sūrat al-Baqarah 2:102.
306 Qur'ān, Sūrah Āl 'Imrān 3:194.
307 Qur'ān, Sūrat al-Qadr 97:1.
308 Qur'ān, Sūrat Ṣād 38:32.
309 Qur'ān, Sūrat Fuṣṣilat 41:35.
310 This example may also be considered the omission of a genitive preposition (*ḥarf al-jarr*).
311 Qur'ān, Sūrat al-Furqān 25:54.
312 This example may be considered the omission of a genitive preposition prior to the object (i.e. him).
313 Qur'ān, Sūrat al-A'rāf 7:155.

***out of** his people."*

xx. Noun or Genitive Preposition (*ḥarf al-jarr*): أَلَا إِنَّ عَادًا كَفَرُوا رَبَّهُمْ – *"Yes indeed! 'Ād rejected their Lord,"*[314] i.e. كَفَرُوا نِعْمَةَ رَبِّهِمْ أَوْ كَفَرُوا بِرَبِّهِمْ – *"Rejected **the favour of** their Lord, or they disbelieved **in** their Lord."*[315]

xxi. *Ḥarf* (Particle, Preposition, Conjunction, Interjection or Letter): تَفْتَأُ – *"You will cease to,"*[316] i.e. لَا تَفْتَأُ – *"You will **not ever** cease to."*[317]

xxii. Verb: مَا نَعْبُدُهُمْ إِلَّا لِيُقَرِّبُونَا إِلَى اللَّهِ زُلْفَى – *"We only worship them so that they may bring us nearer to Allah,"*[318] i.e. يَقُولُونَ مَا نَعْبُدُهُمْ – ***"They say,** 'We only worship them.'"*[319]

xxiii. Object of the verb: إِنَّ الَّذِينَ اتَّخَذُوا الْعِجْلَ – *"As for those who adopted the Calf,"*[320] i.e. إِنَّ الَّذِينَ اتَّخَذُوا الْعِجْلَ إِلَهًا – *"As for those who adopted the Calf **for a god.**"*[321]

xxiv. Part of Sentence: تَأْتُونَنَا عَنِ الْيَمِينِ – *"Come to us from the right side,"*[322] i.e. وَعَنِ الشِّمَالِ – ***"And from the left side."***[323]

xxv. Verb: فَظَلْتُمْ تَفَكَّهُونَ إِنَّا لَمُغْرَمُونَ – *"Then you would begin to lament, 'We are burdened with debt,'"*[324] i.e. تَقُولُونَ إِنَّا لَمُغْرَمُونَ – *"You **would say,** 'We are burdened with debt.'"*[325]

314 Qur'ān, Sūrat Hūd 11:60.

315 In this example, either the possessed/annexed noun 'نِعْمَة – favour' is omitted, or the genitive preposition 'the letter ب'.

316 Qur'ān, Sūrah Yūsuf 12:85.

317 In this example, the word 'لا – not' is omitted rendering the meaning the opposite of what is apparent. This expression would be correctly understood by native Arab speakers but can deceive those who learn the language.

318 Qur'ān, Sūrat az-Zumar 39:3.

319 In this example, the word 'يَقُولُونَ – they say' is omitted.

320 Qur'ān, Sūrat al-A'rāf 7:152.

321 This is an example of the omission of the object.

322 Qur'ān, Sūrat aṣ-Ṣāffāt 37:28.

323 This is an example of the omission of a conjoined word (and a conjunction).

324 Qur'ān, Sūrat al-Wāqi'ah 56:65-66.

325 This example is of the omission of the verb 'تَقُولُونَ – you say'.

xxvi. Adverb: وَلَوْ نَشَآءُ لَجَعَلْنَا مِنكُم مَّلَٰٓئِكَةً – *"And if We please, We could make of you angels,"*[326] i.e. بَدَلًا مِنكُم – *"**In place** of you."*[327]

xxvii. Verb: كَمَا أَخْرَجَكَ رَبُّكَ – *"Just as Your Lord caused you to go out,"*[328] i.e. امْضِ كَمَا أَخْرَجَكَ رَبُّكَ i.e. *"**Go out,** as your Lord caused you to go out."*

Omission of the Predicate of إِنَّ and the Main [Consequent] Clause of a Conditional Sentence, the Object of a Verb, the Subject of a Nominal Sentence and the Like Occur Very Often

One ought to know that the omission of the predicate (*khabar*) of إِنَّ, or of the main (consequent) clause (*jazā'*)[329] of the conditional clause (*sharṭ*)[330], the object of a verb, or the subject (*mubtada'*) of a nominal sentence, etc., when the subsequent word or phrase is suggestive of their omission, happens a great deal in the Noble Qur'ān.

xxviii. An object: فَلَوْ شَاءَ لَهَدَاكُمْ أَجْمَعِينَ – *"If He had willed He would have guided every one of you,"*[331] i.e. فَلَوْ شَاءَ هِدَايَتَكُمْ لَهَدَاكُمْ أَجْمَعِينَ – *"If He had willed **your guidance** He would have guided every one of you."*

xxix. Subject of a Nominal Sentence (*Mubtada'*): اَلْحَقُّ مِن رَّبِّكَ – *"The truth is from your Lord,"*[332] i.e. هَذَا الْحَقُّ مِن رَّبِّكَ – *"**This is** the truth from your Lord."*

xxx. Second Subject of a Verbal Sentence: لَا يَسْتَوِي مِنكُم مَنْ أَنْفَقَ مِنْ قَبْلِ الْفَتْحِ وَقَاتَلَ أُولَٰئِكَ أَعْظَمُ دَرَجَةً مِنَ الَّذِينَ أَنْفَقُوا مِنْ بَعْدُ وَقَاتَلُوا – *"Those of you who gave and fought before the Victory are not the same; they are higher in rank than those who gave and fought afterwards,"*[333] i.e. لَا يَسْتَوِي

326 Qur'ān, Sūrat az-Zukhruf 43:60.

327 This is an example of the omission of the adverbial term 'بَدَلًا – in place of'.

328 Qur'ān, Sūrat al-Anfāl 8:5.

329 Known in Greek as the *apodosis*.

330 Known in Greek as the *protasis*.

331 Qur'ān, Sūrat al-An'ām 6:149.

332 Qur'ān, Sūrat al-Baqarah 2:147.

333 Qur'ān, Sūrat al-Ḥadīd 57:10.

مِنكُمْ مَنْ أَنْفَقَ مِنْ قَبْلِ الْفَتْحِ وَمَنْ أَنْفَقَ مِنْ بَعْدِ الْفَتْحِ – *"Those of you who gave and fought before the Victory are not the same* ***as those who gave and fought after the Victory.****"* The omission of the second subject [i.e. *'those who gave and spent afterwards'*] is indicated by the sentence that follows it, i.e. *'they are higher in rank than those who gave and fought afterwards.'*[334]

xxxi. The main (consequent) clause of a conditional clause: وَإِذَا قِيلَ لَهُمُ اتَّقُوا مَا بَيْنَ أَيْدِيكُمْ وَمَا خَلْفَكُمْ لَعَلَّكُمْ تُرْحَمُونَ، وَمَا تَأْتِيهِمْ مِنْ آيَةٍ مِنْ آيَاتِ رَبِّهِمْ إِلَّا كَانُوا عَنْهَا مُعْرِضِينَ – *"When they are told, 'Have taqwā of what is before you and behind you so that hopefully you will have mercy shown to you.' Not one of your Lord's Signs comes to them without their turning away from it."*[335] i.e. وَإِذَا قِيلَ لَهُمُ اتَّقُوا مَا بَيْنَ أَيْدِيكُمْ وَمَا خَلْفَكُمْ أَعْرَضُوا – *"When they are told, 'Have taqwā of what is before you and behind you,* ***they turn away.****"*[336]

There is No Need to Investigate the Word that Governs the Word 'When (إِذْ)'

One must also note that in His ﷻ words, for example: وَإِذْ قَالَ رَبُّكَ لِلْمَلَائِكَةِ – *"And when your Lord said to the angels,"*[337] and وَإِذْ قَالَ مُوسَى – *"And when Mūsā said,"*[338] the word 'إِذْ (when)' is an adverb (*ẓarf*) for a verb that is here transformed into a sense intending to cause fear and alarm, as when, for instance, someone mentions fearful circumstances or great events in a manner that enumerates them without structuring the sentences or the words being comprised under the compass of declension of the case endings. On the contrary he intends to mention those specific events in order to entrench their imagery in the minds of those who are

334 This is an example of the omission of a second subject – 'and those who spent after the victory' – of the verbal phrase 'they are not the same'.

335 Qur'ān, Sūrat Yā-Sīn 36:45-46.

336 In this example, the word 'أَعْرَضُوا – they turned away' is omitted, which the latter text indicates.

337 Qur'ān, Sūrat al-Baqarah 2:30.

338 Qur'ān, Sūrat al-Baqarah 2:54.

addressed, and thereby to cause fear to enter into their hearts. In such circumstances there is no need to investigate the word that governs [the word 'when']. And Allah ﷻ knows best.

***Omission of the genitive of 'That* (أَنَّ)'**

One ought to know that it is common practice in the Arabic language to omit the genitive preposition (*ḥarf al-jarr*) prior to the infinitive 'أَنْ [or أَنَّ] – that', in which case it takes the meaning of 'لِأَنْ – so that', 'بِأَنْ – because' or 'وَقْتَ أَنْ – at the time that'.

xxxii. The Main [Consequent] Clause of a Conditional Sentence Employing 'If' (*law*)[339]: One ought to know that the principle, for example, in His ﷻ words: وَلَوْ تَرَىٰ إِذِ الظَّالِمُونَ فِي غَمَرَاتِ الْمَوْتِ – *"If you could only see the wrongdoers in the throes of death,"*[340] and His ﷻ words: وَلَوْ يَرَى الَّذِينَ ظَلَمُوا إِذْ يَرَوْنَ الْعَذَابَ – *"If only those who do wrong could see at the time when they see the punishment,"*[341] is that the clause that is the consequence of the conditional clause[342] is omitted, but the Arabs use such a structure with the meaning of wonderment, and hence, there is no need to seek whatever might be omitted here. And Allah ﷻ knows best.

2. Replacement or Substitution (*Ibdāl*)

Ibdāl is an action of many types:

a. Substitution of a Verb for a Verb

He ﷻ may mention a verb in place of another for various reasons – the complete exposition of these reasons is not the purpose of this book – but here are a few examples:

i. أَهَٰذَا الَّذِي يَذْكُرُ آلِهَتَكُمْ – *"Is this the one who makes mention of your*

339 لَوْ is often used rhetorically or to introduce a hypothetical circumstance, sometimes one that is not possible.

340 Qur'ān, Sūrat al-An'ām 6:93.

341 Qur'ān, Sūrat al-Baqarah 2:165.

342 i.e. the apodosis of the protasis.

gods?"[343] i.e. يَسُبُّ آلِهَتَكُمْ – ***"Insults** your gods."* The original expression would have been أَهَذَا الَّذِي يَسُبُّ – *"Is this the one who **insults?"*** but He disliked to mention 'سَبّ – insult' and substituted 'ذِكْر – mention' for it. Many such phrases are used in common language. For example, it is said that 'the enemies of so-and-so have been afflicted with an illness', 'the slaves of Your Reverence honoured us by coming', or 'the slaves of Your Honour are aware of this introduction' meaning 'so-and-so became ill', 'His Grace so-and-so came' and 'His Highness so-and-so is aware', respectively.

ii. وَلَا هُم مِّنَّا يُصْحَبُونَ – *"They will have no companions from Us,"*[344] i.e. وَلَا هُم مِّنَّا يُنْصَرُونَ – *"They **will not be helped** by Us."* That is because help is inconceivable without gathering and companionship, and hence the use of the word 'يُصْحَبُونَ – they will have companions' as a substitute for the word 'يُنْصَرُوْنَ – they will be helped'.

iii. ثَقُلَتْ فِي ٱلسَّمَٰوَٰتِ وَٱلْأَرْضِ – *"It [the Hour] hangs heavy in the heavens and the earth,"*[345] i.e. خَفِيَتْ – *"It is **concealed**,"* because when the knowledge of something is hidden it is burdensome to those in the heavens and the earth.

iv. فَإِنْ طِبْنَ لَكُمْ عَنْ شَيْءٍ مِنْهُ نَفْسًا – *"But if they are happy to give you some of it,"*[346] i.e. فَإِنْ عَفَوْنَ لَكُمْ عَنْ شَيْءٍ مِنْ طَيِّبَةِ أَنْفُسِهِنَّ – *"But if **they forgive you something from the goodness of their selves.**"*[347]

b. Substitution of a Noun for a Noun

Sometimes, He ﷻ mentions a noun in place of another:

v. فَظَلَّتْ أَعْنَاقُهُمْ لَهَا خَاضِعِينَ – *"Before which their heads would be bowed low in*

343 Qur'ān, Sūrat al-Anbiyā' 21:36.
344 Qur'ān, Sūrat al-Anbiyā' 21:43.
345 Qur'ān, Sūrat al-A'rāf 7:187.
346 Qur'ān, Sūrat an-Nisā' 4:4.
347 In this example, 'عَفَوْنَ – they have forgiven' has been substituted by 'طِبْنَ – they were pleased', for it refers to such forgiveness that has been given out of good will.

subjection,"[348] i.e. خَاضِعَةً. [The meaning remains the same.][349]

.iv وَكَانَتْ مِنَ الْقَانِتِينَ – *"And she was one of the obedient,"*[350] i.e مِنَ الْقَانِتَاتِ – *"One of the obedient* ***women.****"*[351]

vii. وَمَا لَهُمْ مِنْ نَاصِرِينَ – *"They will have no helpers,"*[352] i.e. مِنْ نَاصِرٍ – ***"no helper."***[353]

viii. فَمَا مِنْكُمْ مِنْ أَحَدٍ عَنْهُ حَاجِزِينَ – *"And not one of you could have protected him,"*[354] i.e. حَاجِزًا. [The meaning remains the same.][355]

ix. وَالْعَصْرِ، إِنَّ الإِنْسَانَ لَفِي خُسْرٍ – *"By the Late Afternoon, truly man is in loss,"*[356] i.e. ***"The individuals of the sons of Ādam*** *are in loss."* The word is in the singular because it is a generic noun (*ismal-jins*).[357]

x. يَا أَيُّهَا الإِنْسَانُ إِنَّكَ كَادِحٌ إِلَى رَبِّكَ كَدْحًا – *"O Man! You are toiling laboriously towards your Lord,"*[358] meaning ***"O Children of Ādam,"*** and the singular has been used here as a singular because it is a generic noun.

348 Qur'ān, Sūrat ash-Shu'arā' 26:4.

349 The word خَاضِعِينَ is a sound masculine plural. It is used in place of the more grammatically usual broken plural خَاضِعَةً which is feminine singular.

350 Qur'ān, Sūrat at-Taḥrīm 66:12.

351 The word الْقَانِتِينَ is a sound masculine plural. It is used in place of the more grammatically usual sound feminine plural الْقَانِتَات. The sound masculine plural, however, encompasses any number of men or of men and women, whereas the sound feminine plural only comprises women.

352 Qur'ān, Sūrah Āl 'Imrān 3:22.

353 The word نَاصِرِينَ is a sound masculine plural. It is used in place of the more grammatically usual masculine singular نَاصِرٍ.

354 Qur'ān, Sūrat al-Ḥāqqah 69:47.

355 The word حَاجِزِينَ is a sound masculine plural. It is used in place of the more grammatically usual masculine singular حَاجِزًا.

356 Qur'ān, Sūrat al-'Asr 103:1-2.

357 The *ism al-jins* 'generic noun' is a singular noun that designates a species or class. Similarly in English, as well as meaning a single male, man also designates the human race, the human species, *Homo sapiens*, humankind, humanity, human beings, humans, people, mankind.

358 Qur'ān, Sūrat al-Inshiqāq 84:6.

xi. وَحَمَلَهَا الْإِنْسَانُ – *"But man took it on,"*[359] i.e. *"The **individual humans** took it on."*

xii. كَذَّبَتْ قَوْمُ نُوحٍ الْمُرْسَلِينَ – *"The people of Nūḥ rejected the Messengers,"*[360] i.e. ***"They rejected Nūḥ alone."***[361]

xiii. إِنَّا فَتَحْنَا لَكَ – *"Truly We have granted you,"*[362] i.e. إِنِّي فَتَحْتُ لَكَ – ***"Truly I have granted you."***[363]

xiv. إِنَّا لَقَادِرُونَ – *"We have the power,"*[364] i.e. إِنِّي لَقَادِرٌ – ***"I have the power."***

xv. وَلَكِنَّ اللهَ يُسَلِّطُ رُسُلَهُ – *"But Allah gives power to His Messengers,"*[365] i.e. وَلَكِنَّ اللهَ يُسَلِّطُ مُحَمَّدًا – *"But Allah gives power to **Muḥammad** ﷺ"*[366]

xvi. الَّذِينَ قَالَ لَهُمُ النَّاسُ – *"Those to whom people said,"*[367] i.e. *'Those'* were 'Urwah ibn Mas'ūd ath-Thaqafī alone.[368,369]

xvii. فَأَذَاقَهَا اللهُ لِبَاسَ الْجُوعِ – *"So Allah made [the town]*[370] *taste the robes of hunger,"*[371] i.e. طَعْمَ الْجُوعِ – *"The **taste** of hunger."* 'Taste'

359 Qur'ān, Sūrat al-Aḥzāb 33:72.
360 Qur'ān, Sūrat ash-Shu'arā' 26:105.
361 All the messengers taught *tawḥīd*, and hence, to reject one messenger is akin to rejecting them all.
362 Qur'ān, Sūrat al-Fatḥ 48:1.
363 The pronoun *We* is used by Allah ﷻ for Himself in the Qur'ān as the royal 'We' and not as a plural.
364 Qur'ān, Sūrat al-Ma'ārij 70:40.
365 Qur'ān, Sūrat al-Ḥashr 59:6.
366 The context of this *āyah* indicates that 'رُسُلَهُ – His Messengers' means 'رَسُولَهُ – His Messenger', i.e. Muḥammad ﷺ.
367 Qur'ān, Sūrah Āl 'Imrān 3:173.
368 'Urwah ibn Mas'ūd ath-Thaqafī ؓ was a chief of Ṭā'if who was killed by his tribe whilst calling them to Islam. He is thus said to resemble 'Īsā ؑ. (Muslim, *al-Musnad aṣ-Ṣaḥīḥ*, *Kitāb al-Īmān*, *ḥadīth* 423)
369 The word 'هُم – whom' is an attached genitive masculine plural pronoun. However, here it refers to only one person, 'Urwah ibn Mas'ūd ath-Thaqafī ؓ according to al-Qasṭalānī (851 AH/1448 CE – 923 AH/1517 CE) in *Irshād as-Sārī*.
370 Allah ﷻ mentioned the town intending by that the townsfolk.
371 Qur'ān, Sūrat an-Naḥl 16:112.

has been substituted with 'robes' in order to clarify that hunger has effects such as human weakness and feebleness which encompasses the human body like robes do.

xviii. صِبْغَةَ اللهِ – *"The colouring of Allah,"*[372] i.e. دِينَ اللهِ – *"The **dīn** of Allah,"* which was substituted by the word 'صِبْغَة – colouring' in order to make it clear that it is like the colouring by which souls are coloured, or something similar to what the Christians say about the baptismal font.[373]

xix. وَطُورِ سِينِينَ – *"And Mount Sīnīn"*[374] i.e. وَطُورِ سِينَا – *"And Mount* **Sīnā (Sinai)."**

xx. سَلَامٌ عَلَى إِلْ يَاسِينَ – *"Peace be upon Ilyāsīn,"*[375] i.e. سَلَامٌ عَلَى إِلْيَاس – *"Peace be upon **Ilyās**."*

Both nouns [in xix and xx] are altered for the sake of the rhyme.

c. Substitution of One Preposition/Particle for Another

Sometimes, He ﷻ substitutes one preposition/particle for another:

xxi. فَلَمَّا تَجَلَّى رَبُّهُ لِلْجَبَلِ – *"But when His Lord manifested Himself to the mountain,"*[376] i.e. عَلَى الْجَبَلِ – "Upon *the mountain,"* just as He manifested Himself the first time upon the Bush (i.e. the BurningBush).[377]

xxii. هُمْ لَهَا سَابِقُونَ – *"They are the first to reach them,"*[378] i.e. سَابِقُونَ إِلَيْهَا – *"The first* towards *reaching them."*[379]

xxiii. لَا يَخَافُ لَدَيَّ الْمُرْسَلُونَ، إِلَّا مَنْ ظَلَمَ – *"In My Presence the Messengers have*

372 Qur'ān, Sūrat al-Baqarah 2:138.
373 i.e. the Christian rite of baptism which marks the entrance into the Christian religion.
374 Qur'ān, Sūrat at-Tīn 95:2.
375 Qur'ān, Sūrat aṣ-Ṣāffāt 37:130.
376 Qur'ān, Sūrat al-A'rāf 7:143.
377 Qur'ān, Sūrat al-Qaṣaṣ 28:29-30.
378 Qur'ān, Sūrat al-Mu'minūn 23:61.
379 The word 'لَهَا – for/to' has been used to mean 'إِلَيْهَا – to/towards'; the genitive preposition 'ل – for/to' has been used in place of 'إِلَى – to/towards'.

no fear – except for one who did wrong"[380] i.e. لَكِن مَّنْ ظَلَمَ – ***"But,*** *one who did wrong,"* and so it is the inception of a new sentence.[381]

xxiv. لَأُصَلِّبَنَّكُمْ فِي جُذُوعِ النَّخْلِ – *"I will have you crucified in palm trunks,"*[382] i.e. عَلَى جُذُوعِ النَّخْلِ – ***"On*** *palm trunks."*[383]

xxv. أَمْ لَهُمْ سُلَّمٌ يَسْتَمِعُونَ فِيهِ – *"Or do they have a ladder in which they listen?"*[384] i.e. أَمْ لَهُمْ سُلَّمٌ يَسْتَمِعُونَ عَلَيه – "Upon *which they listen."*[385]

xxvi. السَّمَاءُ مُنفَطِرٌ بِهِ – *"[a day] By which heaven will be split apart?"*[386] i.e. مُنفَطِرٌ فِيهِ – *"[a day]* ***In which*** *heaven will be split apart."*[387]

xxvii. مُسْتَكْبِرِينَ بِهِۦ سَـٰمِرًا تَهْجُرُونَ – *"Arrogant towards it, talking arrant nonsense all night long,"*[388] i.e. عَنْهُ – *"Arrogant* ***about*** *it."*[389]

xxviii. أَخَذَتْهُ الْعِزَّةُ بِالْإِثْمِ – *"Pride seized him in wrongdoing,"*[390] i.e. الْعِزَّةُ حَمَلَتْهُ عَلَى الْإِثْمِ – *"Pride* ***carried him off to*** *wrongdoing."*[391]

380 Qur'ān, Sūrat an-Naml 27:10-11.

381 'إِلَّا – *illā*' in the sense of 'except' is an invalid meaning since the messengers are protected from doing major or minor wrong actions. Its usage as 'however/but' beginning a new clause is very common in Qur'ānic Arabic and the Arabic language in general. The complete *āyah* is: إِلَّا مَن ظَلَمَ ثُمَّ بَدَّلَ حُسْنًا بَعْدَ سُوٓءٍ فَإِنِّي غَفُورٌ رَّحِيمٌ – *"However, one who did wrong and then changed evil into good – then I am Ever-Forgiving, Most Merciful."* Qur'ān, Sūrat an-Naml 27:11.

382 Qur'ān, Sūrah Ṭā-Hā 20:71.

383 The genitive preposition 'فِي – in' is used in the place of the genitive preposition 'عَلَى – on'.

384 Qur'ān, Sūrat aṭ-Ṭūr 52:38.

385 Here also, the genitive preposition 'فِي – in' is used in the place of the genitive preposition 'عَلَى – on'.

386 Qur'ān, Sūrat al-Muzzammil 73:18.

387 The genitive preposition 'فِي – in' is replaced with the genitive preposition 'بَاء – by/with'.

388 Qur'ān, Sūrat al-Mu'minūn 23:67.

389 The genitive preposition 'بَاء – by/with' is used in the place of the genitive preposition 'عَنْ – about/regarding'.

390 Qur'ān, Sūrat al-Baqarah 2:206.

391 Here, the genitive preposition 'بَاء – by/with' is used in the place of the genitive preposition 'عَلَى – on/into'. Moreover, 'أَخَذَتْ – take' has the sense

xxix. فَاسْأَلْ بِهِ خَبِيرًا – *"Ask anyone who is informed about Him,"*[392] i.e. فَاسْأَلْ عَنْهُ – *"Ask* ***about*** *Him [anyone who is informed]."*[393]

xxx. لَا تَأْكُلُوا أَمْوَالَهُمْ إِلَى أَمْوَالِكُمْ – *"Do not assimilate their property into your own,"*[394] i.e. مَعَ أَمْوَالِكُمْ – ***"Along with*** *your own."*

xxxi. إِلَى الْمَرَافِقِ – *"To the elbows,"*[395] i.e. مَعَ الْمَرَافِقِ – ***"Along with*** *the elbows."*[396]

xxxii. يَشْرَبُ بِهَا عِبَادُ اللهِ – *"By which Allah's slaves will drink,"*[397] i.e. يَشْرَبُ مِنْهَا عِبَادُ اللهِ – ***"From*** *which Allah's slaves will drink."*[398]

xxxiii. وَمَا قَدَرُوا اللَّهَ حَقَّ قَدْرِهِ إِذْ قَالُوا مَا أَنْزَلَ اللهُ عَلَى بَشَرٍ مِنْ شَيْءٍ – *"They do not measure Allah with His true measure when they say, 'Allah would not send down anything to a mere human being,'"*[399] i.e. أَنْ قَالُوا – ***"That*** *they say."*[400]

d. Substitution of One Sentence for Another

Sometimes, one clause is substituted for another, for example, if one clause indicates the implied outcome of another clause and the reason for its existence, then in such a case, the former replaces the latter, such as:

xxxiv. وَإِنْ تُخَالِطُوهُمْ فَإِخْوَانُكُمْ – *"If you mix [your property] with theirs, they are your brothers,"*[401] i.e. *"If you mix your property with theirs,* ***then there is no harm in that*** because *they are your brothers."* The way with brothers is that they mix their properties.

of 'حَمَلَتْ – carry'.

392 Qur'ān, Sūrat al-Furqān 25:59.

393 The genitive preposition 'بَاء – by/with' is used in the place of the genitive preposition 'عَنْ – about/regarding'.

394 Qur'ān, Sūrat an-Nisā' 4:2.

395 Qur'ān, Sūrat al-Mā'idah 5:6.

396 Both examples (in xxx and xxxi) denote 'إِلَى – to' to mean 'مَعَ – along with'.

397 Qur'ān, Sūrat al-Dahr (*aka* Sūrat al-Insān) 76:6.

398 The genitive preposition 'بَاء – of' is used in the place of the genitive preposition 'مِنْ – from'.

399 Qur'ān, Sūrat al-An'ām 6:91.

400 Here, the conditional word 'إِذْ – since' is used in the place of 'أَنْ – that'.

401 Qur'ān, Sūrat al-Baqarah 2:220.

xxxv. لَمَثُوبَةٌ مِنْ عِنْدِ اللَّهِ خَيْرٌ – *"A reward from Allah is better,"*[402] i.e. ***"They would have found** a reward from Allah to be better."*

xxxvi. إِنْ يَسْرِقْ فَقَدْ سَرَقَ أَخٌ لَهُ مِنْ قَبْلُ – *"If he steals now, his brother stole before,"*[403] i.e. *"If he steals now **then that is no surprise*** for *his brother stole before."*

xxxvii. مَنْ كَانَ عَدُوًّا لِجِبْرِيلَ فَإِنَّهُ نَزَّلَهُ عَلَىٰ قَلْبِكَ بِإِذْنِ اللَّهِ – *"Anyone who is the enemy of Jibrīl, it was he who brought it down upon your heart, by Allah's authority,"*[404] i.e. *"Anyone who is the enemy of Jibrīl, **Allah is an enemy of his**, it was he who brought it down upon your heart, by His authority"* and thus, his enemy deserves the enmity of Allah. *"Allah is an enemy of his"* is omitted due to the following *āyah* [*Anyone who is the enemy of Allah and of His angels, and of His Messengers and of Jibrīl and Mīkā'īl, should know that Allah is the enemy of the unbelievers*], and replaced by *"It was he who brought it down upon your heart."*

e. Substitution of a Definite Noun for an Indefinite Noun

The original speech may require that it be indefinite[405] but He ﷻ varies it by prefixing *lām* (i.e. ال) and ascription of relationship (*iḍāfah*) and so the meaning remains in its original sense of indefiniteness.

xxxviii. وَقِيلِهِ يَا رَبِّ – *"And as for his words, 'My Lord,'"*[406] i.e. وَقِيلٍ لَهُ يَا رَبِّ – *"And as for words **of his**, 'My Lord,'"* which He substituted with 'وَقِيلِهِ – *And as for his words'* because it is more concise.

xxxix. حَقُّ الْيَقِينِ – *"The truth of certainty,"*[407] i.e. حَقٌّ يَقِينٌ – ***"Certain truth."*** It was rendered as a possessive (*iḍāfah*) for ease of pronunciation.

402 Qur'ān, Sūrat al-Baqarah 2:103.
403 Qur'ān, Sūrah Yūsuf 12:777.
404 Qur'ān, Sūrat al-Baqarah 2:97.
405 The indefinite noun is also known as the common noun.
406 Qur'ān, Sūrat az-Zukhruf 43:88.
407 Qur'ān, Sūrat al-Wāqi'ah 56:95.

f. Substitution of Masculine for Feminine, Singular for Plural, etc.

Sometimes, customary usage of natural speech may demand that the pronoun be made masculine or feminine, or singular but He ﷻ alters it from that natural customary usage and makes a feminine into a masculine or vice versa, or uses a plural in place of the singular in order to safeguard the meaning, such as:

xl. فَلَمَّا رَأَى الشَّمْسَ بَازِغَةً قَالَ هَٰذَا رَبِّي هَٰذَا أَكْبَرُ – *"Then when he saw the sun (fem.) come up he said, 'This (masc.) is my Lord! This is greater!'"*[408,409]

xli. مِنَ ٱلْقَوْمِ ٱلظَّٰلِمِينَ – *"From the wrongdoing people."*[410]

xlii. مَثَلُهُمْ كَمَثَلِ الَّذِي اسْتَوْقَدَ نَارًا فَلَمَّا أَضَاءَتْ مَا حَوْلَهُ ذَهَبَ اللَّهُ بِنُورِهِمْ – *"Their likeness is that of one who (sing.) lit a fire, and then when it has lit up all around him, Allah removes their (pl.) light."*[411,412]

g. Substitution of Singular for Dual

Sometimes, a singular is used in the place of a dual, for example:

xliii. إِلَّا أَنْ أَغْنَاهُمُ اللَّهُ وَرَسُولُهُ مِنْ فَضْلِهِ – *"That Allah and His Messenger had enriched them from His bounty."*[413]

xliv. إِنْ كُنْتُ عَلَىٰ بَيِّنَةٍ مِنْ رَبِّي وَآتَانِي رَحْمَةً مِنْ عِنْدِهِ فَعُمِّيَتْ عَلَيْكُمْ – *"If I were to have clear evidence from my Lord and He had given me a mercy direct from Him, but it has been made obscure to you."*[414] In

408 Qur'ān, Sūrat al-An'ām 6:78.

409 The Arabic word 'الشَّمْس – sun' is feminine, as is its predicate 'بَازِغَة – rising'. So the demonstrative pronoun 'هَٰذَا – this (masc.)' ought to have been 'هذه – this (fem.)'. Likewise with the explanatory sentence that follows it: 'هَٰذَا أَكْبَرُ – This is greater' – both words are masculine, though they are in explanation of 'الشَّمْس – the sun', which is feminine.

410 Qur'ān, Sūrat al-Mu'minūn 23:28. In this *āyah*, the plural 'ٱلظَّٰلِمِينَ – wrongdoers' has been used as an adjective for the singular 'ٱلْقَوْم – people'.

411 Qur'ān, Sūrat al-Baqarah 2:17.

412 In this *āyah*, the plural pronoun (in 'بِنُورِهِمْ – with their light') has been used instead of the singular pronoun. One would have expected 'بِنُورِهِ – with his light'.

413 Qur'ān, Sūrat at-Tawbah 9:74. 'مِنْ فَضْلِهِ – His favour' substitutes for 'مِنْ فَضْلِهِمَا – the favour of them both – Allah ﷻ and His Messenger ﷺ'.

414 Qur'ān, Sūrat Hūd 11:28.

this *āyah*, 'فَعُمِّيَتْ – *it has been made obscure*' was 'فَعُمِّيَتَا – ***both*** *[the clear evidence and the mercy] have been made obscure*'; the singular reference has been used because both are as a single thing. Likewise in the case with ٱللَّهُ وَرَسُولُهُ أَعْلَمُ – Allah ﷻ and His Messenger ﷺ know best.[415]

h. Substitution of an Independent Sentence for a Conditional Clause and a Main Consequent Clause, or an Oath and Its Complement

Sometimes, natural speech demands the conditional clause remain the conditional clause, and the consequent clause remain the consequent clause and the consequent clause of the oath remain in its original state, so He ﷻ varies them and makes that portion of the speech an independent clause, starting it afresh to give some structure to the meaning and He establishes something which will indicate it in some way, such as:

xlv. وَٱلنَّٰزِعَٰتِ غَرْقًا، وَٱلنَّٰشِطَٰتِ نَشْطًا، وَٱلسَّٰبِحَٰتِ سَبْحًا، فَٱلسَّٰبِقَٰتِ سَبْقًا، فَٱلْمُدَبِّرَٰتِ أَمْرًا، يَوْمَ تَرْجُفُ ٱلرَّاجِفَةُ – *"By those who pluck out harshly, and those who draw out gently, and those who glide serenely, and those who outrun easily, and those who direct affairs. On the Day the first blast shudders,"*[416] meaning that the Rising [from the dead] and the Gathering (on the Day of Judgement) are real, which His ﷻ words 'يَوْمَ تَرْجُفُ الرَّاجِفَة – *On the Day the first blast shudders*' indicate.

xlvi. وَٱلسَّمَآءِ ذَاتِ ٱلْبُرُوجِ، وَٱلْيَوْمِ ٱلْمَوْعُودِ، وَشَاهِدٍ وَمَشْهُودٍ، قُتِلَ أَصْحَٰبُ ٱلْأُخْدُودِ ، ٱلنَّارِ ذَاتِ ٱلْوَقُودِ *"By Heaven with its Houses of the Zodiac, and the Promised Day, and the witness and the witnessed, cursed be the Companions of the Pit – the fire well stocked with fuel,"*[417] meaning that the

415 Al-Bukhārī, *al-Jāmi' aṣ-Ṣaḥīḥ, Kitāb al-Īmān,* chapter *Adā' al-Khumus min al-Īmān, ḥadīth* 53; Muslim, *al-Musnad aṣ-Ṣaḥīḥ, Kitāb al-Īmān*, chapter 1, *ḥadīth* 93; at-Tibrīzī, *Mishkāt al-Maṣābīḥ, Kitāb al-Īmān, ḥadīth* 2; al-Bayhaqī, *Shu'ab al-Īmān*, Vol. 2, p.281.

416 Qur'ān, Sūrat an-Nāzi'āt 79:1-6.

417 Qur'ān, Sūrat al-Burūj 85:1-5.

recompense for one's deeds is true.[418]

xlvii. إِذَا السَّمَاءُ انْشَقَّتْ، وَأَذِنَتْ لِرَبِّهَا وَحُقَّتْ، وَإِذَا الْأَرْضُ مُدَّتْ، وَأَلْقَتْ مَا فِيهَا وَتَخَلَّتْ، وَأَذِنَتْ لِرَبِّهَا وَحُقَّتْ، يَا أَيُّهَا الْإِنْسَانُ إِنَّكَ كَادِحٌ إِلَىٰ رَبِّكَ كَدْحًا فَمُلَاقِيهِ – *"When the sky bursts open, hearkening to its Lord as it is bound to do! When the earth is flattened out and disgorges what is inside it and empties out, hearkening to its Lord as it is bound to do! O Man! You are toiling laboriously towards your Lord but meet Him you will!"*[419] meaning that the reckoning and recompense will certainly take place.

i. Substitution of the Third Person for the Second Person

Sometimes, Allah ﷻ transforms the method of speech such as, for example, when the method would require direct address but He utilises an indirect form, for example: حَتَّىٰ إِذَا كُنْتُمْ فِي الْفُلْكِ وَجَرَيْنَ بِهِمْ بِرِيحٍ طَيِّبَةٍ – *"When some of you (2nd person) are on a boat, and they (3rd person) are running before a fair wind."*[420]

j. Substitution of Informative for Prescriptive and Vice Versa

He ﷻ may mention the prescriptive in place of the informative and vice versa, such as:

xlviii. فَامْشُوا فِي مَنَاكِبِهَا – *"So walk its broad trails,"*[421] i.e. 'فَتَمْشُوا – *so* ***that you may*** *walk its broad trails.'*[422]

xlix. إِنْ كُنْتُمْ مُؤْمِنِينَ – *"If you are believers,"*[423] i.e. "***your belief requires this.***"

[In the two examples above, the prescriptive sentence has been used in the place of the informative sentence.]

418 The good shall be rewarded whereas the evil shall be punished, as retribution for what they did in the mortal life of this world.

419 Qur'ān, Sūrat al-Inshiqāq 84:1-6.

420 Qur'ān, Sūrat Yūnus 10:22. The word 'بِهِمْ – with them all' has been substituted for 'بِكُمْ – with you all'. Allah ﷻ turns from addressing some specific people to speaking about them.

421 Qur'ān, Sūrat al-Mulk 67:15.

422 This *āyah* uses a performative word but indicates informative meaning. Hence, the command given here refers to permission.

423 Qur'ān, Sūrat al-Baqarah 2:93; Sūrah Āl 'Imrān 3:139, etc.

l. مِنْ أَجْلِ ذَٰلِكَ كَتَبْنَا عَلَىٰ بَنِي إِسْرَائِيلَ – *"On account of that We decreed for the tribe of Isrā'īl,"*[424] i.e. We ordained, basing it on the analogy of the state of the son of Ādam or the similitude of the state of Ādam's son but substituted for it 'مِنْ أَجْلِ ذَٰلِكَ – *On account of that*', because analogy is never without a view to the effective cause (*'illah*) and thus it is as if analogical reasoning is a type of reasoning to discover the effective cause (*ta'līl*).

li. أَرَأَيْتَ – *"Have you seen?"*[425] is originally a question about 'seeing' but it is used here to draw attention to 'listening' to the words that come after it, as is conventionally said, "Do you see?" "Do you hear?"[426]

3. Deferring and Advancing, and Remote Connection[427]

It also becomes difficult to understand the meanings when words are brought forwards, or they are put backwards, as is evident in this famous Arabic couplet:

بُثَيْنَةُ شَأْنُهَا سَلَبَتْ فُؤَادِي . . . بِلَا جُرْمٍ أَتَيْتُ بِهِ سَلَامًا [428]

424 Qur'ān, Sūrat al-Mā'idah 5:32.

425 Qur'ān, Sūrat al-Mā'ūn 107:1.

426 These are questions of a rhetorical nature that emphasise the words that follow them.

427 Remote connection is where a phrase continues its meaning from or connects to something mentioned much earlier.

428 بُثَيْنَةُ is the subject of the verb سَلَبَتْ. It has been brought forwards, and hence it creates a difficulty in understanding the meaning. Another pronunciation is: بُثَيْنَةَ شَأْنُهَا سَلَبَتْ فُؤَادِي ... بِلَا جُرْمٍ أَتَيْتُ بِهِ سَلَامَا, in which case 'بُثَيْنَةَ' is the object of the penultimate word in the second verse 'سَلَا – You two must ask'. This couplet will then be prosed in the following manner: 'سَلَا بُثَيْنَةَ مَا شَأْنُهَا، سَلَبَتْ فُؤَادِي بِلَا جُرْمٍ أَتَيْتُ بِهِ – You two (friends of mine) must ask Buthaynah what is the matter with her because she has stolen my heart without me committing a crime.' In either case, the word 'بُثَيْنَةَ' is so far from its related verb that understanding the meaning without pondering over the grammar is difficult.

"What is the matter with Buthaynah, that she has stolen my heart without me committing any crime? [I pray for her] peace."[429]

A similar case of something that is difficult to understand is that of remote connections, and likewise things of a similar nature, for example:

lii. إِلَّا آلَ لُوطٍ إِنَّا لَمُنَجُّوهُمْ أَجْمَعِينَ، إِلَّا امْرَأَتَهُ – *"With the exception of the family of Lūṭ, all of whom We will save, except for his wife."*[430] In these *āyāt*, an exception [*with the exception of the family of Lūṭ*] precedes another exception [*except for his wife*], and that has caused the complication [in understanding].

liii. فَمَا يُكَذِّبُكَ بَعْدُ بِالدِّينِ – *"What could make you deny the Reckoning after this?"*[431] is connected to His ﷻ words [mentioned previously]: لَقَدْ خَلَقْنَا الْإِنْسَانَ فِي أَحْسَنِ تَقْوِيمٍ – *"We created man in the finest mould."*[432]

liv. يَدْعُو لَمَنْ ضَرُّهُ أَقْرَبُ مِنْ نَفْعِهِ – *"He calls on what is far more likely to harm than help,"*[433] i.e. he calls on someone who harms him.

lv. لَتَنُوءُ بِالْعُصْبَةِ أُولِي الْقُوَّةِ – *"[the keys to which alone] Were a heavy weight for a party of strong men,"*[434] i.e. the party would have been

According to one interpretation, a similar case is that of Sūrat aḍ-Duḥā 93:6-8:
أَلَمْ يَجِدْكَ يَتِيمًا فَآوَىٰ – *"Did He not find you [a succour] and [thus] to orphans He gave shelter [through you]?"*
وَوَجَدَكَ ضَالًّا فَهَدَىٰ – *"And He found you [a guide] and [thus] those astray He guided [through you]?"*
وَوَجَدَكَ عَائِلًا فَأَغْنَىٰ – *"And He found you [compassionate] and [thus] the needy He freed from need [through you]."*
In all three *āyāt*, the object has been brought forward before its verb.

429 This is a couplet by the renowned Arab poet Jamīl ibn Maʿmar al-ʿUdhrī, *aka* Jamīl Buthaynah (d. 81 AH / 701 CE), in his *Dīwān*.

430 Qur'ān, Sūrat al-Ḥijr 15:59-60.

431 Qur'ān, Sūrat at-Tīn 95:7.

432 Qur'ān, Sūrat at-Tīn 95:4.

433 Qur'ān, Sūrat al-Ḥajj 22:13.

434 Qur'ān, Sūrat al-Qaṣaṣ 28:76.

overwhelmed by them.

lvi. وَامْسَحُوا بِرُءُوسِكُمْ وَأَرْجُلَكُمْ – *"And wipe over your heads, and your feet,"*[435] i.e. *"And **wash** your feet."*[436]

lvii. وَلَوْلَا كَلِمَةٌ سَبَقَتْ مِنْ رَبِّكَ لَكَانَ لِزَامًا وَأَجَلٌ مُسَمًّى – *"And were it not for a prior word from your Lord – it would inevitably have already taken place – and [were it not for] a specified term,"*[437] i.e. *"Were it not for a prior word and a specified term, it would inevitably have already taken place."*[438]

lviii. إِلَّا تَفْعَلُوهُ تَكُنْ فِتْنَةٌ – *"If you do not act in this way there will be turmoil,"*[439] is connected to: فَعَلَيْكُمُ النَّصْرُ – *"it is your duty to help them,"*[440] [mentioned in the previous *āyah*].

lix. إِلَّا قَوْلَ إِبْرَاهِيمَ – *"Except for Ibrāhīm's words,"*[441] is connected to [a previous part of the *āyah*]: كَانَتْ لَكُمْ أُسْوَةٌ حَسَنَةٌ فِي إِبْرَاهِيمَ – *"You have an excellent example in Ibrāhīm."*[442]

lx. يَسْأَلُونَكَ كَأَنَّكَ حَفِيٌّ عَنْهَا – *"They will ask you as if you had full knowledge of it,"*[443] i.e. *"They will ask you **of it** as if you had full knowledge."*[444]

4. Additional Wording

There are a few types of words that are additional to the natural

435 Qur'ān, Sūrat al-Mā'idah 5:6.

436 The word 'أَرْجُل – feet' is not in the genitive state, which it would be if it was the object of the verb 'امْسَحُوْا بِ – wipe'; it is in the accusative state, which is due to it being an object of the verb 'اغْسِلُوْا – wash' earlier in the *āyah*.

437 Qur'ān, Sūrat Ṭā-Hā 20:129.

438 The phrase 'وَأَجَلٌ مُسَمًّى – *and a specified term*' is conjoined to 'كَلِمَةٌ – *a word*' and not to 'لِزَامًا – *necessary*'.

439 Qur'ān, Sūrat al-Anfāl 8:73.

440 Qur'ān, Sūrat al-Anfāl 8:72.

441 Qur'ān, Sūrat al-Mumtaḥanah 60:4.

442 Ibid.

443 Qur'ān, Sūrat al-A'rāf 7:187.

444 The phrase 'عَنْهَا – *of it*' which occurs at the end of the *āyah* belongs to the verb 'يَسْأَلُونَكَ – *they will ask you*'.

form of words:

a. Descriptive Additions:

i. وَلَا طَائِرٍ يَطِيرُ بِجَنَاحَيْهِ – *"Or flying creature, flying with its wings."*[445]

ii. إِنَّ الْإِنْسَانَ خُلِقَ هَلُوعًا ، إِذَا مَسَّهُ الشَّرُّ جَزُوعًا ، وَإِذَا مَسَّهُ الْخَيْرُ مَنُوعًا – *"Truly man was created headstrong – desperate when bad things happen, begrudging when good things come."*[446]

b. Additions in Substitution

Additions can be through substitution, such as His ﷻ words:

iii. لِلَّذِينَ اسْتُضْعِفُوا لِمَنْ آمَنَ مِنْهُمْ – *"To those who were oppressed – those among them who believed."*[447]

c. Addition via Explanatory Conjunction

Additions can be through explanatory conjunction such as His ﷻ words:

iv. حَتَّىٰ إِذَا بَلَغَ أَشُدَّهُ وَبَلَغَ أَرْبَعِينَ سَنَةً – *"Then when he achieves his full strength **and** he reaches forty years."*[448]

d. Addition through Repetition

v. وَمَا يَتَّبِعُ الَّذِينَ يَدْعُونَ مِنْ دُونِ اللَّهِ شُرَكَاءَ إِنْ يَتَّبِعُونَ إِلَّا الظَّنَّ – *"Those who call on something other than Allah are not really following their partner-gods. They are only following conjecture."*[449] The primary words are: *"Those who call on something other than Allah are not really following their partner-gods... except conjecture."*

vi. وَلَمَّا جَاءَهُمْ كِتَابٌ مِنْ عِنْدِ اللَّهِ مُصَدِّقٌ لِمَا مَعَهُمْ وَكَانُوا مِنْ قَبْلُ يَسْتَفْتِحُونَ عَلَى الَّذِينَ كَفَرُوا فَلَمَّا جَاءَهُمْ مَا عَرَفُوا كَفَرُوا بِهِ – *"When a Book does come to them from Allah, confirming what is with them – even though before that they were praying for victory over the unbelievers – yet when what they recognise does come to them, they reject it."*[450]

445 Qur'ān, Sūrat al-An'ām 6:38.

446 Qur'ān, Sūrat al-Ma'ārij 70:19-21. '*Headstrong*' is explained by the subsequent two *āyāt* which are descriptive of that term. Ed.

447 Qur'ān, Sūrat al-A'rāf 7:75.

448 Qur'ān, Sūrat al-Aḥqāf 46:15.

449 Qur'ān, Sūrat al-Yūnus 10:66.

450 Qur'ān, Sūrat al-Baqarah 2:89. *"When a Book does come to them from Allah,*

vii. وَلْيَخْشَ الَّذِينَ لَوْ تَرَكُوا مِنْ خَلْفِهِمْ ذُرِّيَّةً ضِعَافًا خَافُوا عَلَيْهِمْ فَلْيَتَّقُوا اللَّهَ – *"People should be afraid in the same way that they would fear for small children if they were to die leaving them behind. They should have taqwā of Allah."*[451,452]

viii. يَسْأَلُونَكَ عَنِ الْأَهِلَّةِ قُلْ هِيَ مَوَاقِيتُ لِلنَّاسِ وَالْحَجِّ – *"They will ask you about the crescent moons. Say, 'They are set times for mankind and for the ḥajj,'"*[453] i.e. they are set times for mankind, because Allah ﷻ legislated that they regulate their times by them, and for the *ḥajj,* because the upshot of setting the fixed times by them is *ḥajj.* If it had been said, 'هِيَ مَوَاقِيتُ لِلنَّاسِ فِي حَجِّهِمْ – They are set times for people **on their *ḥajj,*'** then it would have been more concise but exaggeratedly so.

ix. لِتُنْذِرَ أُمَّ الْقُرَى وَمَنْ حَوْلَهَا وَتُنْذِرَ يَوْمَ الْجَمْعِ – *"So that you may warn the Mother of Cities and those around it, and give warning of the Day of Gathering,"*[454] i.e. *"So that you may warn the Mother of Cities … of the Day of Gathering."*

x. وَتَرَى ٱلْجِبَالَ تَحْسَبُهَا جَامِدَةً – *"You will see the mountains you reckon to be solid,"*[455] i.e. *"You will see the mountains …solid."* 'Seeing' is used in various senses, and so the word 'reckon' has been added [in order to explain that]. What is meant here by 'seeing' is 'reckoning'.

xi. كَانَ ٱلنَّاسُ أُمَّةً وَٰحِدَةً فَبَعَثَ ٱللَّهُ ٱلنَّبِيِّـۧنَ مُبَشِّرِينَ وَمُنذِرِينَ وَأَنزَلَ مَعَهُمُ ٱلْكِتَٰبَ بِٱلْحَقِّ لِيَحْكُمَ بَيْنَ ٱلنَّاسِ فِيمَا ٱخْتَلَفُوا۟ فِيهِ ۚ وَمَا ٱخْتَلَفَ فِيهِ إِلَّا ٱلَّذِينَ أُوتُوهُ مِنۢ بَعْدِ مَا جَآءَتْهُمُ ٱلْبَيِّنَٰتُ بَغْيًۢا بَيْنَهُمْ ۖ فَهَدَى ٱللَّهُ ٱلَّذِينَ ءَامَنُوا۟ لِمَا ٱخْتَلَفُوا۟ فِيهِ مِنَ ٱلْحَقِّ بِإِذْنِهِۦ ۗ وَٱللَّهُ يَهْدِى مَن يَشَآءُ إِلَىٰ صِرَٰطٍ مُّسْتَقِيمٍ – *"Mankind was a single community. Then Allah sent out Prophets bringing good news and giving warning, and with them He sent down*

confirming what is with them… they reject it" is the basic sense imparted and what is in between these two parts is additional to it.

451 Qur'ān, Sūrat an-Nisā' 4:9.

452 This *āyah* contains a repetition of meaning, i.e. 'وَلْيَخْشَ – should be afraid' and 'فَلْيَتَّقُوا – *should have taqwā*'.

453 Qur'ān, Sūrat al-Baqarah 2:189.

454 Qur'ān, Sūrat ash-Shūrā 42:7.

455 Qur'ān, Sūrat an-Naml 27:88.

the Book with truth to decide between people regarding that on which they differed. Only those who were given it differed about it, after the Clear Signs had come to them, envying one another. Then, by His permission, Allah guided those who believe to the truth of that about which they had differed. Allah guides whomever He wills to a straight path."[456] وَمَا اخْتَلَفَ فِيهِ إِلَّا الَّذِينَ أُوتُوهُ – *"Only those who were given it differed about it,"* has been inserted into the multiple levels of structured speech, one part on top of another, in order to explicate the pronoun [they] in 'اخْتَلَفُوا – they differed' and to express that what is meant by 'difference' is the differences that took place in the community of the *da'wah* after the revelation of the Book in that some people believed and others disbelieved.

e. Additional Genitive Particles (*Ḥarf al-Jarr*):

Occasionally, He ﷻ adds a genitive particle (*ḥarf al-jarr*) to the subject or object [of the verb], the addition of that genitive particle rendering it governed by the verb to underscore the connection, such as:

xii. يَوْمَ يُحْمَى عَلَيْهَا – *"On the Day it is heated **upon them** [i.e. the gold and silver],"*[457] i.e. 'هِيَ تُحْمَى – ***they are** heated up*'.[458]

xiii. وَقَفَّيْنَا عَلَىٰٓ ءَاثَٰرِهِم بِعِيسَى ٱبْنِ مَرْيَمَ – *"And We sent 'Īsā son of Maryam following **in their footsteps**,"*[459] i.e. وَقَفَّيْنَاهُمْ بِعِيسَى ٱبْنِ مَرْيَمَ – *"And We sent 'Īsā son of Maryam following them."*[460]

f. The Conjunctive 'و – and'

One ought to understand a point here which is that the letter/particle 'و – *wāw*' is used on many occasions to emphasise the link and not specifically for conjunction, such as in:

xiv. إِذَا وَقَعَتِ ٱلْوَاقِعَةُ لَيْسَ لِوَقْعَتِهَا كَاذِبَةٌ، خَافِضَةٌ رَّافِعَةٌ، إِذَا رُجَّتِ ٱلْأَرْضُ رَجًّا، وَبُسَّتِ ٱلْجِبَالُ بَسًّا، فَكَانَتْ

456 Qur'ān, Sūrat al-Baqarah 2:213.
457 Qur'ān, Sūrat at-Tawbah 9:35.
458 The 'عَلَىٰ – on' in 'عَلَيْهَا' is additional.
459 Qur'ān, Sūrat al-Mā'idah 5:46.
460 'عَلَىٰ آثَار' is additional in this *āyah*.

هَبَآءً مُّنۢبَثًّا، وَكُنتُمْ أَزْوَٰجًا ثَلَٰثَةً – *"When the Great Event occurs, none will deny its occurrence; bringing low, raising high. When the earth is convulsed and the mountains are crushed and become scattered dust in the air and you will be classed into three."*[461]

xv. حَتَّىٰٓ إِذَا جَآءُوهَا فُتِحَتْ أَبْوَٰبُهَا وَقَالَ لَهُمْ خَزَنَتُهَا – *"When they arrive there. Its gates are opened,* and *its keepers say to them."*[462]

xvi. وَلِيُمَحِّصَ ٱللَّهُ ٱلَّذِينَ ءَامَنُوا۟ – *"And so that Allah can purge those who believe."*[463]

g. The Conjunctive 'ف – so/then'

Similarly the 'ف – *fā'* is also used in augmentation. In the commentary on the book of *Ḥajj*, the chapter on "When the *'Umrah* pilgrim does *ṭawāf* (circumambulation) for the *'Umrah* and then leaves, does that suffice him for the *ṭawāf al-wadā'* (the farewell circumambulation)?", Al-Qasṭalānī[464] writes: "It is permissible to insert a letter of conjunction (*ḥarf al-'aṭf*) between the adjective and the noun it qualifies in order to emphasise its connection to the noun that is qualified. For example: إِذْ يَقُولُ ٱلْمُنَٰفِقُونَ وَٱلَّذِينَ فِى قُلُوبِهِم مَّرَضٌ – *"And when the hypocrites and those with sickness in*

461 Qur'ān, Sūrat al-Wāqi'ah 56:1-7. The last و – *wāw* is extra, i.e. *"When the Great Event occurs…you will be classed into three."*

462 Qur'ān, Sūrat az-Zumar 39:71. The و – *wāw* is extra, i.e. *"When they arrive there. Its gates are opened,* ***and*** *its keepers say to them."*

463 Qur'ān, Sūrah Āl 'Imrān 3:141. The initial و – *wāw* is extra, i.e. *"So that Allah can purge those who believe."*

464 Al-Qasṭalānī: He is Imām Shihāb ad-Dīn Abu'l-'Abbās Aḥmad ibn Muḥammad ibn Abū Bakr ibn 'Abd al-Malik ibn Aḥmad ibn Muḥammad ibn al-Ḥusayn ibn 'Alī al-Qasṭalānī al-Miṣrī ash-Shāfi'ī (851 AH/1448 CE – 923 AH/1517 CE). He was a great scholar, a contemporary of Imām as-Suyūṭī (848 AH/1445 CE – 911 AH/1505 CE), and spent much time in Makkah and Madīnah. He authored many beneficial scholarly works, such as *Irshād as-Sārī fī Sharḥ Ṣaḥīḥ al-Bukhārī*, *al-Māwahib al-Ladunniyyah bi al-Minaḥ al-Muḥammadiyyah* and *Sīrat ar-Rasūl* ﷺ.

their hearts said"[465] Sībawayh[466] said, "That is similar to saying, 'I passed by Zayd and your colleague' when by 'your colleague' one means 'Zayd'."

Az-Zamaksharī[467] said about His ﷻ words: وَمَا أَهْلَكْنَا مِن قَرْيَةٍ إِلَّا وَلَهَا كِتَابٌ مَعْلُومٌ – *"We did not destroy any city without it having a set time."*[468] "In this *āyah* [the part 'إِلَّا وَلَهَا كِتَابٌ مَعْلُومٌ – *without it having a set time*'] is a clause that occurs as a description of 'قَرْيَة – city', though the rule indicates there should not be a 'و – *wāw*' between them, as in His ﷻ words: وَمَا أَهْلَكْنَا مِن قَرْيَةٍ إِلَّا لَهَا مُنذِرُونَ – *"We have never destroyed a city without it having warners."*[469] It [the 'و – *wāw*'] only interposes [in the former *āyah*] to emphasise the connection between the description and what it describes, as is said in the case of a 'حال – circumstantial expression': جَاءَنِي زَيْدٌ عَلَيْهِ ثَوْبٌ – 'Zayd came to me upon him there were clothes' or جَاءَنِي زَيْدٌ وَعَلَيْهِ ثَوْبٌ – 'Zayd came to me and upon him there were clothes.'"

h. Diffusion of Pronouns, and Intending Two Different Meanings by One Word

465 Qur'ān, Sūrat al-Anfāl 8:49. In this *āyah*, 'الْمُنَافِقُونَ – the hypocrites' are qualified by 'الَّذِينَ – those who' i.e. *"And when the hypocrites, those with sickness in their hearts."* The letter و – *wāw* is not conjunctive but concomitant emphasis.

466 Sībawayh (or Sībūyeh) an-Naḥwī (the Grammarian). He is Abū Bishr 'Amr ibn 'Uthmān Qanbar (142 AH/760 CE – 183 AH/796 CE). He was of Persian origin and grew up in Baṣra (Iraq). He was an influential linguist and grammarian. He authored *al-Kitāb*, a book on Arabic grammar.

467 Az-Zamakhsharī: He is Abu'l-Qāsim Maḥmūd ibn 'Umar az-Zamakhsharī, also called Jārullāh (God's Neighbour) (464 AH/1075 CE – 538 AH/1144 CE). He was an Arabic scholar, grammarian and theologian of Persian origin whose chief work is *al-Kashshāf 'an Ḥaqā'iq at-Tanzīl – The Discoverer of Revealed Truths*, his exhaustive linguistic commentary on Qur'ān. Although a *mu'tazilī*, his works are unparalleled in their knowledge of Arabic and thus are widely studied and cited.

468 Qur'ān, Sūrat al-Ḥijr 15:4.

469 Qur'ān, Sūrat ash-Shu'arā' 26:208.

Occasionally, the diffusion of the pronouns and the application of two or more meanings using one word becomes a cause of complexity in the comprehension of the text. For example:

xvii. وَإِنَّهُمْ لَيَصُدُّونَهُمْ عَنِ السَّبِيلِ وَيَحْسَبُونَ أَنَّهُم مُّهْتَدُونَ – *"And they debar them from the path, yet they still think they are guided,"*[470] meaning that the *shayṭāns* debar people from the path, and the people think they are guided.[471]

xviii. وَقَالَ قَرِينُهُ – *"His inseparable comrade will say."*[472] In one location [50:27], the word 'comrade' means 'the *shayṭān*', and in the other [20:23], it means 'the angel'.[473]

xix. يَسْأَلُونَكَ مَاذَا يُنفِقُونَ قُلْ مَآ أَنفَقْتُم مِّنْ خَيْرٍ – *"They will ask you what they should give away. Say, 'Any wealth you give away...'"*[474] and His ﷻ words: يَسْأَلُونَكَ مَاذَا يُنفِقُونَ قُلِ الْعَفْوَ – *"They will ask you what they should give away. Say, 'Whatever is surplus to your needs.'"*[475] As for the first, it means 'whatever you expend' and 'whatever type of thing you expend', and is true with respect to asking about the mode of expending because expending becomes of numerous types with regards to the modes of expenditure. The second means 'what wealth should you spend?'

i. 'جَعَلَ' and 'شَيْءٌ'

Of this type, are the words 'شَيْءٌ', 'جَعَلَ' etc. which are used with numerous meanings:

xx. جَعَلَ is sometimes used for 'خَلَقَ – He created' as in وَجَعَلَ الظُّلُمَٰتِ

470 Qur'ān, Sūrat az-Zukhruf 43:37.

471 The pronoun 'هُمْ – they' (attached to إِنَّ) represents the 'الشَّيَاطِيْن – *shayṭāns*', the hidden pronoun in 'يَحْسَبُوْنَ – they reckon' indicates the people. The pronoun 'هُمْ – they' (attached to أَنَّ) indicates, again, the people. This is an illustration of the diffusion of pronouns.

472 Qur'ān, Sūrat Qāf 50:23, 27.

473 This is an example of using one word for two meanings, when both are relatively close to one another.

474 Qur'ān, Sūrat al-Baqarah 2:215.

475 Qur'ān, Sūrat al-Baqarah 2:219.

وَالنُّورَ– *"He created the darknesses and the light."*[476]

xxi. It can sometimes be in the sense of 'اِعْتَقَدَ – he believed' as in وَجَعَلُوا لِلَّهِ مِمَّا ذَرَأَ – *"They assign to Allah of that He has created."*[477]

As for the word شَيْء, it is sometimes used in place of the subject or the object and with other uses:

xxii. أَمْ خُلِقُوا مِنْ غَيْرِ شَيْءٍ – *"Or were they created without any thing?"*[478] i.e. without a Creator?

xxiii. فَلَا تَسْأَلْنِي عَنْ شَيْءٍ – *"Do not question me about a thing,"*[479] i.e. do not question me regarding anything of my affair about which you are unclear.

j. النَّبَأُ, الأَمْرُ and الخَطْبُ

The words 'النَّبَأُ', 'الأَمْرُ' and 'الخَطْبُ' [three synonyms meaning 'affair, business or matter'] sometimes refer to that which one has been informed about, such as: هُوَ نَبَأٌ عَظِيمٌ – *"This is momentous news,"*[480] i.e. it is an astonishing story.

k. 'الخَيْرُ – Good' and 'الشَّرُّ – Evil'

Likewise, the meanings of 'الخَيْرُ – good' and 'الشَّرُّ – evil', and words synonymous with them, vary in their intended meanings in accordance with their contexts and locations.

l. Bringing Forward or Putting the *Āyāt* Back in their Order

Of this sort also there is the diffuse nature of the *āyāt*:

xxiv. He ﷻ may move straight away to the principle topic of an *āyah* after citing the story and mention it before completing the story and then return to the story and complete it. It is possible that a particular *āyah* was revealed at a prior stage in time, yet in the sequence of recitation it may be

476 Qur'ān, Sūrat al-An'ām 6:1.

477 Qur'ān, Sūrat al-An'ām 6:136. In *"They assign to Allah a share of the crops and livestock He has created"* the word 'assign' means that they 'believe' that Allah has a share of the crops and livestock He has created.

478 Qur'ān, Sūrat aṭ-Ṭūr 52:35.

479 Qur'ān, Sūrat al-Kahf 18:70.

480 Qur'ān, Sūrat aṣ-Ṣād 38:67.

delayed. For example, قَدْ نَرَىٰ تَقَلُّبَ وَجْهِكَ فِي السَّمَاءِ – "*We have seen you looking up into heaven*"[481] was revealed prior to سَيَقُولُ السُّفَهَاءُ مِنَ النَّاسِ – "*The fools among the people will ask,*"[482] but the order in recitation is the opposite.

xxv. The reply may be inserted amidst the speech of disbelievers, as in His ﷻ words: وَلَا تُؤْمِنُوا إِلَّا لِمَنْ تَبِعَ دِينَكُمْ قُلْ إِنَّ الْهُدَىٰ هُدَى اللَّهِ أَنْ يُؤْتَىٰ أَحَدٌ مِثْلَ مَا أُوتِيتُمْ – "*'Do not trust anyone except for those who follow your dīn.' Say, 'Allah's guidance is true guidance.' '[Do not believe] that anyone could be given the like of what you were given.'*"[483]

In short, these discussions demand great detail, but there is sufficient detail in what I have mentioned. If the student learns the Qur'ān from blessed people and keeps these issues in mind when reciting it, he will grasp the purpose of the speech with the minimum of contemplation. Moreover, he will understand affairs and issues not mentioned, by reasoning analogically from that which is mentioned and will thus move from one example to other examples.

5. On the Decisive (*Muḥkam*), the Allegorical (*Mutashābih*), Indirect Expression (*Kināyah*), Allusion (*Ta'rīḍ*) and Conceptual Metaphor (*Majāz 'Aqlī*)

a. The Decisive (*Muḥkam*)

One should know that the Decisive (*Muḥkam*) is that in which the person knowledgeable of the language will take only one particular meaning from that speech. The criterion is the understanding of the early Arabs, not of contemporary investigators of minute issues who split hairs, because this idle minute investigation is a chronic illness that renders what is decisive allegorical, and renders what

481 Qur'ān, Sūrat al-Baqarah 2:144.

482 Qur'ān, Sūrat al-Baqarah 2:142.

483 Qur'ān, Sūrah Āl 'Imrān 3:73. The words cited from the Jews, "*Do not trust anyone except for those who follow your dīn, [do not believe] that anyone could be given the like of what you were given*" are interrupted by the command: "*Say, 'Allah's guidance is true guidance.'*"

is well-known unknown.

b. Allegorical (*Mutashābih*)

The Allegorical (*Mutashābih*) is that which is capable of two (or more) meanings, either due to:

1. The possibility of a pronoun referring to two or more nouns as a man said, "أَمَّا إِنَّ الأَمِيرَ أَمَرَنِي أَنْ أَلْعَنَ فُلَانًا ، لَعَنَهُ اللهُ – The amir has ordered me to curse so-and-so, may Allah curse him."[484]
2. The word may convey two or more meanings such as His ﷻ words "لَمَسْتُمُ – *touched*"[485] which has the sense of 'sexual intercourse' as well as 'touching (with the hand)'.
3. The conjunction may apply to [words that are] both near and distant as with His ﷻ words "وَامْسَحُوا بِرُءُوسِكُمْ وَأَرْجُلِكُمْ – *and wipe your heads and your feet*[486] *to the ankles*"[487] in the recitation with the *kasrah* [on the *arjuli* – feet].[488]
4. It may be used for either a conjunction or for initiating a sentence (*isti'nāf*) as in His ﷻ words "وَمَا يَعْلَمُ تَأْوِيلَهُ إِلَّا اللهُ وَالرَّاسِخُونَ فِي الْعِلْمِ يَقُولُونَ – *No one knows its inner meaning but Allah. As for those firmly rooted in knowledge say.*"[489,490]

484 In this example, an ambiguity arises as to whom the curse of the speaker is directed against: so-and-so or the amir.

485 Qur'ān, Sūrat an-Nisā' 4:43; Sūrat al-Mā'idah 5:6.

486 A *kasrah* which renders the last term 'وَأَرْجُلِكُمْ', and which thus makes the 'feet' the object of the verb 'wipe' along with the 'heads', hence applying the meaning of 'wiping' to the 'feet' also. Thus, the conjunction 'و – *wāw*' can refer back to the distant verb 'wash' or to the verb which is closer 'wipe'.

487 Qur'ān, Sūrat al-Mā'idah 5:6.

488 This recitation is not permissible according to the scholars of the four *madhhabs*, and the resultant *fiqh* position is thus not acceptable. It was, however, an admissible recitation and an acceptable *fiqh* judgement according to the *madhhab* of aṭ-Ṭabarī who was an imam in Qur'ān recitation, *tafsīr, 'aqīdah* and in fiqh. Nevertheless, his madhhab is now extinct. Ed.

489 Qur'ān, Sūrah Āl 'Imrān 3:7.

490 The 'و – *wāw*' may either function as a conjunction, and thus the *āyah*

c. Indirect Expression (*Kināyah*)

Indirect expression (*kināyah*) is that one affirms a matter but does not intend the affirmation of that matter specifically but intends to divert the attention of the person addressed towards something inherent in it, either customarily (*'ādah*) or intellectually (*'aql*), just as one understands being much given to showing hospitality from their saying "عَظِيمُ الرَّمَادِ – abundant in ashes"[491] and the sense of liberal generosity is understood from "بَلْ يَدَاهُ مَبْسُوطَتَانِ – *No! Both His hands are open wide.*"[492]

Picturing the Intended Meaning with a Sensory Image

Picturing the intended meaning with a sensory image is also of this type [i.e. *kināyah*]. This is a vast area within Arabic poetry and orations, and the Tremendous Qur'ān and the Sunnah of our Prophet ﷺ are replete with it, such as:

i. His ﷻ words "وَأَجْلِبْ عَلَيْهِم بِخَيْلِكَ وَرَجِلِكَ – *and rally against them your cavalry and your infantry*"[493] which likens *Shayṭān* to a highway robber, as he bellows to his comrades saying, "Attack from this point and get in from that direction."

ii. And His ﷻ words "وَجَعَلْنَا مِن بَيْنِ أَيْدِيهِمْ سَدًّا وَمِنْ خَلْفِهِمْ سَدًّا – *We have placed a barrier in front of them and a barrier behind them,*"[494] and His ﷻ words "جَعَلْنَا فِي أَعْنَاقِهِمْ أَغْلَالًا - *We have put iron collars*

is translated as *"No one knows its inner meaning but Allah and those firmly rooted in knowledge"*, or the 'و – *wāw*' may serve inceptively and be used to start a fresh sentence, and be translated thus *"No one knows its inner meaning but Allah. Those firmly rooted in knowledge say."* In the latter case, the reciter stops before the conjunction. The dominant majority choose the latter recitation and its meaning. Among those who chose the former were Ibn Rushd (520 AH/1126 CE – 595 AH/1198 CE), the author of *Bidāyat al-Mujtahid*. Ed.

491 i.e. the generous host will have his fire lit a great deal in cooking food and thus will have abundant ashes.

492 Qur'ān, Sūrat al-Mā'idah 5:64.

493 Qur'ān, Sūrat al-Isrā' 17:64.

494 Qur'ān, Sūrah Yā-Sīn 36:9.

round their necks."[495] He likens the disbelievers' turning away in aversion from contemplating the *āyāt* to a man whose hands have been shackled, or around whom walls have been erected so that he is completely unable to see anything.

iii. And His ﷻ words "وَاضْمُمْ إِلَيْكَ جَنَاحَكَ مِنَ الرَّهْبِ – *And hug your arms to your sides to still your fear*"[496] meaning gather your thoughts, and keep doubts and anxiety away.

Examples of that in common usage

If we were to describe the bravery of a particular individual, we could take a sword and strike towards this direction and that direction just to indicate his overpowering people in every direction with his quality of courage, even if he had never once taken hold of a sword in his life.

Or they say, "So-and-so says, 'I do not know of anyone in the world to compete with me,' or he says 'so-and-so does thus and thus,'" indicating the deportment of a contestant at the time of defeating his opponent, even though the individual in question may never have said or done that.

Or they say, "So-and-so choked me," or, "he took the morsel out of my mouth."[497]

d. Allusion (*Ta'rīḍ*)

Allusion (*ta'rīḍ*) occurs when Allah ﷻ mentions a general ruling or reprehensible matter aiming to describe the state of a specific individual, or warning against the state of a specific man, reproducing in the speech some of that individual's particularities which will acquaint those addressed as to who he is. Thus, the reciter will become absorbed in places such as this but will need that narrative. When the Prophet ﷺ wished to repudiate someone,

495 Qur'ān, Sūrah Yā-Sīn 36:8.

496 Qur'ān, Sūrat al-Qaṣaṣ 28:32.

497 All these are figurative expressions that are not literally true.

he would say: "مَا بَالُ أَقْوَامٍ يَفْعَلُونَ كَذَا وَكَذَا – What is wrong with people that dosuch-and-such?"[498]

And in the case of His ﷻ words "وَمَا كَانَ لِمُؤْمِنٍ وَلَا مُؤْمِنَةٍ إِذَا قَضَى اللَّهُ وَرَسُولُهُ أَمْرًا أَنْ يَكُونَ لَهُمُ الْخِيَرَةُ مِنْ أَمْرِهِمْ – *When Allah and His Messenger have decided something it is not for any man or woman of the believers to have a choice about it,*"[499] they allude to the episode of Zaynab [bint Jaḥsh][500] and her brother.[501]

And His ﷻ words "وَلَا يَأْتَلِ أُوْلُوا۟ ٱلْفَضْلِ مِنكُمْ وَٱلسَّعَةِ – *Those of you possessing affluence and ample wealth should not make oaths*"[502] allude to Abū

498 Ḥadīths with similar meanings and references: Al-Bukhārī, *al-Jāmiʿ aṣ-Ṣaḥīḥ, Kitāb ash-Shurūṭ*; al-Bukhārī, *al-Jāmiʿ aṣ-Ṣaḥīḥ, Kitāb al-Adab*; al-Bukhārī, *al-Jāmiʿ aṣ-Ṣaḥīḥ, Kitāb al-Iʿtiṣām bi'l-Kitāb wa's-Sunnah*; Muslim, *al-Musnad aṣ-Ṣaḥīḥ, Kitāb an-Nikāḥ*; Muslim, *al-Musnad aṣ-Ṣaḥīḥ, Kitāb al-ʿItq*; Muslim, *al-Musnad aṣ-Ṣaḥīḥ, Kitāb al-Faḍā'il*; at-Tirmidhī, *al-Jāmiʿ al-Kabīr, Kitāb al-Waṣāyā ʿan Rasūl Allāh* ﷺ; Ibn Mājah, *as-Sunan, al-Muqaddamah*; Ibn Mājah, *as-Sunan, Kitāb aṭ-Ṭalāq*; Abū Dāwūd, *as-Sunan, Kitāb aṣ-Ṣalāh*; Abū Dāwūd, *as-Sunan, Kitāb al-Adab*; an-Nasa'ī, *as-Sunan, Kitāb Iftitāḥ aṣ-Ṣalāh*; an-Nasa'ī, *as-Sunan, Kitāb Ṣifat aṣ-Ṣalāh*; an-Nasa'ī, *as-Sunan, Kitāb az-Zakāh*; an-Nasa'ī, *as-Sunan, Kitāb aṭ-Ṭalāq*; and an-Nasa'ī, *as-Sunan, Kitāb al-Buyūʿ*.

499 Qur'ān, Sūrat al-Aḥzāb 33:36.

500 She is Zaynab bint Jaḥsh (31 BH/593 CE – 22 AH/643 CE) the daughter of the Prophet's paternal aunt Umaymah bint ʿAbdulmuṭṭalib. She was first married to Zayd ibn Ḥārithah (36 BH/588 CE – 7 AH/629 CE). He was the slave of the wife of the Prophet Muḥammad ﷺ, Khadījah bint Khuwaylid (70 BH/555 CE – 4 BH/619 CE), whom she gifted to the Prophet ﷺ on their wedding. Zayd was later freed by the Prophet and treated as his own son. It is said that he was a descendant of the famous Arab poet Imru' al-Qays (d. 60 BH / 565 CE). Then later Zaynab was married to the Prophet Muḥammad ﷺ after her divorce from Zayd.

501 When the Prophet ﷺ sought Zaynab's hand for Zayd in marriage, she and her brother, ʿAbdullāh ibn Jaḥsh (d. 3 AH/625 CE in the Battle of Uḥud) at first refused because Zayd was not her equal in standing. This was the 'choice' referred to in the *āyah*.

502 Qur'ān, Sūrat an-Nūr 24:22 "وَلَا يَأْتَلِ أُوْلُوا۟ ٱلْفَضْلِ مِنكُمْ وَٱلسَّعَةِ أَن يُؤْتُوٓا۟ أُو۟لِى ٱلْقُرْبَىٰ وَٱلْمَسَٰكِينَ وَٱلْمُهَٰجِرِينَ فِى سَبِيلِ ٱللَّهِ ۖ وَلْيَعْفُوا۟ وَلْيَصْفَحُوٓا۟ ۗ أَلَا تُحِبُّونَ أَن يَغْفِرَ ٱللَّهُ لَكُمْ ۗ وَٱللَّهُ غَفُورٌ رَّحِيمٌ – *Those of you possessing affluence and ample wealth should not make oaths that they will not*

Bakr aṣ-Ṣiddīq[503,504]

In circumstances such as these, it is impossible to understand the meanings unless the background narrative is known.

e. Conceptual Metaphor (*Majāz 'Aqlī*)

Conceptual Metaphor (*majāz 'aqlī*) is to attribute an action to an individual who is not its doer, or to render something its object that is not in reality its object because of the connection of the similarity between the two[505], and that the speaker claims it to be of the same genus and an example of it, as when it is said 'an amir built a palace', whereas it was the builders who built it[506], or 'Spring brought forth vegetation', whereas it was really brought forth by Allah ﷻ in the season of Spring. And Allah ﷻ knows best.

give to their relatives and the very poor and those who have made hijra in the way of Allah. They should rather pardon and overlook. Would you not love Allah to forgive you? Allah is Ever-Forgiving, Most Merciful."

503 He is 'Abdullāh ibn Abī Quḥāfah (52 BH/573 CE – 13 AH/634 CE) *aka* Abū Bakr; the first Muslim amongst free men, and the first *khalīfah* after the Prophet Muḥammad ﷺ. He is known by the title aṣ-Ṣiddīq (Utterly Truthful) and is believed to be the best of mankind after the prophets and messengers. (Al-Bayhaqī, *al-Jāmi' li-Shu'ab al-Īmān*, 1:18)

504 He had been helping one of the men, Misṭah ibn Uthāthah, who later slandered 'Ā'ishah and then vowed to cut off his support. (Al-Bukhārī, *al-Jāmi' aṣ-Ṣaḥīḥ, Kitāb ash-Shahādāt, ḥadīth* 2661)

505 i.e. the assimilated connection between the real subject and the substituted subject, or between the real object and the substituted object. There always remains a circumstantial indicator that prevents the real meaning from being intended.

506 The builders built it at the command of the amir.

PART 3

The Subtleties of the Qur'ān's Composition and Explanation of Its Marvellous Approach

Chapter 1

The Structure of the Noble Qur'ān and the Styles of the *Sūrahs* in it

The Noble Qur'ān has not been arranged in chapters and sections like those of other books in which each discussion is described in a different chapter or section. On the contrary, the Qur'ān assumes a structure similar to a collection of ordinances; just as a king issues an edict to his subjects according to the requisites of the circumstances, and after a time a second edict and so on, and eventually it becomes an amalgamation of many edicts. Someone then collects them all and makes an orderly 'anthology' of them. In a similar manner, the Absolute King, Allah ﷻ, revealed *sūrahs* of the Qur'ān to His Prophet ﷺ, one after another, as and when required, for the guidance of His slaves.

During the prophetic era, each *sūrah* was preserved and compiled separately, then during the era of Abū Bakr and 'Umar ؓ all the *sūrahs* were incorporated into one volume in a specific sequence.[507]

507 It has been reported that Zayd ibn Thābit (13 BH/610 CE – 39 AH/660 CE) ؓ said: Abū Bakr ؓ sent for me after the slaughter of people in the Battle of Yamāmah. 'Umar ؓ was with him. Abū Bakr ؓ said, "Umar came to me and said, 'Many Qur'ān memorisers were killed in the Battle

This collection was named the *Muṣḥaf* (collection of sheets).

With the Companions ﷺ, the *sūrahs* were categorised as four types:

1. *As-Sab' aṭ-Ṭiwāl* (the Seven Long *Sūrahs*)[508] – these are the longest *sūrahs*.
2. *Mi'ūn*[509] (Hundreds) – those that have a hundred, or slightly

of Yamāmah, and I fear that heavy casualties will be inflicted on the Qur'ān memorisers in other places and therefore much of the Qur'ān will be lost. I think that you should order the collection of the Qur'ān.'" "Abū Bakr said, 'I said to 'Umar, "How can you do something which the Messenger of Allah ﷺ did not do?" 'Umar said, "By Allah, it is good." 'Umar kept on at me about it until Allah opened my breast to that. I think the same as 'Umar thinks about it.'"
Zayd continued: Abū Bakr said, "You are an intelligent young man and we have no doubts about you. You used to write down the revelation for the Messenger of Allah ﷺ. Therefore, seek out the Qur'ān and collect it." By Allah, if he had obliged me to move one of the mountains, that would not have been weightier for me than what he ordered me to do of collecting the Qur'ān. I said, "How can you do something which the Messenger of Allah ﷺ did not do?" Abū Bakr said, "By Allah, it is good." Abū Bakr kept on at me until Allah opened my breast to that which Allah had opened the breasts of Abū Bakr and 'Umar. So I began to search out the Qur'ān and collect it from palm stalks, thin white stones, and the breasts of men until I found the end portion of Sūrat at-Tawbah with Abū Khuzaymah al-Anṣārī which I did not find with anyone else: *"A Messenger has come to you from among yourselves. Your suffering is distressing to him."* (Qur'ān, Sūrat at-Tawbah 9:128-129) (This copy of the Qur'ān) remained in the possession of Abū Bakr ﷺ until Allah took him, and then it was with 'Umar during his lifetime, and then it was with Hafṣah bint 'Umar. (Al-Bukhārī, *al-Jāmi' aṣ-Ṣaḥīḥ, Kitāb Faḍā'il al-Qur'ān, ḥadīth* 4986)

508 The *as-Sab' aṭ-Ṭiwāl* or *aṭ-Ṭuwal* (Seven Long *Sūrahs*) are: 1. al-Baqarah (2), 2. Āl 'Imrān (3), 3. an-Nisā' (4), 4. al-Mā'idah (5), 5. al-An'ām (6), 6. al-A'rāf (7) and 7. al-Anfāl (8) plus at-Tawbah (9) together, or Yūnus (10). (Al-Bayhaqī, *Shu'ab al-Īmān*, chapter *Dhikr as-Sab' aṭ-Ṭiwāl*, *ḥadīths* 2417 – 2419)

509 Pronounced *Mi'īn* in the genitive case.

more than a hundred *āyāt*.

3. *Mathānī* (Oft-Repeated)[510] – they have less than one hundred *āyāt*.
4. *Mufaṣṣal* (Distinct).[511]

In the sequence of the Noble Qur'ān, two or three *mathānī sūrahs* have been included among the *mi'ūn sūrahs*, and that is because their context corresponded to that of those *mi'ūn sūrahs*. Likewise, in the other categories there are some instances of a similar nature.

Based on this *muṣḥaf*, 'Uthmān[512] ﷺ had some copies made that he sent to the different provinces in order that the Muslims could derive benefit from them and so that they would not incline towards any other arrangement.[513]

510 These chapters are so called because they are recited more often than the Seven Long *Sūrahs* and the Hundreds.

511 It was reported by Wāthilah ibn al-Asqa' ﷺ who said: The Prophet ﷺ said, "I have been given in lieu of the Torah (Tawrāh), the Seven Long *Sūrahs* (*as-Sab' aṭ-Ṭiwāl*); in lieu of the Psalms (Zabūr), the Hundreds (*al-Mi'īn*); and in lieu of the Injīl, the Oft-Repeated *Sūrahs* (*al-Mathānī*), and I have been singled out for the Distinct *Sūrahs* (*al-Mufaṣṣal*)." (Al-Bayhaqī, *Shu'ab al-Īmān*, chapter *Dhikr as-Sab' aṭ-Ṭiwāl*, *ḥadīth* 2415)

512 He is 'Uthmān ibn ʿAffān ﷺ (45 BH/579 CE – 35 AH/656 CE), the third *khalīfah* after the Prophet ﷺ. He is known as *Dhu'n-Nūrayn* (Possessor of the Two Lights), for having been honoured with consecutively marrying two of the daughters of the Prophet Muḥammad ﷺ.

513 Anas ibn Mālik ﷺ reported that Ḥudhayfah ibn al-Yamān came to 'Uthmān when the people of Syria were conquering Armenia and Azerbaijan with the people of Iraq. Ḥudhayfah was alarmed by the differences in their recitation. Ḥudhayfah said to 'Uthmān, "Amīr al-Mu'minīn! Save this community before they disagree about the Book as the Jews and Christians differed!" So 'Uthmān sent a message to Ḥafṣah, saying, "Send us the manuscripts (in your possession) and we will copy them and then return them to you." So Ḥafṣah sent them to 'Uthmān. He ordered Zayd ibn Thābit, 'Abdullāh ibn az-Zubayr, Sa'īd ibn al-'Āṣ, and 'Abd ar-Raḥmān ibn al-Ḥārith ibn Hishām to transcribe copies.

The Beginnings and Conclusions of the *Sūrahs* are Like Royal Edicts

Since there is a perfect relationship between the styles of the *sūrahs* and the style of royal edicts, at the beginning and the end, the method of correspondence was adhered to. For just as they begin some of them with praise of Allah ﷻ, and some with explanation of the purpose of the dictation, and some with the name of the sender and the one to whom the letter is sent, some are brief messages and fragments without any specific topic, and some are lengthy while others are brief, likewise, Allah ﷻ begins some chapters with praise and glorification, and others with explanation of the purpose of the revelation:

ذَلِكَ الْكِتَابُ لَا رَيْبَ فِيهِ هُدًى لِلْمُتَّقِينَ

"That is the Book, without any doubt.
In it is guidance for the God-fearing"[514]

and His ﷻ words:

سُورَةٌ أَنْزَلْنَاهَا وَفَرَضْنَاهَا

"A sūrah We have sent down and imposed."[515]

This category of *sūrah* resembles that which they write, such as:

'Uthmān said to the group of the three Qurayshīs, "When you and Zayd ibn Thābit disagree about any portion of the Qur'ān, write it in the dialect of the Quraysh for it was revealed in their language." They did just that. When they had made many copies from it, 'Uthmān returned the manuscripts to Ḥafṣah and he sent a copy of what they had copied out to every region and commanded that every sheet or copy which had any other form of the Qur'ān should be burned. (Al-Bukhārī, *al-Jāmi' aṣ-Ṣaḥīḥ, Kitāb Faḍā'il al-Qur'ān, ḥadīth* 4984; *Kitāb Nazala al-Qur'ān bi-Lisān Quraysh, ḥadīth* 3506)

514 Qur'ān, Sūrat al-Baqarah 2:2.

515 Qur'ān, Sūrat an-Nūr 24:1.

"This is what so-and-so has agreed with so-and-so" and "This is what so-and-so has bequeathed." And the Prophet ﷺ wrote at the Treaty of Ḥudaybiyyah:

هَذَا مَا قَاضَى عَلَيْهِ مُحَمَّدٌ رَسُولُ اللَّهِ

"This is that what Muḥammad the Messenger of Allah ﷺ brings suit on the basis of..."[516]

Some Qur'ānic *āyat* begin with the name of the sender or the addressee, as He ﷻ said:

تَنزِيلُ ٱلْكِتَٰبِ مِنَ ٱللَّهِ ٱلْعَزِيزِ ٱلْحَكِيمِ

"The revelation of the Book is from Allah, the Almighty, the All-Wise"[517]

and He ﷻ said:

كِتَٰبٌ أُحْكِمَتْ ءَايَٰتُهُۥ ثُمَّ فُصِّلَتْ مِن لَّدُنْ حَكِيمٍ خَبِيرٍ

"A Book whose āyāt are perfectly constructed, and then demarcated, coming directly from One who is All-Wise, All-Aware."[518]

This category resembles that which they write: 'This edict is issued by the Royal Office of ...' or when they write: 'This is an announcement from His Highness the Khalīfah to the inhabitants of such-and-such a city...'

The Prophet ﷺ had written:

مِنْ مُحَمَّدٍ عَبْدِ اللَّهِ وَرَسُولِهِ إِلَى هِرَقْلَ عَظِيمِ الرُّومِ

"From Muḥammad, the slave of Allah and His Messenger,

516 Al-Bukhārī, *al-Jāmi' aṣ-Ṣaḥīḥ*, *Kitāb aṣ-Ṣulḥ*, chapter 6, *ḥadīth* 2699.
517 Qur'ān, Sūrat az-Zumar 39:1.
518 Qur'ān, Sūrat Hūd 11:1.

to Heraclius[519], Emperor of the Byzantines."[520]

Some of them begin in the manner of brief messages and fragments without specific topics, as He ﷻ said:

إِذَا جَآءَكَ ٱلْمُنَٰفِقُونَ

"When the hypocrites come to you"[521]

and He ﷻ said:

قَدْ سَمِعَ ٱللَّهُ قَوْلَ ٱلَّتِى تُجَٰدِلُكَ فِى زَوْجِهَا

"Allah has heard the words of the woman who disputes with you about herhusband"[522]

and He ﷻ said:

يَٰٓأَيُّهَا ٱلنَّبِىُّ لِمَ تُحَرِّمُ مَآ أَحَلَّ ٱللَّهُ لَكَ

"O Prophet! Why do you make ḥarām what Allah has made ḥalāl foryou."[523]

Poetic Format of the Beginning of Some *Sūrahs*

Since the epitome of Arab eloquence is in their odes, and it was one of their old traditions in the commencement of their odes that they would rhapsodise about amazing places and extraordinary events, then Allah ﷻ adopted this mode in some *sūrahs*, as He ﷻ said:

519 Heraclius (49 BH/575 CE – 20 AH/641 CE).

520 Al-Bukhārī, *al-Jāmi' aṣ-Ṣaḥīḥ, Kitāb Bad' al-Waḥy, ḥadīth* 7; *Kitāb al-Jihād, ḥadīth* 2941.

521 Qur'ān, Sūrat al-Munāfiqūn 63:1.

522 Qur'ān, Sūrat al-Mujādilah 58:1.

523 Qur'ān, Sūrat at-Taḥrīm 66:1.

وَٱلصَّـٰٓفَّـٰتِ صَفًّا، فَٱلزَّٰجِرَٰتِ زَجْرًا، فَٱلتَّـٰلِيَـٰتِ ذِكْرًا

"By those drawn up in ranks, and by the warners crying warning, and by the reciters of the Reminder"[524]

and He ﷻ said:

وَٱلذَّٰرِيَـٰتِ ذَرْوًا، فَٱلْحَـٰمِلَـٰتِ وِقْرًا

"By the scatterers scattering, and those bearing weighty loads"[525]

and He ﷻ said:

إِذَا ٱلشَّمْسُ كُوِّرَتْ، وَإِذَا ٱلنُّجُومُ ٱنكَدَرَتْ

"When the sun is compacted in blackness, when the stars fall in rapid succession."[526]

Concluding Parts of *Sūrahs* According to the Mode of Edicts

Just as kings conclude their edicts with concise comprehensive statements, excellent counsels, emphasis on holding fast to the aforementioned commands, and severe warnings against those who oppose them, likewise, Allah ﷻ concluded the *sūrahs* with concise comprehensive words, springs of wisdom, eloquent emphasis and stern admonitions.

Interspersal of Eloquent Words in the Middle of the *Sūrahs*

Occasionally, within the *sūrah*, an eloquent statement of an extremely beneficial and wonderful nature occurs, comprising all sorts of praise and glorification [of Allah ﷻ] or the expression of [Divine] favours and reminders of [His] blessings, for example: As He ﷻ commenced to state the difference in the statuses of the

524 Qur'ān, Sūrat aṣ-Ṣāffāt 37:1-3.
525 Qur'ān, Sūrat adh-Dhāriyat 51:1-2.
526 Qur'ān, Sūrat at-Takwīr 81:1-2.

Creator and the creatures in His ﷻ words:

قُلِ ٱلْحَمْدُ لِلَّهِ وَسَلَـٰمٌ عَلَىٰ عِبَادِهِ ٱلَّذِينَ ٱصْطَفَىٰٓ
ءَآللَّهُ خَيْرٌ أَمَّا يُشْرِكُونَ

"Say: 'Praise be to Allah and peace be upon His slaves whom He has chosen.' Is Allah better, or what they associate with Him?"[527]

Then, He elucidated this subject in five *āyāt* in the most eloquent mannerandwithanamazingmethod.[528]

Allah ﷻ commenced the argument with Banī Isrā'īl that takes place throughout Sūrat al-Baqarah (2) with His words:

527 Qur'ān, Sūrat an-Naml 27:59.

528 Qur'ān, Sūrat an-Naml 27:60-64:
أَمَّنْ خَلَقَ ٱلسَّمَـٰوَٰتِ وَٱلْأَرْضَ وَأَنزَلَ لَكُم مِّنَ ٱلسَّمَآءِ مَآءً فَأَنۢبَتْنَا بِهِۦ حَدَآئِقَ ذَاتَ بَهْجَةٍ مَّا كَانَ لَكُمْ أَن تُنۢبِتُوا۟
شَجَرَهَآ ۗ أَءِلَـٰهٌ مَّعَ ٱللَّهِ ۚ بَلْ هُمْ قَوْمٌ يَعْدِلُونَ أَمَّن جَعَلَ ٱلْأَرْضَ قَرَارًا وَجَعَلَ خِلَـٰلَهَآ أَنْهَـٰرًا وَجَعَلَ لَهَا رَوَٰسِىَ وَجَعَلَ
بَيْنَ ٱلْبَحْرَيْنِ حَاجِزًا ۗ أَءِلَـٰهٌ مَّعَ ٱللَّهِ ۚ بَلْ أَكْثَرُهُمْ لَا يَعْلَمُونَ أَمَّن يُجِيبُ ٱلْمُضْطَرَّ إِذَا دَعَاهُ وَيَكْشِفُ ٱلسُّوٓءَ وَيَجْعَلُكُمْ
خُلَفَآءَ ٱلْأَرْضِ ۗ أَءِلَـٰهٌ مَّعَ ٱللَّهِ ۚ قَلِيلًا مَّا تَذَكَّرُونَ أَمَّن يَهْدِيكُمْ فِى ظُلُمَـٰتِ ٱلْبَرِّ وَٱلْبَحْرِ وَمَن يُرْسِلُ ٱلرِّيَـٰحَ بُشْرًۢا بَيْنَ يَدَىْ
رَحْمَتِهِۦٓ ۗ أَءِلَـٰهٌ مَّعَ ٱللَّهِ ۚ تَعَـٰلَى ٱللَّهُ عَمَّا يُشْرِكُونَ أَمَّن يَبْدَؤُا۟ ٱلْخَلْقَ ثُمَّ يُعِيدُهُۥ وَمَن يَرْزُقُكُم مِّنَ ٱلسَّمَآءِ وَٱلْأَرْضِ ۗ أَءِلَـٰهٌ
مَّعَ ٱللَّهِ ۚ قُلْ هَاتُوا۟ بُرْهَـٰنَكُمْ إِن كُنتُمْ صَـٰدِقِينَ

"He Who created the heavens and the earth and sends down water for you from the sky by which We make luxuriant gardens grow – you could never make their trees grow. Is there another god besides Allah? No indeed, but they are people who equate others with Him! He Who made the earth a stable dwelling place and appointed rivers flowing through its midst and placed firmly embedded mountains on it and set a barrier between the two seas. Is there another god besides Allah? No indeed, but most of them do not know it! He Who responds to the oppressed when they call on Him and removes their distress, and has appointed you as khalīfahs on the earth. Is there another god besides Allah? How little you pay heed! He Who guides you in the darkness of land and sea and sends out the winds bringing advance news of His mercy. Is there another god besides Allah? Exalted is Allah above what they associate with Him! He Who originates creation and then regenerates it and provides for you from out of heaven and earth. Is there another god besides Allah? Say: 'Bring your proof if you are being truthful.'"

يَـٰبَنِىٓ إِسْرَٰٓءِيلَ ٱذْكُرُوا۟ نِعْمَتِىَ ٱلَّتِىٓ أَنْعَمْتُ عَلَيْكُمْ

"Tribe of Israel! remember the blessing I conferred on you"[529]

and then He concludes the argument with the same words:

يَـٰبَنِىٓ إِسْرَٰٓءِيلَ ٱذْكُرُوا۟ نِعْمَتِىَ ٱلَّتِىٓ أَنْعَمْتُ عَلَيْكُمْ

"Tribe of Israel! remember the blessing I conferred on you."[530]

In Arab rhetoric, to conclude an argument with the very words that it commenced with is held in high regard.

Similarly, He ﷻ begins the polemic with the People of the Book (*Ahl al-Kitāb*)[531] in Sūrah Āl 'Imrān (3) with His words:

إِنَّ ٱلدِّينَ عِندَ ٱللَّهِ ٱلْإِسْلَـٰمُ

"The dīn in the sight of Allah is Islam"[532]

so that the cause of the dispute is clear, and the subsequent discourse restricted to that claim. And Allah ﷻ knows best.

529 Qur'ān, Sūrat al-Baqarah 2:40.

530 Qur'ān, Sūrat al-Baqarah 2:47.

531 *Ahl al-Kitāb*: the People of the Book, referring to the Jews and Christians. Some other religions are treated analogously with them, but not in all respects. For example, although Zoroastrians are accorded some of the same rights under Islamic governance as Jews and Christians, Muslims may not eat their meat or marry them. Ed.

532 Qur'ān, Sūrah Āl 'Imrān 3:19.

Chapter 2

Division of the *Sūrahs* into *Āyāt* and Their Unique Mode of Expression

The practice of Allah ﷻ in most *sūrahs* is to divide them into *āyāt* just as the poets ordinarily divide poems up into verses.

The Difference between *Āyāt* and Verses

The limit of what can be said about the difference between them is that in both of them the voice is raised in recitation in order to give pleasure to both the persons of the declaimer and the listener, but that verses are restricted by the rules of versification and rhyme which Khalīl ibn Aḥmad [an-Naḥwī][533] recorded and from whom the poets received them. The *āyāt* are based on overall metre and rhyme that resemble natural flow very much, and not on [metres such as] أفاعيل (*afā'īl*) and تفاعيل (*tafā'īl*)[534] nor on specific

533 He is 'Abd ar-Raḥmān al-Khalīl ibn Aḥmad al-Farāhīdī (110 AH/718 CE – 175 AH/791 CE), inventor of the Science of Prosody (*'Ilm al-'Arūḍ*) and founder of Arabic Lexicography. He was the grammar (*naḥw*) teacher of Sībawayh/Sībūyeh, of al-Aṣma'ī and of the grammarians of Baṣra. He wrote the *Kitāb al-'Ayn*, considered to be the first Arabic lexicon.

534 These are the metres of a poem – they are four; 1. فَعُوْلُنْ (*fa'ūlun*), 2. مَفَاعِيْلُنْ (*mafā'īlun*), 3. مَفَاعِلَتُنْ (*mafā'ilatun*), 4. فَاعِلَاتُنْ (*fā'ilātun*) – all other metres are

rhymes, etc., which are matters of craft and terminology.

WHAT *ĀYĀT* AND VERSES HAVE IN COMMON

As for reviewing that which *āyāt* and verses of poetry have in common – and we express that universal matter as the voice being raised in recitation, then apprehension of those matters that were adhered to in the *āyāt* and that have the rank of section marking – then all of that requires some detail, and Allah ﷻ is the Guardian of success.

The detail of this summary is that a sound innate natural disposition (*fiṭrah salīmah*) experiences a certain type of enjoyment and sweetness in listening to rhyming and well-measured poems and fine *rajaz*-poetry[535]. If one considers the cause of that perception of sweetness, one realises that the soul of the person addressed tastes a special sweetness in speech, part of which is in harmony with another part and it makes him anticipate other speech of a similar nature. When he hears another couplet, whose parts are similarly balanced and harmonious, and what he anticipated is realised, his pleasure is multiplied. If both verses have corresponding rhymes too, the pleasure is multiplied thrice-fold. Thus, enjoying and finding pleasure in verses with this secret is a part of primordial human nature with which humans have been created. All people of sound temperaments from moderate climates agree unanimously about that.

Then after that, different schools and methods came about with respect to the harmony of different metres in every verse and similarly on the conditions of the rhymes between verses.

The Arabs follow particular rules and principles which al-Khalīl clarified, and the Indians follow a different method that corresponds to their linguistic disposition and their natural genius.

derived from these four.

535 *rajaz*: classical Arabic musical poetry with a simple metre that is often recited in military/war chants.

Similarly, people of each epoch devised a specific technique and they travelled a distinct route.

Approximate Concordance is the Matter that Different Types of Composed Speech Have in Common

If we were to seek a common uniting factor in their differing forms and traditions, and we considered the all-encompassing secret in them, we would discover that it is 'approximate concordance' and nothing else. For example, the Arabs sometimes use مَفَاعِلُنْ (*mafāʿilun*) and مُفْتَعِلُنْ (*muftaʿilun*) in place of مُسْتَفْعِلُنْ (*mustafʿilun*), and they consider فَعْلَاتُنْ (*fuʿlātun*) a substitute for فَاعِلَاتُنْ (*fāʿilātun*) according to the rule, and they believe it important for the last foot[536] of the second hemistich of a verse to correspond with the last foot of the second hemistich of another verse, and likewise the last foot of the first hemistich of a verse to correspond with the last foot of the first hemistich of another verse. In the portion of a hemistich between the first and last foot (*ḥashw*),[537] they permit much elision and omission (*ziḥāf*),[538] contrary to the poets of Persia who consider elision and omission ugly.

Similarly, the Arabs consider it good to use مُنيراً in the second verse, if the first verse contains قبوراً, contrary to non-Arab poets. Arab poets consider the words دَاخِلُ ,حَاصِلُ and نَازِلُ to be of the same category, contrary to non-Arab poets.

The use of a word in a manner such that it falls between the two hemistichs of the verse and such that a half is at the beginning [of the second hemistich] and a half is in the tail [of the first hemistich] is considered correct by the Arabs but not by non-Arabs.

In brief, the common factor between Arabic and Persian prosody

536 This is the caesurae.

537 *ḥashw*: metrical interpolation of words into a text.

538 زِحَاف pl. زِحَافَات (*ziḥāf*) consists in the omission of a letter or a vowel or both for the sake of the rhyme.

is approximate concordance and not exact concordance.

Indian Metres

The Indians based the metres of their poetry on the number of letters, without taking into consideration the measures of the vowels and the consonants. They also give us a sense of pleasure. We have heard the tunes that some villagers sing and take pleasure in and it is speech that has approximate concordance or a *radīf*[539] that may be of only one word or a combination of many words. They sing these like poems and derive pleasure from them. Every people has specific procedures in their prosody.

Similarly, all nations are agreed on seeking pleasure from tunes and melodies, but the difference lies in their manner of singing and its rules.

Greek Tunes

The Greeks have formulated some metres that they call '*al-Maqāmāt*' (a system of modes that divides an octave into tones) from which they have derived certain tones and subdivisions and they have developed an extremely fine and detailed art for themselves.

Indian Tunes

The Indians developed six modes (*naghamāt*), from which they developed smaller modes. We have seen that in the village, people who are oblivious of these terminologies were intelligent enough to compose words and give them melodies according to their own inbuilt dispositions, which they sing without defining their principles or restricting their particular issues.

If we hazard an opinion after these observations, we do not find the common factor to be anything but approximate concordance, and the intellect has no goal but that summary extract and it has

539 *radīf*: rhythmic ending of two or more verses, with one or more words.

no concern for the details of connected complementary rhymes. Good taste desires only the pure sweetness and does not concern itself with the *ṭawīl* (long) and *madīd* (extended) *baḥrs*[540].

Qur'ānic Observance of this Common Universal Beauty

When the Creator ﷻ wanted to address man, who is created from a handful of clay, He only considered that comprehensive common beauty and did not consider those forms that some people, but not others, think of as beautiful. Then when the King of Kings ﷻ wanted to speak in the manner of human beings He paid attention to that simple principle and shared secret and did not observe the rules that change with the changing of times and circumstances.

In reality, the basis for a strict adoption of terminological rules is incapacity and ignorance, and the attainment of this summary and artistic beauty without the medium of those rules – such that eloquence does not change in the lowlands and the highlands and speech does not become lost in the plains and the mountains – is a miracle that is dumbfounding. I will extract a foundation from the flow of the Truth, exalted is He, according to that usage, and formulate a principle from it: that in most of the *sūrahs* Allah ﷻ has observed the extent of the breath and not *ṭawīl* and *madīd* measures. Similarly, during pauses between *āyāt*, He ﷻ has observed the cessation of breath on the long-vowels, or on that which a long-vowel stops, not the rules of the art of versification. This principle demands further expansion and detail, and so let the reader pay close attention to what I say.

The entrance of the breath into the human windpipe and

540 *baḥr*: fixed metrical lines in Arabic poetry. In Arabic poetry, these total nineteen; *ṭawīl*, *madīd*, *basīṭ*, *wāfir*, *kāmil*, *hazaj*, *rajaz*, *muqtaḍab*, *ramal*, *munsariḥ*, *muḍāri'*, *mujtathth*, *sarī'*, *jadīd*, *qarīb*, *khafīf*, *mushākil*, *mutaqārib* and *mutadārik*. (Shipley, Joseph Twadell, ed. *Dictionary of World Literature: Criticism, Forms, Technique.* London: George Routledge & Sons Ltd., 1943, p.430)

its exit is a natural matter in man even if its prolongation or shortening is a part of what is destined. However, if it is left to its natural disposition, it only has a limited prolongation. When man breathes he experiences animation, and then that animation diminishes gradually until it disappears completely, and then he needs a second fresh breath. This prolongation is a matter that is limited to an unknown degree and it is fixed to a common measure, inasmuch as it does no harm to omit two or three words, or indeed, a third or a quarter of its extent. Similarly, it does not take one beyond the limit to add two or three words, nor indeed the increase of a third or a quarter. One is permitted to differentiate between the number of three-letter words (*watid*[541]) and two-letter words (*sabab*[542]), and it is also allowed to bring some of the 'feet' (*rukn*[543]) forward before others. This prolongation of the breath has been made a metre, and divided into three:

i. long (*ṭawīl*) – e.g. Sūrat an-Nisā' (4)

ii. medium (*mutawassiṭ*) – e.g. Sūrat al-A'rāf (7) and Sūrat al-An'ām (6)

iii. short (*qaṣīr*) – e.g. Sūrat ash-Shu'arā' (26) and Sūrat ad-Dukhān (44)

Qur'ānic Rhymes

Concluding the breath on a prolongation that relies on a letter is the sufficient rhyme from whose repetition again and again one's nature derives much pleasure, irrespective of whether those [final] letters are the quiescent letters (*maddah*) ا (*alif*) in one place, و (*wāw*) in another place, and ي (*yā'*) in yet another, or whether that final letter is the [consonant] ب (*bā'*) in one place, ج (*jīm*) in

541 *watid*: a 'peg' of a verse, it is an Arabic word of three letters the first of which is voweled and the second or third of which is silent.

542 *sabab*: a 'cord' of a verse, it is an Arabic word composed of only two letters the latter of which is either voweled or silent.

543 *rukn*: 'foot' in a verse of poetry. The foot is the basic metrical unit that generates a line of verse.

another place and ق (*qāf*) in another. Thus, according to this rule, the words: يَعْلَمُونَ ، مُؤْمِنِينَ and مُسْتَقِيمٌ all rhyme and مَرِيجٌ ، تَجِيدُ ، تَبَارٌ ، فَوَاقٌ ، خُرُوجٌ and عُجَابٌ are all according to the rule.

Suffixing an Alif

Likewise, the occurrence of ا – *alif* at the end of the word is a sufficient rhyme – its repetition delights even though the last quiescent letter of the rhyming word (*rawī*)[544] is different, as in one place He ﷻ says, 'كَرِيمًا', in another 'حَدِيثًا' and again 'بَصِيرًا'. If the rhyme of the last letter of each verse was binding here, it would be akin to binding oneself to something unnecessary, such as that which occurs at the beginnings of Sūrah Maryam (19) and Sūrat al-Furqān (25).

Concordance of the Āyāt on the Same Letter

Rhyming of *āyāt* on the same letter, such as the letter م (*mīm*) in Sūrat al-Qitāl (47)[545], and the letter ن (*nūn*) in Sūrat ar-Raḥmān (55) – affords pleasure and sweetness. Likewise, the repetition of a phrase after a portion of speech is also very appealing, such as those in Sūrat ash-Shuʿarā' (26), Sūrat al-Qamar (54), Sūrat ar-Raḥmān (55) and Sūrat al-Mursalāt (77).

Sometimes, the rhyme at the end of the *sūrah* may be exchanged for the first part in order to stimulate the listener and in order to draw attention to the gracefulness of the speech, for example, as in 'إِدًّا' and 'هَدًّا' towards the end of Sūrah Maryam (19), and 'سَلَامًا' and 'كِرَامًا' towards the end of Sūrat al-Furqān (25), and 'سَاجِدِينَ', 'طِينٍ' and 'مُنظَرِينَ' towards the end of Sūrah Ṣād (38) along with the fact that the rhymes at the beginnings of these *sūrahs* differ from them, as is clear.[546]

In most *sūrahs*, such metres and rhymes as we have indicated

544 *rawī*: the last quiescent letter of a verse.

545 Qur'ān, Sūrat al-Qitāl (47) is also known as Sūrah Muḥammad.

546 They later adopt endings to their *āyāt* different from the endings of the earlier *āyāt*.

are understood to be significant. If there is a word at the end of an *āyah* that is appropriate for a rhyme then that is what is done, otherwise it is connected to a phrase or clause that expresses the favours of Allah (*ālā'ullāh*), or one that issues a warning to those addressed. For example:

i. وَهُوَ الْحَكِيمُ الْخَبِيرُ – *"He is the All-Wise, the All-Aware."*[547]
ii. وَكَانَ اللَّهُ عَلِيمًا حَكِيمًا – *"And Allah is All-Knowing, All-Wise."*[548]
iii. كَانَ اللَّهُ بِمَا تَعْمَلُونَ خَبِيرًا – *"Allah is Aware of what you do."*[549]
iv. لَعَلَّكُمْ تَتَّقُونَ – *"So that hopefully you will be God-fearing."*[550]
v. إِنَّ فِي ذَلِكَ لَذِكْرَى لِأُولِي الْأَلْبَابِ – *"There is a reminder in that for people of intelligence."*[551]
vi. إِنَّ فِي ذَلِكَ لَآيَاتٍ لِقَوْمٍ يَتَفَكَّرُونَ – *"There are certainly Signs in that for people who reflect."*[552]

Sometimes, exaggeration is required in such situations, for example "فَاسْأَلْ بِهِ خَبِيرًا – *Ask anyone who is informed about Him*"[553] and bringing forward or putting back in the word order is sometimes employed, and at other times there may be transposition of letters or an addition, such as "إِلْ يَاسِينَ i.e. إِلْيَاسَ – (The prophet) Ilyās"[554] and "وَطُورِ سِينِينَ i.e سِينَاء – *and Mount Sinai.*"[555]

The Secret Behind Harmonising Long *Āyāt* with Shorter *Āyāt* and Vice-versa

Here one ought to know that the harmony of speech and its ease on the tongue – for example because of the fact that it flows or because of its repetition in the *āyah* – puts long phrases in balance

547 Qur'ān, Sūrat al-An'ām 6:18.
548 Qur'ān, Sūrat an-Nisā' 4:17.
549 Qur'ān, Sūrat al-Fatḥ 48:11.
550 Qur'ān, Sūrat al-A'rāf 7:171.
551 Qur'ān, Sūrat az-Zumar 39:21.
552 Qur'ān, Sūrat ar-Rūm 30:21.
553 Qur'ān, Sūrat al-Furqān 25:59.
554 Qur'ān, Sūrat aṣ-Ṣāffāt 37:130.
555 Qur'ān, Sūrat at-Tīn 95:2.

with short phrases.

Occasionally, first clauses may be shorter and tighter than subsequent clauses, something which gives the words sweetness, for example, in His ﷻ words:

خُذُوهُ فَغُلُّوهُ، ثُمَّ ٱلْجَحِيمَ صَلُّوهُ، ثُمَّ فِى سِلْسِلَةٍ ذَرْعُهَا سَبْعُونَ ذِرَاعًا فَٱسْلُكُوهُ

"Seize him and truss him up. Then roast him in the Blazing Fire. Then bind him in a chain which is seventy cubits long."[556]

It is as if the Speaker conceals within himself in the like of such speech that the first phrase [*seize him and truss him up*] along with the second [*then roast him in the Blazing Fire*] are in one pan [of the balance] and the third phrase alone [*then bind him in a chain which is seventy cubits long*] is in another pan.

Qur'ānic *Āyāt* with Three Main Supports

Occasionally *āyāt* may have three main supports, such as His ﷻ words:

يَوْمَ تَبْيَضُّ وُجُوهٌ وَتَسْوَدُّ وُجُوهٌ فَأَمَّا ٱلَّذِينَ ٱسْوَدَّتْ وُجُوهُهُمْ أَكَفَرْتُم بَعْدَ إِيمَٰنِكُمْ فَذُوقُوا ٱلْعَذَابَ بِمَا كُنتُمْ تَكْفُرُونَ وَأَمَّا ٱلَّذِينَ ٱبْيَضَّتْ وُجُوهُهُمْ فَفِى رَحْمَةِ ٱللَّهِ هُمْ فِيهَا خَٰلِدُونَ

"On the Day when faces are whitened and faces are blackened. As for those whose faces are blackened: 'What! Did you disbelieve after having believed? Taste the punishment for your unbelief!'

As for those whose faces are whitened, they are in Allah's mercy,

556 Qur'ān, Sūrat al-Ḥāqqah 69:30-32.

remaining in it timelessly, for ever."[557]

[There are two *āyāt* here.] Ordinary people amalgamate the first with the second and consider it a long one.

Qur'ānic *Āyāt* with Two Metrical Feet

There may at times occur two rhymes within the same *āyah*, as is found in the following couplet:

كَالزَّهْرِ فِي تَرَفٍ وَالْبَدْرِ فِي شَرَفٍ   وَالْبَحْرِ فِي كَرَمٍ وَالدَّهْرِ فِي هِمَمِ

(The Prophet ﷺ) is like a blooming flower in freshness and the full moon in splendour,

And the ocean in generosity and time in its fearless courage.[558]

The Reason Behind a Longer *Āyah* Being with Other Short Ones

Occasionally, a single *āyah* might appear that is longer than all the other *āyāt*. The secret in it is that if the beauty of the speech which arose from close approximation of metre and the excitement of the anticipated matter, i.e. the rhyme, were to be placed in one pan, and the beauty of the speech that arose from ease of delivery and accordance with the nature of the speech without any alteration in it were to be placed in another pan, sound natures would consider the aspect of meaning [i.e. the second case] to be weightier and would disregard one of the two anticipations and would round out the truth by awaiting the second.

Other Modes of Expression in the *Sūrahs*

As for that which we said at the beginning of this discussion, that the Sunnah of Allah ﷻ has been thus in *most* of the Qur'ānic

557 Qur'ān, Sūrah Āl 'Imrān 3:106-107.

558 Al-Būṣīrī, Sharafuddīn Muḥammad ibn Sa'īd (607 AH/1211 CE – 693 AH/1294 CE), *Qaṣidat al-Burdah (al-Kawākib ad-Durriyyah fi Madḥ Khayr al-Bariyyah)*, Chapter 3 – On Praising the Prophet ﷺ, couplet 55.

sūrahs, that is because some of them do not exhibit such metres or rhymes. Hence, some of these Qur'ānic *sūrahs* are on the model of public speakers' orations and sages' parables. You may have heard of the conversation of the women that is narrated by our lady ʿĀ'ishah[559], and you may know well its rhymes. In some *sūrahs*, the speech occurs according to the fashion of the writings of the Arabs without attending to any [structure], such as the conversations of people between themselves, except that all speech is concluded with something that makes it clear that it is its conclusion.

The secret here is that the pause in the Arabic language occurs where one's breath ends and when the statement runs out of vitality. It is preferable to end speech on a quiescent letter[560]. It is for this reason that the Speech takes the form of *āyāt*.

This is what Allah has opened up to this incapable person in this area. And Allah ﷻ knows best.

The Reason for Choosing New Metres and Rhymes

If they ask: Why did He ﷻ not choose those metres and rhymes which the poets acknowledge and which are more pleasurable than this? Then we would say: the fact of them being more pleasurable differs with differing people and understandings, and even if we accepted [your assumption], the origination of methods of metres and rhymes on the tongue of the Messenger of Allah ﷺ – while he was *ummī* (untutored by any person) – is a clear sign of his prophethood ﷺ.

If the Qur'ān had been revealed according to the metres of the poets and their rhymes, the *kuffār* (disbelievers) would have thought that it is the same poetry as is well known and famous among the Arabs and would have gained no benefit from that

559 A *ḥadīth* of Sayyidah 'Ā'ishah in which eleven women adopt rhyming schemes when describing their husbands. (Al-Bukhārī, *al-Jāmi' aṣ-Ṣaḥīḥ, Kitāb an-Nikāḥ*, chapter 83, *ḥadīth* 5189)

560 The quiescent letters are: ا (*alif*), و (*wāw*) and ي (*yā'*).

thought, just as when eloquent poets and writers try to show their superiority over their peers in front of witnesses, they derive new forms and issue the challenge "Is there anyone who can write poetry like me, or write a treatise like me?" If such people had proceeded according to the old paradigms their proficiency would only have been obvious to others who are themselves proficient and consummate.

Chapter 3

The Logic Behind the Repetition of the Five Sciences and the Lack of Order in Explaining Them

Firstly, if they ask the reason as to why the five sciences in the Noble Qur'ān have been mentioned repeatedly, and why He ﷻ did not suffice Himself with one particular location, we say:

There are two degrees of what we want to disclose to the reader:

1. The purpose here is only to teach something unknown. In the case of a person addressed who knows none of the rulings and whose intellect grasps none of it, when he hears this speech that of which he had been ignorant becomes known.
2. The purpose is to make the image of that knowledge present in his faculty of perception so that he may find complete sweetness in it and so that his heart and his faculty of perception might be totally engrossed in that knowledge, and the colour of that knowledge might overwhelm all of his faculties until they are, as it were, tinted with them, in the same way as we recite poetry whose meaning we know and yet every time we find a new pleasure and so we love the repetition for this reason.

Both degrees are intended in the Tremendous Qur'ān when

investigating the five sciences: for those ignorant, it is intended to teach them what they do not know, and for the person of knowledge, repetition is adopted in order to permeate them with these sciences.

However, most of the discussions on rulings are not repeated because the second degree was not sought.

For this reason, Allah, exalted is He, orders us to recite [the Noble Qur'ān] repeatedly and a great deal, and does not suffice Himself with our simply understanding it.

However, He ﷻ observed this measure of differentiation along with this repetition that He chose in most circumstances to repeat these issues with fresh expressions and new methods so that they would have more impact on people and would be more forceful arguments for their intellects. If He ﷻ had simply repeated one expression it would have been like the *wird*[561] which they repeat. As for using different expressions and varying the methods, then the intellect and thoughts will go deeply and fully into those issues.

Secondly, if they ask: why are these issues spread throughout the Tremendous Qur'ān without any attention to order and structure such as mentioning the blessings of Allah first and giving them their due, then mentioning the Days of Allah and completing them, and then embarking on dialectic with the disbelievers? Then we say that even if the power of Allah, blessed is He and exalted, encompasses all conceivable things, nevertheless what is decisive in these subject matters is wisdom. Wisdom entails the harmony of that which is sent to them both linguistically and in the methods of explanation, and this sense is indicated in His ﷻ words:

561 A *wird* is any portion of *dhikr* (invocation and remembrance of Allah ﷻ), Qur'ān and *du'ā* that is recited regularly.

لَّقَالُوا۟ لَوْلَا فُصِّلَتْ ءَايَـٰتُهُۥٓ ءَا۬عْجَمِىٌّ وَعَرَبِىٌّ

"They would have said, 'Why have its Signs not been made plain? What! A foreign language for an Arab?' "[562]

The Arabs had no book up until the time of the revelation of the Qur'ān, neither a Divine Book nor one of human authorship. The kind of structures which authors have invented today would not have been recognised by the Arabs. If you have any doubt about this then contemplate the poems of the poets whose lives spanned pre-Islamic *jāhiliyyah* (the Era of Ignorance) and Islam, and read the letters of the Noble Prophet ﷺ, the correspondence of 'Umar al-Fārūq ؓ and this reality will become clear to you. Thus if the Speech had come with some other method of rhetoric than they were familiar with they would have fallen into bewilderment, and something they were unfamiliar with would have reached their hearing and it would have confused their minds.

Also, the purpose is not merely to acquaint them with something they do not know, rather the purpose is to acquaint them, along with evocation and repetition and that this sense be found abundantly without any particular order in the strongest possible way and the most complete form.

562 Qur'ān, Sūrah Fuṣṣilat 41:44.

Chapter 4

The Inimitable Nature of the Noble Qur'ān

If they ask how the Noble Qur'ān could be classified as inimitable, then we may respond by saying that according to us, the inimitable nature of the Noble Qur'ān is multifaceted, for example:

1. Its mode of expression – the Arabs had many areas of rhetoric in which they would compete with their contemporaries in eloquence: poetry (*qaṣīdah*[563]), speeches, epistles and dialogues. The Arabs were not familiar with any other modes of expression than these four, nor had they the capacity to invent any other mode. The origination of a mode of expression totally distinct from those existing modes, upon the tongue of the *ummī* Prophet ﷺ was sufficient miracle.
2. Its informing us about the histories and the rulings of previous religions in such a way as affirmed previously revealed Divine scriptures without having learnt that from anyone.
3. Its informing us about circumstances yet to come about, and thus whenever any of that is found to be true and in accordance

563 A *qaṣīdah* is poetry comprising a good number of verses, which have two hemistichs. It is usually sung.

with those predictions a new miracle has appeared.

4. Its highest degree of eloquence, which is beyond the capacity of a human being. However, since we come after the first Arabs we are unable to reach its essence. But the measure which we know is that the employment of lucid words and sweet constructions gracefully and without affectation that we find in the Tremendous Qur'ān is to be found nowhere else in any of the poetry of the earlier or later peoples. This is a matter of taste that only highly skilled poets grasp, as ought to be the case, and which the generality of people do not.

We also know that, with respect to the three types of reminder and the dispute with the disbelievers, in every place the issues are clothed according to the method of the *sūrah* in fresh new clothes whose hems the hands of the insolent and presumptuous cannot even reach.

If anyone is unable to understand that, he ought to study the narratives of the prophets mentioned in [Sūrats] al-A'rāf (7), Hūd (11) and ash-Shu'arā' (26), then study them as mentioned in aṣ-Ṣāffāt (37), and then read these stories themselves in adh-Dhāriyāt (51)[564] so that the difference may become clear.

It is similar with respect to mention of the punishment of the wrongdoing and disobedient unjust ones and the reward of the right-acting obedient ones, which is mentioned in every place in the Noble Qur'ān in a new way, as is also the case with the quarrelling of the people of the Fire with each other, which appears each time in a new guise, but to talk about this would be too lengthy.

We also understand that tending the requirement of the situation, the detail of which is found in knowledge of the meanings (*'ilm al-ma'ānī* – syntactical subtlety) and in discussion of that, and the use of metaphors and allusions that the science of rhetoric (*'ilm al-*

564 Qur'ān, Sūrat adh-Dhāriyāt (51).

bayān) has undertaken to make clear, whilst bearing in mind the states of those addressed who are illiterate and unaware of these artifices, cannot be imagined in a better form than is found in the Tremendous Qur'ān. This is because what is sought in the Noble Qur'ān is that those points that are clear and understandable to the generality of mankind but pleasing to the elect should be placed in wholesome addresses that everybody would recognise. This is like uniting two opposites, which is not possible for a human being, but Allah is able to do all things. How excellently the poet has said:

يَزِيدُكَ وَجْهُهُ حُسْناً

إِذَا مَا زِدْتَهُ نَظَراً

His face appears ever the more beautiful to you,
The more you behold it.[565]

Miracle of Qur'ānic Legislation

There is a reason that it is not easy to understand except for people who contemplate the secrets of the laws, and that is that the five sciences themselves point to the fact that the Qur'ān has come down from the presence of Allah, exalted is He, for the guidance of the children of Adam, in the same way as when the

565 This couplet is attributed to the famous poet Abū Nuwās al-Ḥasan ibn Hānī Al-Ḥakamī (138 AH/756 CE in Ahvaz, Persia – 198 AH/814 CE in Baghdad). He was one of the greatest of the classical Arabic poets, who also composed in Persian. He was a master of all the contemporary genres of Arabic poetry. Abū Nuwās has entered the folkloric tradition, and he appears several times in *The Book of One Thousand and One Nights* (*Alf Laylah wa Laylah*). A crater on the planet Mercury is named in his honour. It is said he was surnamed Abū Nuwās due to two locks of hair which hung down on his shoulders. (Ibn Khallikān (607 AH/1211 CE – 680 AH/1282 CE), *Wafayāt al-A'yān* (Biographical Dictionary), p.394)

medical scientist looks into the *Canon of Medicine* [of Ibn Sīnā][566], which beautifully describes illnesses, their causes, symptoms and medications, he will not doubt that its author is most competent in the science of medicine. Likewise, when the person who is knowledgeable of the secrets of the laws knows the things that people ought to be taught to educate them and then contemplates the five sciences, he will know without any doubt that these sciences have come about in such a way that one cannot imagine anything better than it:

> The radiant sun itself is evidence of itself
> If you need evidence,
> then do not turn your face away from it.

566 This is *al-Qānūn fī aṭ-Ṭibb*, authored by Abū 'Alī al-Ḥusayn ibn 'Abdullāh ibn 'Alī Sīnā (*aka* Avicenna) (370 AH/980 CE (Bukhārā) – 428 AH/1037 CE (Hamadān, Iran)). He was a Persian Muslim polymath who is said to have authored almost 450 treatises. His magnum opus is *al-Qānūn fī aṭ-Ṭibb* (*The Canon of Medicine*), comprising fourteen volumes, and used as the standard medical text in Europe and the Islamic world up until the eighteenth century CE.

PART 4A

The Varieties of Qur'ānic *Tafsīr* and the Differences Between the *Tafsīr* of the Companions and the Successors

رضي الله عنهم

Chapter 1

The Schools of the Commentators

One ought to know that there are different schools with regards to the art of Qur'ānic *tafsīr*:

1. The *Tafsīr* of *Muḥaddithūn* (Hadith Scholars)

A group intend the narrations of those reports that relate to Qur'ānic *āyāt*, whether those reports are ascribed with connected *isnāds* to the Prophet Muḥammad ﷺ (*marfū'*[567]) or stop at the Companions ﷺ (*mawqūf*[568]), the statement of a Successor (*maqṭū'*) or even Isrā'īliyyāt[569] traditions (Judaica) – this school is that of the *Muḥaddithūn* (*ḥadīth* scholars)

2. The *Tafsīr* of Muslim Scholars of *Kalām*

A group intend to interpret the *āyāt* on the Divine names and attributes, such that those that do agree with the school

567 *marfū'*: a *ḥadīth* that is traced directly back to the Prophet Muḥammad ﷺ.

568 *mawqūf*: a *ḥadīth* that is traced back to a Companion of the Prophet Muḥammad ﷺ. It was often the practice of the Companions to narrate *ḥadīth* of the Prophet ﷺ in this fashion for fear of attributing something to him inaccurately.

569 *Isrā'īliyyāt* (Judaica) are traditions that the People of the Book narrate about events and personages mentioned in the Qur'ān that are also to be found in their books.

of exaltation of Allah above the association of partners or any imperfection or resemblance to created form (*tanzīh*), they turn them away from their literal meanings. They refute the objections raised by those who differ with some Qur'ānic *āyāt* – this is the way of the Muslim Scholars of *Kalām* (Scholastic Theology).

3. The *Tafsīr* of Experts in Juristic Principles

A group are concerned with the derivation of *fiqh* rulings and with finding the weightiest *ijtihād* judgements and answering the positions of those who differ – and this is the school of the *fuqahā'* who are knowledgeable in the principles of *fiqh* (*uṣūl al-fiqh*).

4. The *Tafsīr* of Grammarians and Lexicographers

A group elucidate the case endings [of the words] of the Qur'ān and its linguistic usages, and present numerous evidences from the speech of the Arabs in each category – this is the school of the grammarians and lexicographers.

5. The *Tafsīr* of Master Litterateurs

A party mention the fine points of meaning and rhetorical usage in detail, and they glory in this category – and this is the way of men of letters.

6. The *Tafsīr* of Skilled Reciters

Some of them are concerned for the transmissions of the recitations that have been narrated from their teachers and they do not leave anything big or small in this category without narrating it – and this is the characteristic of the Qur'ān reciters.

7. The *Tafsīr* of the *Ṣūfīs*

Some of them talk about points connected to knowledge of travelling the path (*sulūk*) or knowledge of the realities (*ḥaqā'iq*)[570]

570 *Taṣawwuf* is the science of *iḥsān* and is based on sincerity of intention and honesty of action according to the teachings of Islam, with overwhelming

at the least excuse – and this is the school of the *Ṣūfis*.

In brief, the field is vast, and each of them intends to make the meanings of the Noble Qur'ān understood, has delved into a particular discipline, has explained it according to the measure of his own eloquence and understanding, and took the school of his colleagues as the most obvious. For that reason the domain of *tafsīr* expanded to an unimaginable extent and innumerable books were compiled on it.

Some commentators desired to amalgamate all of that in their commentaries. Some of them spoke in Arabic and some in Persian. They differed in their abridging or in elaborating but they greatly expanded the extent of knowledge.

What Allah has Bestowed Upon me of Knowledge of *Tafsīr*

This needy one – with the praise of Allah ﷻ and through His granting of success – has obtained a relationship to every one of these disciplines, and I have grasped most of their principles and a substantial number of their branches. I have also won a type of minute inquiry and independence in all of their categories in a manner comparable to the exercise of independent legal reason within a particular school of thought (*ijtihād fī madhhab*).[571]

I have been made aware of two or three further disciplines from the limitless ocean of Divine bounty over and above the aforementioned. If you ask me honestly, I am a pupil of the Noble Qur'ān directly [without intermediary], just as I am a direct Uwaysī disciple of the spirit of the Prophet ﷺ[572], a direct beneficiary of

awareness of the omniscience of Allah ﷻ.

571 i.e. he had reached the degree of being independent of other Qur'ānic commentators.

572 The term Uwaysī is applied to someone who gains spiritual knowledge and/or blessings directly from a spiritual doctor, or even from the Prophet Muḥammad ﷺ, without the need for physical interaction. This

the Beautiful Ka'bah and am directly influenced by the Greater *Ṣalāh* without intermediary.

وَلَوْ أَنَّ لِي فِي كُلِّ مَنْبَتِ شَعْرَةٍ
لِسَاناً لَمَا اسْتَوْفَيْتُ وَاجِبَ حَمْدِهِ

"Even if I had a tongue at the root of every hair,
I still could not have fulfilled the obligation
of praising Him."

I deem it essential to write many words on those disciplines in this epistle.

term is derived from Uways ibn 'Āmir al-Qarnī (30 BH/594 CE (Yemen) – 36 AH/657 CE (Syria)) who became Muslim during the lifetime of the Prophet Muḥammad ﷺ but he was never honoured with meeting him. (Muslim, *al-Musnad aṣ-Ṣaḥīḥ, Kitāb Faḍā'il aṣ-Ṣaḥābah*, chapter on the Merits of Uways al-Qarnī, *ḥadīths* 6490 – 6492)

Chapter 2

The Reports in the Commentaries of the *Muḥaddithūn* (Hadith Scholars)

Describing the reports that are cited in the commentaries of the *ḥadīth* scholars, etc., some reports relate to the causes of revelations.

There are two kinds of cause of revelation:

1. That an event has taken place that has distinguished the *īmān* of the believers from the hypocrisy of the hypocrites as happened during the battles of Uḥud and al-Aḥzāb, and so Allah ﷻ revealed praise of those [believers] and condemnation of those [hypocrites] in order to differentiate between the two groups. Throughout the mention of the event there are many allusions with all their particularities, so that it is necessary that the event be explained with some brief words so that the context of the words is clear to the reader.
2. That in which the meaning of the *āyah* is complete as it is without need of knowing the story that is the cause of revelation since the point is in the general meaning of the words not the particular nature of the cause. Earlier commentators had mentioned that event in order to contain all those traditions that are relevant to the *āyah*, or possibly intending to clarify

what the general sense of the *āyah* confirms, even though it is unnecessary to mention this kind.

On the Saying 'نَزَلَتِ الآيَةُ فِي كَذَا – the *Āyah* was Revealed About Such-and-such'

It has been verified by this needy one that many of the Companions and the Successors ﷺ would often say: 'نَزَلَتِ الآيَةُ فِي كَذَا – the *āyah* was revealed about such-and-such.'

By this, they intended to portray the meaning of what the *āyah* substantiated or to mention some of the circumstances which the *āyah* encompassed in its general meaning, whether or not the story preceded the revelation of the *āyah* or came later than it, or the story was Isrā'īlī (Judaica) or from the Era of Ignorance or the time of Islam, or is applicable to all of the conditions of the *āyah* or just some of them. And Allah ﷻ knows best.

Understanding the Backdrop of Revelations via Independent Reasoning (*Ijtihād*)

One knows from this careful investigation that independent reasoning (*ijtihād*) also has a part to play in this type [i.e that of semantically understanding the cause of revelation] and there is a sphere for stories. He who keeps these points in mind will be capable of treating the differences concerning the causes of revelation with minimum effort.[573]

Useless matters in tafsīr

An example of this is detailing a story whose source is alluded to in the Qur'ān and thus the commentators go to the utmost in producing details from the traditions of the Banī Isrā'īl or from the books on the *sīrah* (biographies, *especially* of the Prophet

573 With respect to some *āyāt*, the commentators of the Qur'ān differed with regards to what occasioned their revelation or how they were revealed, and hence, the author emphasises that the reader should bear in mind the points of scrutiny so that he may easily find the solution.

Muḥammad ﷺ) and they cite them with all of their constituent parts.

In this there is some detail: if the *āyah* contains an allusion to a story in such a manner that the person knowledgeable in the language is brought to a halt and will research into it, then mention of it is one of the functions of the commentator. It is futile [to mention] any event that is extraneous to this type (of explanation), such as whether Banī Isrā'īl's cow[574] was male or female, or whether the dog of the Fellows of the Cave[575] was spotted or red in colour. Mentioning this is of the things that do not concern one. The Companions ﷺ used to detest such discussions and deemed them a waste of time.

One ought to bear in mind two points here:

1. When transmitting events, they should be narrated just as they have been heard without resorting to reasoning. As for a party of earlier Qur'ānic commentators, they directed their attention to that allusion and assigned an appropriate interpretation to it and interpreted it according to the most probable interpretation, whereas the matter appeared doubtful to later generations. Since the methods of explanation were not refined in that age, it often happened that a probable explanation became confused with a definite explanation, and so they mentioned one of them in place of the other. This is an issue of independent exertion of judgement (*ijtihād*) – there is enough room in it for reasoning and for speculation, and racing the horses of "someone said and he said" is possible.

If one bears this point in mind, he will be able to decide between many of the differences of the commentators. Moreover, he may come to know that many of the discussions and exchanges of views of the Companions ﷺ were not their absolute positions, but rather their scholarly researches which those capable of exercise

574 Qur'ān, Sūrat al-Baqarah 2:67-71.
575 Qur'ān, Sūrat al-Kahf 18:22.

of independent judgement (*mujtahid*) discuss among themselves.[576]

In this manner, this weak slave interprets the saying of Ibn 'Abbās ﵄:

لَا أَجِدُ فِي كِتَابِ اللهِ إِلَّا الْمَسْحَ ، لَكِنَّهُمْ أَبَوْ إِلَّا الْغَسلَ

"I do not find anything in the Book of Allah ﷻ but wiping, but they refused (anything) but washing, i.e. they understood it to mean 'washing'"

to explain the *āyah*:

يَـٰٓأَيُّهَا ٱلَّذِينَ ءَامَنُوٓاْ إِذَا قُمۡتُمۡ إِلَى ٱلصَّلَوٰةِ
فَٱغۡسِلُواْ وُجُوهَكُمۡ وَأَيۡدِيَكُمۡ إِلَى ٱلۡمَرَافِقِ
وَٱمۡسَحُواْ بِرُءُوسِكُمۡ وَأَرۡجُلَكُمۡ إِلَى ٱلۡكَعۡبَيۡنِ

"You who believe! when you get up to do the prayer,
wash your faces and your hands and your arms to the elbows,
and wipe over your heads, and (wash) your feet to the ankles."[577]

This needy one understands that this is not his taking the position that wiping is obligatory, nor is there in it a decisive interpretation of the *āyah* to mean that wiping is a fundamental pillar [of *wuḍū'*]. On the contrary, the verdict of Ibn Abbās ﵄ is that the feet ought to be washed, but he confirms that there is an

576 At times, some Companions ﵃ would narrate from others by way of discussion and not to endorse any particular position. These discussions have been mentioned by various *fuqahā'* merely as academic references, but some readers may consider them to be the absolute stances of the respective Companion ﵃. It is therefore imperative for the reader of a *tafsīr* of Qur'ān to understand the difference between probable and definite explanations, and the role of independent reasoning, so as to avoid such confusion.

577 Qur'ān, Sūrat al-Mā'idah 5:6.

anomaly here and presents a probability so as to see which path the scholars contemporary with him would adopt in resolving this contradiction.

However, those who fail to understand the discussions of the earlier scholars (*salaf*), misunderstood this to be the verdict and *madhhab* of Ibn Abbās ,[578] but far be it for him to have taken this position!

2. Narrating Isrā'īliyyāt is a plot that has crept into our *dīn* after the rule had been neither to accept them nor to reject them:

$$ لَا تُصَدِّقُوا أَهْلَ الْكِتَابِ وَلَا تُكَذِّبُوهُمْ $$

"Neither affirm the People of the Book nor deny them."[579]

Because one of two things is necessary:

i. As long as the allusion of the Noble Qur'ān can be explained using the Sunnah of our Prophet ﷺ, Isrā'īliyyāt must not be used. For example, as long as there is found an interpretation in the prophetic Sunnah for:

---

578 i.e. that the feet ought to be wiped over with wet hands and not washed. In all the accepted readings, the words 'وَأَرْجُلَكَ – and your feet' and the words 'وُجُوهَكُمْ وَأَيْدِيَكُمْ – your faces and your hands' – are all three objects of the verb 'فَاغْسِلُوا – then wash'. Only the word 'بِرُؤُوسِكُمْ – your heads' is the item related to the verb 'وَامْسَحُوا – and wipe'. However, the commentator aṭ-Ṭabarī alone considered 'وَأَرْجُلِكَ – and your feet' should have a *kasrah* indicating that it was also the object of the verb 'وَامْسَحُوا – and wipe', and according to his *fiqh* it was acceptable to wipe the feet rather than wash them.

579 It was reported by Abū Hurayrah ﷺ, who said: The People of the Book used to recite the Torah in Hebrew and explain it in Arabic to the Muslims. On that the Messenger of Allah ﷺ said, "Do not affirm the People of the Book or deny them, but say: *'We believe in Allāh and what is revealed to us.'* (Qur'ān, Sūrat al-Baqarah 2:136)" (Al-Bukhārī, *al-Jāmi' aṣ-Ṣaḥīḥ*, *Kitāb Tafsīr al-Qur'ān*, chapter 11, *ḥadīth* 4485; also 7362 and 7542)

وَلَقَدْ فَتَنَّا سُلَيْمَـٰنَ وَأَلْقَيْنَا عَلَىٰ كُرْسِيِّهِۦ جَسَدًا ثُمَّ أَنَابَ

"We tested Sulaymān and placed a lifeless body on his throne. Then he turned (to Allah)"[580]

which refers to his omitting to say '*in shā'Allāh – Allah-willing*',[581] and being taken to task for that particular reason[582] then why should the story of the evil Ṣakhr[583] be mentioned?

580 Qur'ān, Sūrah Ṣād 38:34.

581 The saying of Allah ﷻ *'And indeed We put Sulaymān to task.'* (Qur'ān, Sūrah Ṣād 38:34) i.e. We first tasked him with worldly striving, and then, secondly, We placed an empty body on his throne. (Al-Qārī, al-Mullā 'Alī (d.1014 AH/1605 CE), *Sharḥ ash-Shifā'* of *al-Qāḍī 'Iyāḍ* (475 AH/1083 CE – 544 AH/1149 CE), 2 volumes (Beirut, 1421 AH/2001 CE), Vol.2, p.282) Allah ﷻ tested Sulaymān ﵇, i.e. He afflicted him with something, about which there is a difference of opinion: it is said that He adopted seclusion from the people and so Allah ﷻ reprimanded him for that, and it is also said that he fell in love with a king's beautiful daughter called Jarādah, who secretly worshipped an idol. When Sulaymān ﵇ became aware of that, he burned it down. (Al-Khafājī, Shahābuddīn Aḥmad, *Nasīm ar-Riyāḍ fī Sharḥ Shifā' al-Qāḍī 'Iyāḍ* (475 AH/1083 CE – 544 AH/1149 CE), 5 volumes (Beirut, 1421AH /2001 CE), Vol.5, p.385)

582 This has been explained in *ḥadīths* such as: It is reported by Abū Hurayrah ﵁ that the Messenger of Allah ﷺ said, "Sulaymān, the son of Dāwūd – peace be upon them both – said, 'I will go around tonight to a hundred wives – or ninety-nine – and each of them will bear a warrior who will strive in the way of Allah ﷻ.' His companion said to him, 'Say, "*in shā'Allāh* (if Allah wills)."' (But) he did not say '*in shā'Allāh*' and so, none of those wives conceived except for one who bore half a man. By the One in Whose power is the soul of Muḥammad, if he had said, '*in shā'Allāh*', they would all have been striving, as warriors, in the way of Allah." (Al-Bukhārī, *al-Jāmi' aṣ-Ṣaḥīḥ*, *Kitāb* 23, *ḥadīth* 2819, etc.)

583 According to some narrations, the frail body placed upon the throne of Sulaymān ﵇ was a devil named Ṣakhr. A story has been narrated by Qatādah that Sulaymān ﵇ ordered the Bayt al-Maqdis to be built, one that would not echo the sound of iron. He strove but it was not possible. He was told of a jinn who lived in the ocean, who could build

ii. That one speaks only according to the degree that the allusion requires, with a view to the general principle 'what is vitally necessary is estimated according to the extent of the vital necessity', in order that it be possible to confirm it according to the evidence of the Qur'ān and so that one can restrain oneself from more than that.

Qur'ānic *Tafsīr* by Means of the Noble Qur'ān

There is an extremely subtle point here that it is vital to know: in some parts of the Noble Qur'ān an event has been mentioned in summary fashion, but in another place in detail, as Allah ﷻ says:

قَالَ إِنِّيٓ أَعْلَمُ مَا لَا تَعْلَمُونَ

"He [Allah] said, 'I know what you do not know.'"[584]

Then at another place, He says:

such a colossal structure according to the intended design. That jinn was captured and spellbound. To cut the rocks, he would use a diamond (and that helped get rid of the sound of iron). Whenever Sulaymān ﷺ would enter the washroom, he would remove his signet ring – it was engraved with the Greatest Name *(al-Ism al-A'ẓam)* of Allah ﷻ and was used to rule over the various dominions of creation. One day, he removed his ring and gave it to the jinn to hold until he returned from the washroom. The jinn hurled it into the sea and it was subsequently swallowed by a fish. Sulaymān ﷺ lost his kingdom and his authority (for it was vested in the ring bearing the Greatest Name of Allah ﷻ), and the jinn assumed his appearance, ruling over the dominion of what was once under Sulaymān ﷺ and only the wives of Sulaymān ﷺ were protected from that jinn. This continued for up to forty days until he found his signet ring in the belly of a fish. He wore it and regained his kingdom. The name of that jinn was Ṣakhr. (*Tafsīr Ibn Kathīr*, commentary on the Qur'ān, Sūrah 38, *āyah* 34; also in the commentary upon the same *āyah* in *Tafsīr aṭ-Ṭabarī* and *ad-Durr al-Manthūr*) Many Qur'ānic commentators and scholars have refuted this narration as being an Isrā'īliyyah that is totally farfetched.

584 Qur'ān, Sūrat al-Baqarah 2:30.

أَلَمْ أَقُل لَّكُمْ إِنِّىٓ أَعْلَمُ غَيْبَ ٱلسَّمَٰوَٰتِ وَٱلْأَرْضِ
وَأَعْلَمُ مَا تُبْدُونَ وَمَا كُنتُمْ تَكْتُمُونَ

"Did I not tell you I know (all) the hidden realities of the heavens and the earth and I also know all that you disclose and all that you conceal?"[585]

The latter statement *is* the former but in detail hence it is possible to know the *tafsīr* of that summary and to proceed from the summary to the more detailed.

For another example, the story of 'Īsā ﷺ has been mentioned in summary form in Sūrah Maryam (19) in which He says:

وَلِنَجْعَلَهُۥٓ ءَايَةً لِّلنَّاسِ وَرَحْمَةً مِّنَّا ۚ وَكَانَ أَمْرًا مَّقْضِيًّا

"'It is so that We can make him a Sign for mankind and a mercy from Us.' It is a matter already decreed."[586]

Then it is detailed in Sūrah Āl 'Imrān (3):

وَرَسُولًا إِلَىٰ بَنِىٓ إِسْرَٰٓءِيلَ أَنِّى قَدْ جِئْتُكُم بِـَٔايَةٍ مِّن رَّبِّكُمْ

"[We will make him] a Messenger to the tribe of Israel [and he will say]: 'I have brought you a Sign from your Lord.'"[587]

The former text contains glad tidings in summary whereas the latter mentions the glad tidings in detail. Thus this weak slave[588] takes this *āyah* to mean:

585 Qur'ān, Sūrat al-Baqarah 2:33.
586 Qur'ān, Sūrah Maryam 19:21.
587 Qur'ān, Sūrah Āl 'Imrān 3:49.
588 Shāh Waliyyullāh al-Muḥaddith ad-Dihlawī, may Allah be merciful to him.

وَرَسُولًا إِلَى بَنِي إِسْرَائِيلَ مُخْبِراً بِأَنِّي قَدْ جِئْتُكُم

"[We will make him] a Messenger to the tribe of Israel ***informing that:*** *'I have brought you...."'*

The subject matter of all these is good news, without the need for an implicitly understood attachment such as that which as-Suyūṭī indicated, when he said, "When Allah sent him to the Children of Isrā'īl he said to them: إِنِّي رَسُولُ اللهِ إِلَيْكُمْ بِأَنِّي قَدْ جِئْتُكُمْ "I am the messenger of Allah to you in that I have brought you."[589]

And Allah ﷻ knows best.

TAFSĪR OF UNUSUAL EXPRESSIONS USED IN THE NOBLE QUR'ĀN

There is also the *tafsīr* of unusual expressions[590], something that is based either on following up the Arabic language or on grasping the thread of the *āyah* or the preceding *āyah* and recognising the relationship of a word to the parts of the clause in which it occurs.

Introduction of Independent Reasoning in Explaining Unusual Expressions

Here also the intellect has a role and there is room for difference of opinion, for one word may be used for multifarious meanings in

589 When Allah ﷻ sent him to the Banī Isrā'īl, he said to them, "I am the messenger of Allah to you all." 'أَنِّي – That I' meaning, 'بِأَنِّي – Because, I', 'قَدْ جِئْتُكُمْ بِآيَةٍ – *I have brought you a Sign*' – an indication of my integrity – this comes in sequence after an omission which is implicit and whose measure is explained by as-Suyūṭī's saying 'فَلَمَّا بَعَثَهُ اللهُ – *and when Allah sent him* ' – which alludes to the story of his message, after mentioning the story of his being foretold, of his being conceived and of his birth – 'مِنْ رَبِّكُمْ – *from your Lord*'. (Aṣ-Ṣāwī, *Ḥāshiyat aṣ-Ṣāwī 'alā Tafsīr al-Jalālayn*, 5 volumes, Vol.1, p.155, commentary on Sūrah Āl 'Imrān 3:49)

590 *gharā'ib*, singular *gharīb*: something strange or rare. In the case of Qur'ānic *tafsīr*, *gharīb al-qur'ān* is a text of Qur'ān that is rarely used in the Arabic language; the science is said to have a distinct and meritorious status.

Arabic. Intellects differ in their researches when following up the usages of the Arabs and understanding of the relationship of what precedes and what follows, which resulted in the different views of the Companions and the Successors ﷺ, each one of whom followed his own method.

A diligent commentator ought to weigh the explanation of unusual expressions twice: first, with respect to the usages of the Arabs, so as to understand which aspect of them is stronger and more likely, and second, with respect to the relationship of preceding and succeeding [words and *āyāt*] until he knows which of the two [approaches] is more appropriate and more firmly established.

After researching the organisation of the principles of the science of *tafsīr* deeply as well as their sources, and also studying the relevant *ḥadīths*, this needy one has derived fresh discoveries whose subtlety and fineness are apparent to all except capricious coarse people.

For example:

كُتِبَ عَلَيْكُمُ ٱلْقِصَاصُ فِى ٱلْقَتْلَى

"Retaliation is prescribed for you in the case of people killed"[591,592]

591 Qur'ān, Sūrat al-Baqarah 2:178.

592 Most commentators of Qur'ān see *qiṣāṣ* as synonymous with '*qawad* retaliation' in this *āyah*, and they take *qatlā* to be the plural of '*qatīl* the person killed'. In this case, the equivalence of '*female for female* (*al-unthā bi'l-unthā*)' is not premature. However, the author has presented a new and fine interpretation of this *āyah*. He said that *qiṣāṣ* means 'equality, similarity, retaliation, *diyah* and wounding', whereas *qatlā* only means 'those killed'; it does not include the murderers. In such a case, the *āyah* means 'It has been enjoined on you to adopt similarity and equality with regards to those killed in such a manner that the slain are categorised as the freemen, slaves, males and females, and that each individual has an opposite number in the other group. The following qualities will not be reckoned: wealth, social status or nobility.' As such, the freeman

I take to mean the equivalence of those killed and that some of them share with others in a single ruling. So, in the *tafsīr* of:

وَٱلْأُنثَىٰ بِٱلْأُنثَىٰ

"and female for female"[593]

one does not need the inconvenience of abrogation, nor is one compelled to pursue such interpretations as bear little weight. Similarly, I interpret His words, exalted is He:

يَسْـَٔلُونَكَ عَنِ ٱلْأَهِلَّةِ

"They ask you about the new moons"[594]

to mean: يَسْأَلُونَكَ عَنِ الْأَشْهُرِ "They ask you about the months" i.e. the months of *ḥajj* – and so He, exalted is He, says:

هِىَ مَوَٰقِيتُ لِلنَّاسِ وَٱلْحَجِّ

"They are set times for mankind and for the ḥajj."[595]

Similarly, His words, exalted is He:

هُوَ ٱلَّذِىٓ أَخْرَجَ ٱلَّذِينَ كَفَرُوا۟ مِنْ أَهْلِ ٱلْكِتَـٰبِ مِن دِيَـٰرِهِمْ لِأَوَّلِ ٱلْحَشْرِ

"It is He who expelled those who disbelieved among the People of the Book from their homes to the first gathering-place"[596]

is equal to another freeman, and consequently, the slave is not equal to the freeman, etc. (Aṣ-Ṣāwī, *Ḥāshiyat aṣ-Ṣāwī 'alā Tafsīr al-Jalālayn*, 5 volumes, Vol.1, p.80, commentary on Sūrat al-Baqarah 2:178)

593 Qur'ān, Sūrat al-Baqarah 2:178.

594 Qur'ān, Sūrat al-Baqarah 2:189.

595 *Ibid.*

596 Qur'ān, Sūrat al-Ḥashr 59:2.

i.e. [لِأَوَّلِ الحَشْرِ] means لِأَوَّلِ جَمعِ الجُنُودِ – "for the first collection of the groups/gathering of the armies", because Allah ﷻ says:

وَٱبْعَثْ فِى ٱلْمَدَآئِنِ حَـٰشِرِينَ

"And send out marshals to the cities"[597]

and:

وَحُشِرَ لِسُلَيْمَـٰنَ جُنُودُهُۥ

"Sulayman's troops were assembled for him."[598]

This is more in accord with the story of Banū Naḍīr[599], and a stronger explanation of the blessing.

The Differing Interpretations of the Earlier and Later Generations of the Meaning of Abrogation in Such a Way as Necessitate Different Views on the Number of Abrogated *Āyāt*

Of that there is also the explanation of the abrogating (*nāsikh*) and the abrogated (*mansūkh*). At this stage, one ought to bear in mind two points:

1. The Noble Companions ﷺ and the Successors would use the term '*naskh* (abrogation)' with a meaning different from the well known technical term of the theoreticians, and that was closer to the more literal meaning of '*izālah* – removal, elimination', and the meaning of *naskh* according to them was

597 Qur'ān, Sūrat al-A'rāf 7:111.

598 Qur'ān, Sūrat an-Naml 27:17.

599 Banū Naḍīr was a Jewish tribe who lived in Madīnah during the early seventh century CE. They conspired to attack the Prophet Muḥammad ﷺ and the Muslims of Madīnah. This was a betrayal of the treaty between them and, as a result, they were expelled. They later allied with the pagans against the Muslims in the Battle of the Trench and also participated in the Battle of Khaybar.

'to eliminate some aspects of the former *āyah* by the latter *āyah*', be that:

a.   to express the ending of the period of its application

b.   to divert the statement from the obvious meaning to another less obvious

c.   to make clear the existence of a restriction that has been introduced

d.   to particularise something general

e.   to express the fact that there exists a difference between the text and what has been treated as analogous to it outwardly

f.   to declare the termination of a pre-Islamic custom

g.   to express the abrogation of a previous sacred law, etc. etc.

This is a vast area in which the intellect has its place and it is possible for there to be difference of opinion, and thus they consider the number of abrogated *āyāt* to amount to as many as five hundred.[600]

2. Primarily the explanation of abrogation in the technical sense of the term is in knowledge of the history of the revelation, but sometimes they consider the consensus of the right-acting first generations or the agreement of the majority (of the scholars) as a sign of *naskh*, and they pass verdict on that basis. Many *fuqahā'* have done that, even though it is possible in many such instances that that which an *āyah* applies may be something other than that which consensus is compatible with.

In short, following up the traditions that inform us about abrogation would use up a lifetime, and hence it is intensely difficult to reach the depths of the matter.

Hadith scholars have other things apart from these matters which they transmit in their *tafsīrs*, for example:

a.   the discussions of the Companions 🙵 on an issue and their producing an *āyah* as evidence

---

600   Deeper investigation will reveal *āyāt* of this type to be almost innumerable.

b. their producing an *āyah* as an example
c. their [citing the] recitation of the Prophet ﷺ of an *āyah*
d. [their] narration of a *ḥadīth* that corresponds to the *āyah* in its original meaning
e. [their citing] the mode of pronunciation [of the word] that is reported from the Prophet ﷺ, or from his Companions ﷺ.

Chapter 3

Remaining Subtle Points in this Category

DEDUCING LEGAL RULINGS

Deduction of legal rulings is an area that is vast. There is ample room for the intellect in examination of the import of the *āyāt*, their allusions and what necessarily follows from them. Differing and differences of opinions are also to be found in it. Allah, exalted is He, has cast into the mind of this needy one the enumeration of these deductions as ten types and their order, and this is a tremendous set of scales with which to weigh many deduced legal rulings.

TAWJĪH (RESOLUTION OF APPARENT PROBLEMS)

Tawjīh (resolution of apparent problems) is a skill with many branches. It is used by commentators in explaining texts, and their acumen and mental precision is tested by it, which exposes the differences in their degrees of understanding.

Sayings of the Companions ﷺ on *Tawjīh*

The Companions ﷺ spoke – even though the rules of resolution of apparent problems (*tawjīh*) had not yet been refined – on the resolution of apparent problems in the noble *āyāt*, and they said a great deal. The reality of *tawjīh* is that if the commentator finds some difficulty (in understanding) the words of an author, he pauses there until he has solved it. Since those who recite the Noble Qur'ān are not all of the same degree of intelligence, the *tawjīh* is not all of the same degree. The *tawjīh* of beginners is not the same as that of experts, since sometimes a difficulty in understanding occurs to the mind of the expert commentator and thus he needs to solve it, whereas the novice remains totally unaware of that difficulty – in fact, he cannot grasp it.[601] There is much whose explanation is difficult for the novice but not for the expert. The one who encompasses all aspects of intellect will tend the state of the ordinary reader, and speak according to his level of understanding.

The Main Issue of *Tawjīh*

1. In *āyāt* relating to polemic (*āyāt al-mukhāṣamah*) it is to expose the schools of the false sects and to review the ways of compelling people to accept a proof.
2. In *āyāt* of legal rulings (*āyāt al-aḥkām*), it is to create a picture of the form of the case, explain the benefits that exist in the restrictions, such as caution and other things.
3. In *āyāt* reminding [people of] the Favours of Allah (*at-tadhkīr bi ālā'illāh*), it is by painting a picture of those favours and explaining their particular passages.
4. In *āyāt* reminding of the Days of Allah (*at-tadhkīr bi ayyām Allāh*), it is to show the dependence of stories on each other, and to give full due to the allusions that exists in the narration of a story.
5. In reminding of death and what follows it (*at-tadhkīr bi'l-*

601 Those unacquainted with arduous circumstances, in whatever sphere, may come across a difficulty and not even realise its existence, whereas experts would anticipate it.

mawt wa mā ba'da-hu), it is to create pictures of those matters and confirm those states.

Types of *Tawjīh*

1. Bringing any matter that is unfathomable due to its unfamiliarity closer to understanding
2. Removal of any contradiction existing between two evidences, or two expositions or between what is rational and what is transmitted
3. Differentiating between two matters that become mixed up
4. Correlating two things that differ
5. Explaining the truth of the promise indicated in the *āyah*
6. Explaining how the Prophet ﷺ put into practice the commands he was given in the Noble Qur'ān.

In summary, the commentaries of the Companions ﷺ contain an abundant share of *tawjīh* but the commentator will not have discharged his duty until he explains the aspect of difficulty in detail and then talks about resolution of the difficulty in detail and then weighs up their verdicts fairly.

THE EXCESSES OF THE SCHOLARS OF *KALĀM*

The excesses to which the Scholars of *Kalām* (Scholastic Theologians) go in interpreting the allegorical *āyāt* (*mutashābihāt*) and in explaining the reality of the Divine Attributes is not my way. My way, in this regards, is the way of Mālik[602], ath-

---

602 He is Mālik ibn Anas ibn Mālik ibn 'Āmr al-Aṣbaḥī (93 AH/711 CE – 179 AH/795 CE), *also known as* Imām al-Mālik. He was an expert in Qur'ānic sciences, prophetic tradition and jurisprudence. His teachers include Imām Ja'far aṣ-Ṣādiq (83 AH/702 CE – 148 AH/765 CE). He and Imām Abū Ḥanīfah (80 AH/699 CE – 148 AH/767 CE) met each other. He is one of the three in the Golden Chain of *ḥadīth* narrators, i.e. Mālik from Nāfi' (d. 117 AH/735 CE) from 'Abdullāh ibn 'Umar (9 BH/614 CE – 73 AH/693 CE). He is the founder of the Mālikī *madhhab*.

Thawrī[603], Ibn al-Mubārak[604] and all the predecessors, which is to allow allegorical *āyāt* to pass according to their apparent outward meaning and to give up plunging into their interpretation.

Polemic in the Qur'ān

Debating over deduced legal rulings, treating one's own legal school carefully and demolishing others' legal schools, and using tricks to defend against Qur'ānic evidence is not correct in my view and I fear that it might become a kind of repudiation of the Qur'ān. The only thing that is necessary is that one seek the meaning of the *āyāt* and takes that as one's *madhhab* whether or not those who agree with you take it as their *madhhab* or those who differ with you.

The Linguistic Usages of the Qur'ān

As for the Qur'ānic language one ought to take it from the usages of the first generations of Arabs, and rely completely on the reports and sayings of the Companions and the Successors ﵃.

The Syntax of the Qur'ān

The syntax of the Noble Qur'ān has suffered a strange damage, for one particular group of commentators have adopted the school of Sībawayh, and they interpret whatever contradicts his school even if the interpretation is implausible. In my view this is not sound, but on the contrary one ought to follow the stronger view and that which is more in harmony with the preceding and subsequent [words and phrases] whether that is according to the

603 He is Sufyān ibn Sa'īd ath-Thawrī (98 AH/716 CE – 161 AH/778 CE). He was a Successor to the Companions ﵃, an Islamic scholar and a legal expert. He founded the Thawrī *madhhab*, which later became extinct.

604 He is 'Abdullāh ibn al-Mubārak (118 AH/736 CE – 181 AH/797 CE). He was an Islamic scholar from Khorāsān, and a *ḥadīth* expert with a strong memory. His teachers include Imāms Abū Ḥanīfah, Mālik and ath-Thawrī.

school of Sībawayh or al-Farrā'[605].

Declension of المقيمين الصلاة

'Uthmān ibn 'Affān ﷺ said regarding the likes of the *āyah*:

ج

وَٱلْمُقِيمِينَ ٱلصَّلَوٰةَ وَٱلْمُؤْتُونَ ٱلزَّكَوٰةَ

"Those who establish the ṣalāh and pay zakāh,"[606]

سَتُقِيمُهَا الْعَرَبُ بِأَلْسِنَتِهَا

"The Arabs will establish it with their tongues."

In my view, the proof of this phrase is that the contradiction of well-known expressions are also valid. Very often the early Arabs agreed that that which contradicted grammatical principles was used whenever they spoke in orations or in discussions. Then since the Qur'ān was revealed in the language of the early Arabs, it is no surprise that a letter ي – *yā'* might sometimes occur in place of a letter و – *wāw*, or a singular might occur in place of the dual, or the feminine in place of the masculine. What I have verified is that وَالْمُقِيمِينَ الصَّلَاةَ should be explained as being in the nominative (*marfū'*) case, and Allah ﷻ knows best.

The Knowledge of Semantics and Rhetoric

As for the science of semantics and rhetoric (or syntactical study and figurative usage), it is a recent science that developed after the era of the Companions and Successors ﷺ. As for those issues that have been understood in the tradition of the majority of the Arabs, then that is well and good, but with regards to those

605 Al-Farrā': He is Abū Zakariyyā Yaḥyā ibn Ziyād al-Farrā' (144 AH/760 CE – 207 AH/822 CE) – the expert grammarian and philologist from Kūfa (Iraq). He was given the title *'Amīr al-Mu'minīn fī an-Naḥw* (Leader of the Believers in Grammar)'.

606 Qur'ān, Sūrat an-Nisā' 4:162.

hidden matters that none can grasp save for those masters of these sciences who go very deeply [into these matters], we do not accept them to be [the thing that is] sought in the Noble Qur'ān.

Sufic Indications (*Ishārāt*)

Sufic indications and their reflections are not, in reality, a part of the science of Qur'ānic *tafsīr.* Indeed, when listening to the Noble Qur'ān, some truths dawn upon the heart of the person who travels the path with knowledge (*sālik*). Those things are produced in his heart in between the Qur'ānic composition and the spiritual state with which he is characterised or the gnosis which he possesses.[607] For example, someone hears the love story of Laylā and Majnūn,[608] and it reminds him of his beloved and he recalls his memories of her.

There is a useful and important benefit that one must be aware of, and that is that the Prophet ﷺ reckoned reflection and drawing a moral to be important. He himself performed that in order that reflection would become a Sunnah for the Muslim Ummah and an opening of the door of Divinely bestowed knowledge (*al-'ulūm al-mawhūbah*) for them: just as the Prophet ﷺ cited His words, exalted is He:

فَأَمَّا مَنْ أَعْطَىٰ وَاتَّقَىٰ

"As for him who gives out and is God-fearing"[609]

in reference to the debate on the Decree even though what the

607 These are extrinsic spiritually ecstatic matters based on one's own taste and experience – they are not *tafsīr* of Qur'ān, though they may be helpful in understanding it.

608 The love story of Laylā and Majnūn, (a story with similarities to Romeo and Juliet, Shīrīn and Farhād, and Heer and Rānjhā) and said to have happened during the seventh century CE in the region of present day Iraq.

609 Qur'ān, Sūrat al-Layl 92:5.

āyah articulates is that "whosoever does such-and-such actions We shall guide him to the path to the Garden and bliss, and but whoever does the opposite of that We will open up to him the path to the Fire and punishment." However, it is possible that one will come by the path of reflection to know that Allah, exalted is He, created everyone for a particular condition which befalls him, whether or not he knows from whence. Hence, by means of this reflection this *āyah* has a connection to the issue of the Decree.

A similar case is His words, exalted is He:

وَنَفْسٍ وَمَا سَوَّىٰهَا
فَأَلْهَمَهَا فُجُورَهَا وَتَقْوَىٰهَا

"And the self and what proportioned it
and inspired it with depravity or taqwā"[610]

for the meaning articulated by this noble *āyah* is that Allah ﷻ has acquainted every soul with what is good and what is evil. However, since there is a resemblance in a general manner between the creation of the scientific form of good and evil and between the good and evil which exist at the moment of the breathing of the *rūḥ* (spirit), then it is possible to derive evidence from this *āyah* in the case of the decree by means of the path of reflection. And Allah ﷻ knows best.

610 Qur'ān, Sūrat ash-Shams 91:7-8.

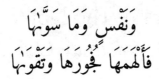

Chapter 4

Wonders of the Noble Qur'ān (*Gharā'ib al-Qur'ān*)

Wonders of the Noble Qur'ān[611] which have been singled out in *ḥadīths* for extra attention and to show their merit are of various types:

1. Wonders in the science of reminding about the favours of Allah ﷻ such as *āyāt* that comprehensively sum up a large number of the attributes of the Truth (*al-Ḥaqq*) ﷻ inside them, e.g. the *Āyat al-Kursī*[612], Sūrat al-Ikhlāṣ[613], the last *āyāt* of Sūrat al-Ḥashr[614] and the opening *āyāt* of Sūrat al-Mu'min[615].
2. A wonder with respect to the science related to reminding [people] of the days of Allah ﷻ, is an *āyah* which either clarifies a rare story, or a well-known story but with all its detail, or a story with important benefits worthy of reflection.

611 Known as *Gharīb al-Qur'ān* (*plural: Gharā'ib al-Qur'ān*), it is ordinarily reserved as technical term for a word used in Qur'ān but rarely used in the Arabic language. However, here the author uses it in the sense of something extraordinary or wondrous.

612 Qur'ān, Sūrat al-Baqarah 2:255.

613 Qur'ān, Sūrat al-Ikhlāṣ 112.

614 Qur'ān, Sūrat al-Ḥashr 59.

615 Qur'ān, Sūrat al-Mu'min 40, is also known as Sūrat al-Ghāfir.

This is the reason why, regarding the story of the encounter of Mūsā ﷺ with Khaḍir, the Prophet Muḥammad ﷺ said: "وَدِدْنَا أَنَّ مُوسَى كَانَ صَبَرَ حَتَّى يَقُصَّ اللهُ عَلَيْنَا مِنْ خَبَرِهِمَا – We wish that Mūsā had been patient with Khaḍir until Allah ﷻ had told their story to us."[616]

3. A wonder in the science of reminding [people of] death and what comes after it is a comprehensive *āyah* about the circumstances of the Rising [from the Dead], and thus it occurs in the noble *ḥadīth*: "مَنْ سَرَّهُ أَنْ يَنْظُرَ إِلَى يَوْمِ الْقِيَامَةِ كَأَنَّهُ رَأْيُ عَيْنٍ ، فَلْيَقْرَأْ: إِذَا الشَّمْسُ كُوِّرَتْ، إِذَا السَّمَاءُ انْفَطَرَتْ، إِذَا السَّمَاءُ انْشَقَّتْ – Whoever wishes to look at the Day of Rising as if with his own eyes should recite *'When the sun is compacted in blackness,*[617] *When the sky is split apart,*[618] *When the sky bursts open.'*"[619,620]
4. A wonder in the science of legal rulings is an *āyah* which contains clarification of the *ḥadd* limits [and punishments for contraventions of the limits] and specification of particular statutes such as the specification of one hundred lashes for the *ḥadd* transgression of fornication, the specification of three periods of menstruation[621] – or three periods of purity[622] – for the divorcée's post-divorce waiting period (*'iddah*) and the specification of the shares of inheritance.
5. A wonder in the science of polemic is an *āyah* in which a response is given in such an articulate and conclusive manner

616 Al-Bukhārī, *al-Jāmi' aṣ-Ṣaḥīḥ*, *Kitāb Tafsīr al-Qur'ān*, chapter 18, *ḥadīth* 4725; also *Kitāb al-'Ilm*, chapter 45.

617 Qur'ān, Sūrat at-Takwīr 81

618 Qur'ān, Sūrat al-Infiṭār 82.

619 Qur'ān, Sūrat al-Inshiqāq 84.

620 At-Tirmidhī, *al-Jāmi' al-Kabīr*, *Tafsīr al-Qur'ān 'an Rasūl Allāh* ﷺ, chapter *Min Sūrat Idha'sh-Shamsu Kuwwirat…* (Sūrat at-Takwīr), *ḥadīth* 3333.

621 According to the Ḥanafī school, the *'iddah* (the waiting period before she can marry again) of the divorcée is three periods of menstruation.

622 According to the Mālikī, Shāfi'ī and Ḥanbalī schools, the *'iddah* of the divorcée is three periods of purity.

that it obliterates all doubts and suspicions, or clarifies the state of one of these groups with a clear example, such as His ﷻ words: "مَثَلُهُمْ كَمَثَلِ الَّذِي اسْتَوْقَدَ نَارًا – *Their likeness is that of people who light a fire*"[623] and similarly, one which explains with wonderful metaphors the repulsive nature of worshipping idols, and the difference between the rank of the Creator and that which is created and between the Owner and he who is owned, or which explains in the most eloquent manner the invalidation of the deeds of those who are guilty of ostentation and seeking worldly fame.

6. The wonders of the Noble Qur'ān are not confined to these particular categories alone. Sometimes a wonder is wondrous with respect to the eloquence of the Qur'ān and the elegance of its method such as Sūrat ar-Raḥmān[624] – hence its title 'the Bride of the Qur'ān (*'Arūs al-Qur'ān*) in *ḥadīths*'.[625] Sometimes, the wonders are wondrous with respect to the portrayal of the form of the joyous and the wretched.

623 Qur'ān, Sūrat al-Baqarah 2:17.
624 Qur'ān, Sūrat ar-Raḥmān 55.
625 Al-Bayhaqī, *Shu'ab al-Īmān*, *ḥadīth* 2494; at-Tibrīzī, *Mishkāt al-Maṣābīḥ*, *Kitāb Faḍā'il al-Qur'ān*, section 3, *ḥadīth* 2180.

Chapter 5

The Outer and Inner States of the Noble Qur'ān

A noble *ḥadīth* states:

أُنْزِلَ الْقُرْآنُ عَلَى سَبْعَةِ أَحْرُفٍ ،
لِكُلِّ آيَةٍ مِنْهَا ظَهْرٌ وَبَطْنٌ ، وَلِكُلِّ حَرْفٍ حَدٌّ،
وَلِكُلِّ حَدٍّ مُطَّلَعٌ

"The Noble Qur'ān, was revealed in seven modes. Each *āyah* has an outward (*ẓahr*) and an inward (*baṭn*)[626]. Every mode has a limit (*ḥadd*). Every limit has a place to ascend to (*muṭṭala'*)."[627]

626 There are many interpretations of these two terms, *ẓahr* – 'outward' and *baṭn* – 'inward', such as 'a verbal expression and interpretation', 'a verbal expression and meaning', 'an apparent and known interpretation and an intrinsic interpretation', 'a narration and an admonition' and 'a reading and an understanding'. Ed.

627 It was narrated by 'Abdullāh ibn Mas'ūd (d. 29 AH/650 CE); at-Tibrīzī, *Mishkāt al-Maṣābīḥ*, *Kitāb al-'Ilm*, section 2, *ḥadīth* 238. The terms *ḥadd* – 'limit' and *muṭṭala'*– 'place to ascend to' are translated according to the meanings given by Ibn al-Athīr (d. 630 AH/1232 CE) in his *an-Nihāyah*.

One must know that the outward of all five sciences is that which is the evidence of the speech and articulated by it. And the interpretation is:

1. In reminding of the favours of Allah ﷾, it is to ponder over the favours of Allah ﷾, and to be vigilantly watchful for the Truth (*al-Ḥaqq*) ﷾.
2. In reminding of the Days of Allah ﷾, it is to recognise and know the object of praise and blame, punishment and reward in those stories, and to derive lessons and warning from them.
3. In reminding of the Garden and the Fire, it is the manifestation of fear and hope, and to consider those matters as if right in front of one's eyes.
4. In the *āyāt* containing legal rulings, it is derivation of hidden rulings by means of the meanings and indications.
5. In the polemic against false sects, it is to recognise the source of those ugly matters and to connect the likes of them to them.

The place of ascent (*muṭṭala'*) of the outward is knowledge and recognition of the language and usages of the Arabs and the transmitted traditions connected to the science of *tafsīr*.

The place of ascent (*muṭṭala'*) of the inward is the fineness of the mind and an upright understanding along with the light of the inward and tranquility of the heart. And Allah ﷾ knows best.

Chapter 6

Some Divinely-Gifted Sciences

Interpretation of the Stories of the Prophets

1. Among the Divinely-gifted sciences, in addition to those sciences of *tafsīr* that we have given an account of, there is also the interpretation (i.e. *ta'wīl*) of the stories of the prophets. This needy one has authored a treatise in this field entitled *Ta'wīl al-Aḥadīth* (Interpretation of Events). By *ta'wīl* what is meant is that every story which happened has as its starting point the preparation of the Messenger and the preparation of his people according to Allah's directing which He ﷻ intended in that moment. It is as if He indicated this meaning in His words, exalted is He: "وَيُعَلِّمُكَ مِن تَأْوِيلِ ٱلْأَحَادِيثِ – *And He will teach you the true meaning of events.*"[628]
2. There is also, for example, revision of the five sciences which have been articulated by the Noble Qur'ān, and which we have previously looked at in detail at the beginning of this treatise, so refer to the relevant section.
3. There is also the translation of the Noble Qur'ān into Persian in a way that comes close to the Arabic text in the measure of the words, and in particularisation and generalisation. I called it *Fatḥ ar-Raḥmān fī Tarjamat al-Qur'ān*. I omitted this

628 Qur'ān, Sūrah Yūsuf 12:6.

stipulation in some places fearing without detail the reader's lack of understanding.

4. There is also the science of the special properties of the Noble Qur'ān (*khawāṣṣ al-Qur'ān*). A group of our predecessors spoke about the special properties of the Qur'ān from two points of view: an aspect which resembles *du'ā*, and an aspect which resembles sorcery – I seek refuge with Allah from it! However, Allah ﷻ has opened a category for this needy one beyond what has been transmitted of the special properties of the Qur'ān, and He placed in my lap all of the Divine Names, the greatest *āyāt* (*al-Āyāt al-'Uẓmā*) and the blessed *du'ās* at one go and He said: "This is a gift from Us for use,"
5. Except that each Divine Name, *āyah* and invocation is stipulated with conditions that are independent of any regulations. Our only instruction is that one ought to anticipate an indication from the world of the Unseen – as that in the Prayer for Seeking Good (*Ṣalāt al-Istikhārah*) – when one awaits which Qur'ānic *āyah* or Divine Name is hinted from the Unseen. Thereafter, one ought to recite the relevant *āyah*, or pronounce the respective Divine Name as is fixed by the proponents of that particular skill.[629]

These are the topics that we intended to discuss in this epistle.

All praise is due to Allah ﷻ, the First, The Last, the Outward, the Inward.

Blessing and salutations upon our master Muḥammad, all his Progeny and all his Companions.

629 This final paragraph deals with the inner meanings of the divine names and attributes of the Creator ﷻ, about which the author instructs us to seek help from Allah ﷻ through *Ṣalāt al-Istikhārah* and awaiting His aid in disclosing the intended meaning via indications. Thereafter, one interprets that indicated meaning in light of the relevant field, i.e. of legal commands, beliefs and divine favours.

PART 4B

Abbreviated Letters

Of the sciences that Allah ﷻ has bestowed upon this weak slave there is a science by means of which the veil is removed from the abbreviated letters in the Noble Qur'ān (*al-ḥurūf al-muqaṭṭaʿāt*). In order to explain this, we need an introduction.

Introduction

One should know that every letter of the alphabet from which Arabic words are composed has its own simple meaning, something that can only be expressed by means of subtle and enigmatic indications. It has been observed here that many of the closely related roots[630] either agree in meaning or do so approximately, as some of the more acute writers have mentioned. For example, in a word whose first letter is ن and whose next is ف e.g.: نفر , نفث , نفخ , نفح , نفق , نفد , نفذ their combination gives, in one sense or another, the meaning of *khurūj* (going out).

In a word whose first letter is ف and the second ل, e.g.: , فلز , فلد فلق , فلح , فلج their combination gives, in one sense or another, the meaning of *shaqq* (splitting) and *fatḥ* (opening).

It is from this point of view that adept men of letters know that the Arabs often pronounce one word in different ways by substituting letters that are close, e.g.: دك and دق or ز and ج.

In short, there is a great deal of evidence for what we have stated, but we only intend to draw attention to it. This is all Arabic, even though real Arabic Arabs do not grasp it and even if the grammarians do not get to the core of it. This is just like when you ask Arabs about the understanding of the definition of

630 *Mawādd* sing. *māddah* are the roots of the words, e.g. the root of *kitāb* كتاب comprises the three letters *kāf*, *tā'* and *bā'*.

the genus and particular idioms, they are unable to explain them even though they employ and use them.[631] Moreover, those who investigate the Arabic language in detail are not of equal status; some of them are more intelligent than others. In that respect you see a group of the most eloquent expounding meanings that others do not grasp, even though this is also one of the sciences of their Arabic language. Many plunge into this ocean with its numerous waves but do not manage to elucidate this obscure understanding.

One ought to know that the abbreviated letters at the commencement of the *sūrahs* are their distinguishing marks which indicate in a summary fashion the meanings which the *sūrah* expands upon in detail. This is just as when authors and compilers name their compositions and compilations in such a way that those books' names direct the reader's mind to the meanings they contain. For example, Imām al-Bukhārī named his compilation *al-Jāmi' aṣ-Ṣaḥīḥ al-Musnad fī Ḥadīth Rasūl Allāh* ﷺ.[632]

Thus, the meaning of الٓمٓ (Alif Lām Mīm)[633] is that which is hidden (*ghayb*) that is not seen (*ghayr muta'ayyan*) with regards to the sullied visible world, because the أ and the ه both give the meaning of that which is hidden, with the only difference being that the ه gives the meaning of that which is hidden of this world[634]

631 It seems that many native speakers of any particular language are unaware of the grammatical terms and the structural principles of their mother tongues, even though they speak it perfectly well on a regular basis without ever planning or pre-structuring their words.

632 It is *al-Jāmi' al-Musnad aṣ-Ṣaḥīḥ al-Mukhtaṣar min Umūr Rasūli'llāhi wa Sunani-hī wa Ayyāmi-hī* (The Abridged Collection of Connected Chains of Authentic Hadiths regarding Matters Pertaining to the Messenger of Allah ﷺ, His Practices and His Times), *aka Ṣaḥīḥ al-Bukhārī* (referred to in this book as *al-Jāmi' aṣ-Ṣaḥīḥ*), regarded as the most authentic collection of Prophetic traditions (*ḥadīths*).

633 Qur'ān, Sūrat al-Baqarah 2:1; Sūrat al-'Ankabūt 29:1; Sūrat ar-Rūm 30:1; Sūrah Luqmān 31:1; Sūrat as-Sajdah 32:1.

634 'World' here is *'ālam* not *dunyā*. Ed.

and the ا gives the meaning of that which is hidden of the pure world. Therefore, the Arabs use the words أم and أو at the time of interrogation, and at the time of conjunction أو, because the affairs which one seeks to understand are very widespread, and are hidden relative to that which is seen. Similarly that about which one has some doubt is hidden. And the ء 'hamzah' is prefixed to the beginnings of the imperative in order to indicate the meaning imagined in the mind of the speaker[635], and its details are entrusted to its root. From the pronouns, they chose the ه because it is that which is hidden of this world, and the seen gains a summary of the whole. The ل indicates the meaning of specification, and it is from this perspective that they add the ل in order to render the noun definite. With respect to its pronunciation by the meeting of the lips, the م indicates the sullied primordial substance in which many different realities gather, are limited and return from pure space to the prison of limitation and isolation.

الٓمٓ, therefore, alludes to the pure superabundance that is limited to the world of being set apart and isolated, and that has been destined according to their customs and their sciences. It clashed against the harshness of their hearts with the reminder, and it clashed against their false verdicts and their dull actions with argument and by defining goodness and wrongdoing for them. The *sūrah* in its entirety details this summary and clarifies this obscurity.

الٓر (Alif Lām Rā)[636] is similar to الٓمٓ, except that the ر in it indicates hesitation, so that it indicates an unseen that is specified and another time is sullied.

Similarly, the م along with the ر, as in الٓمٓر (Alif Lām Mīm Rā)[637], again and again indicates the specific sullied unseens. This is an

635 '*Mutakallim* – the one who is speaking' is the 'first person' in grammar.

636 Qur'ān, Sūrah Yūnus 10:1; Sūrah Hūd 11:1; Sūrah Yūsuf 12:1; Sūrah Ibrāhīm 14:1; Sūrat al-Ḥijr 15:1.

637 Qur'ān, Sūrat ar-Ra'd 13:1.

allusion to the sciences that again and again clash against the ugly wrongdoing of the children of Adam. This is realised by what is recited in this *sūrah*, time after time, of the stories of the prophets and their sayings, with repeated questions and answers.

ط (Ṭā') and ص (Ṣād)[638] indicate the movement of rising from the sullied world to the higher world; but the ط refers to the greatness and eminence of that which moves, together with it being stained and sullied whereas the ص refers to its good qualities and its fineness.

س (Sīn) indicates diffusion, disappearance and its spreading over all the horizons.

طه (Ṭā Hā)[639] are the stations of the prophets which are the traces of their directing their attention to the higher world, in such a manner that an unseen form may come into existence for them with a comprehensive clarification. They have been mentioned in the Books.

Similar to it is طسم (Ṭā Sīn Mīm)[640] the stations of the prophets that are traces of their higher movements that circulated throughout the sullied world and became scattered across the horizons.

The meaning of ح (Ḥā') is similar to that of ه (Hā') except that when it is accompanied by radiance, manifestation and being set-apart, these meanings are expressed by ح (Ḥā').

Thus, the meaning of حم (Ḥā Mīm)[641] indicates a radiantly luminous summing up which connects to those false beliefs and corrupt deeds which the sullied world is singled out with, and indicates the refutation of their statements and the manifestation of the truth in ambivalent matters and debates and that which

638 Qur'ān, Sūrah Ṣād 38:1.
639 Qur'ān, Sūrat Ṭā-Hā 20:1.
640 Qur'ān, Sūrat ash-Shu'arā' 26:1; Sūrat al-Qaṣaṣ 28:1.
641 Qur'ān, Sūrat al-Mu'min (*aka* al-Ghāfir) 40:1; Sūrah Fuṣṣilat (*aka* Ḥā-Mīm as-Sajdah) 41:1; Sūrat ash-Shūrā 42:1; Sūrat az-Zukhruf 43:1; Sūrat ad-Dukhān 44:1; Sūrat al-Jāthiyah 45:1; Sūrat al-Aḥqāf 46:1.

they have adopted of customs.

ع ('Ayn) indicates seeing and beautiful manifestation.

ق (Qāf) like م indicates this world but from the perspective of strength and severity, whereas م (Mīm) [indicates this world] from the perspective of the collection of the forms in it and their accumulation.

Thus, عٓسٓقٓ ('Ayn Sīn Qāf)[642] means a radiant reality circulating in the defiled world.

نٓ (Nūn)[643] indicates the light that spreads and disperses the darkness, akin to the manner that is seen just prior to the true dawn or near sunset.

ي (Yā') indicates something similar except that the light it denotes is less than that which ن indicates. Likewise, the specification that ي indicates is less than than that of ه.

Thus يسٓ (Yā Sīn)[644], symbolises meanings widely spread throughout the world.

صٓ (Ṣād)[645] indicates a condition that comes about through natural disposition[646] and acquisition (i.e. worked for) when the prophets direct themselves to their Lord ﷻ.

ق (Qāf) is an allusion to strength and severity and the disapproval of specification in this world, as is said "The object of my intention is a form which came into being in this world by fracture and collision."

ك (Kāf) is similar to ق except that the meaning in it of strength is less than in that of ق .

Thus the meaning of كهيعص (Kāf Hā Yā 'Ayn Ṣād)[647] is a defiled world possessing darkness in which some luminous sciences and

642 Qur'ān, Sūrat ash-Shūrā 42:2.
643 Qur'ān, Sūrat al-Qalam 68:1.
644 Qur'ān, Sūrah Yā-Sīn 36:1.
645 Qur'ān, Sūrah Ṣād 38:1.
646 i.e. naturally.
647 Qur'ān, Sūrah Maryam 19:1.

others are specifically required for the return to their Most High Lord.

In summary, the meanings of these abbreviated letters have been cast into my heart by means of my personal taste. It is not possible to make these general meanings clearer than the words we have used in describing them, but these words are insufficient in approaching the essence of that which we want to explain, indeed, from one point of view if not others, they are even quite different.

And Allah ﷻ knows best.

Initial translation completed on:

Friday 2nd September 2011/4th Shawwāl 1432 AH after fajr prayer
(318th Hijrī birthday of Shāh Waliyyullāh al-Muḥaddith ad-Dihlawī,
raḥmatu'llāhi ta'ālā 'alayhi)

This ends the English translation of four out of five parts of
al-Fawz al-Kabīr fī Uṣūl at-Tafsīr.

We intend to translate/publish Part 5 as a separate volume *in shā'Allāh.*

Glossary

A

'ādah	habit, custom, something done regularly.
adīb	litterateur, man of letters.
aḥkām	*see ḥukm*
Ahl al-Kitāb	People of the Book; includes Christians, Jews and Sabians, who believe in a revealed book and a prophet sent by Allah ﷻ.
'āmm	general.
'aql	intellect.
'ārif	gnostic, one who knows and recognises Allah ﷻ. *See ma'rifah.*
'arūḍ	rhythm, stress and intonation of speech (*linguistics*), measures in poetry, the science of poetic metre, prosody; the final *taf'ilah*, or the final part of the first hemistich of a poetic verse (*poetry*) (see *ḍarb*).
asbāb	*see sabab*
aṣl (*pl. uṣūl*)	syllable (*poetry*); source (*leg.*); root.
'aṭf	conjunction, such as 'and', 'but' and 'or' (*grammar*).
awtād	*see watad/watid*
awzān	*see wazn*
āyah (*pl. āyāt*)	sign; smallest unit of the Noble Qur'ān.
āyāt adh-dhikr	*āyāt* of remembrance.

āyāt al-aḥkām Qur'ānic *āyāt* relating to divine statutes, statutory *āyāt*.

āyāt al-jadal Qur'ānic *āyāt* relating to disputation, *āyāt* of the Noble Qur'ān that debate with those of incorrect beliefs.

B

baḥr in classical Arabic poetry, the poetic form is based on fixed metrical lines, known as (*pl. buḥūr*) – there are nineteen in total.

baḥīrah a she-camel that had given birth to five offspring and which was set free as a part of a pre-Islamic pagan rite.

balāghah rhetoric (*see 'ilm al-balāghah*).

basīṭ a compound metre in classical Arabic poetry. Its form follows the pattern: two long syllables and one short syllable followed by one long syllable and then one long, one short, one long syllable. They are repeated for the first line.

Bible The Christian Holy Book, divided into sections, the Old and the New Testaments, the former containing the older books of the Children of Israel including much historical and traditional material, and the latter containing what are currently believed to be books, the Gospels, that have some remnants of the *Injīl* that was revealed to the prophet 'Īsā (Jesus) ﷺ as well as letters and works from other people.

C

D

Dābbat al-Arḍ Beast of the earth – that will appear near the Last Day.

ḍarb	to strike; the final *taf'īlah*, or the final part of the second hemistich of a poetic verse (*poetry*) (*see 'arūḍ*); pause in a line of verse dictated by sense or natural speech rhythm rather than by metrics, caesura.
dhabḥ	slaughter for the mundane purpose of the consumption of meat.
dhikr	remembrance, invocation.
dhimmī	non-Muslim living under Islamic governance.
dīn	comprehensive way of life including those elements that are referred to as 'religion'.
Dīn Ḥanīf	the *dīn* of the natural inclination to the truth – that which was given by Allah ﷻ and adhered to by all the prophets.
dirāyah	the use of intellectual and rational abilities to form an opinion-oriented explanation; objective exegesis (esp. of the Noble Qur'ān).

E

F

fann	skill, art, science, trait.
fann at-tawjīh	mode of orientation; tracing the cause.
faqīh	someone knowledgeable in *fiqh*.
fāṣilah	distance; metrical foot (*poetry*).
fiqh	understanding, particularly in terms of the *dīn* whether an action or word is obligatory, recommended, permissible, abhorrent or forbidden.
fiṭrah	nature, inborn natural predisposition.
fiṭrah salīmah	sound natural disposition, innate pure and sound instinct (esp. to recognise the oneness of Allah ﷻ).

G

ghā'ib absent, third person (*grammar*).

gharīb strange, foreign, unusual, obscure, rare.

Gharib al-Ḥadīth words or texts in *ḥadīths* that are obscure and not easy to understand, possibly because they are used rarely.

Gharīb al-Qur'ān words or texts in the Noble Qur'ān that are obscure and not easy to understand, possibly because they are used rarely.

ghassāq discharges of dirty wounds; of the pus of the inmates of Hell.

ghazal a poem, often of an amorous nature, consisting of couplets and a refrain, similar to a sonnet.

H

ḥāḍir present; second person (*grammar*) (*see mukhāṭab*).

ḥadīth modern (*adjective*); event, occurrence, occasion; tradition; account of a saying, doing, tacit approval or quality of the Prophet Muḥammad ﷺ – it is not the same as *sunnah*.

ḥadīth ṣaḥīḥ authentic prophetic tradition whose *isnād* is unbroken and consists entirely of narrators of impeccable integrity and memory.

ḥajj pilgrimage to the Ka'bah in Makkah consisting of verbal, physical and financial rites – it is enjoined on the qualified individual once in his lifetime.

ḥām, or *ḥāmī* a male camel employed for breeding purposes, and then released in the name of an idol after having produced a certain number of young.

ḥamīm boiling hot water; in the Qur'ān it is mentioned as being given to the inmates of Hell to drink.

ḥanīf one who is by nature upright and inclines to the

	true path.
Ḥaram	the area surrounding the Sacred Mosques in Makkah and Madīnah.
ḥarām	forbidden and unlawful which is proven to be so by way of conclusive evidence.
ḥarf	letter, particle, preposition.
ḥarf jārr	genitive preposition.
ḥashw	padding, to fill (*lit.*); the collective name of the parts of the verse other than the *'arūḍ* and interpolation of textual material into a hemistich or between hemistichs, metrical filler.
ḥukm (*pl. aḥkām*)	judgement, command, rule, directive, law.

I

'ibādah (*pl. 'ibādāt*)	worship; the relationship of slavehood with the Creator.
iḍāfah	possessive; annexation, accreditation (*grammar*).
'iddah	waiting period; the probationary period before a divorcée or widow may marry again.
iftirā'	falsity, fabrication, slander.
ijtihād	juridical deduction in the Sharī'ah by personal effort (*see taqlīd*), either upon the basis of the Book and the Sunnah and the other *uṣūl* (principles) of *fiqh* or on the basis of previous positions adopted by expert people of *ijtihād* (*see ijtihād fi'l-madhhab*).
ijtihād fi'l-madhhab	juridical deduction in the Sharī'ah by personal effort based on the methodological principles of the school one adheres to.
'illah	effective cause.
'ilm	knowledge, science.
'ilm al-balāghah	science of rhetoric.

'ilm al-bayān science or study of figurative usage.
'ilm ladunī knowledge directly from the Divine presence that is acquired by the creation without any effort but inspired in them by Allah ﷻ (also known as *'ilm mawhūb* – knowledge granted as a gift).
'ilm al-ma'ānī science or study of syntactical subtlety.
'ilm mawhūb *see 'ilm ladunī.*
ism noun (*grammar*), name.
ism al-ishārah demonstrative pronoun.
ism al-jins generic noun, a noun that covers an entire species or class (*grammar*).
istiḥsān juristic preference.
isti'ārah *lit.*: 'borrowing', a type of metaphor.
isti'ārah makniyyah allusive metaphor where the object of comparison (*mushabbah bihī*) is dropped and is alluded to by one of its necessary qualities.
isti'ārah tashrīḥiyyah expressed metaphorical borrowing where the word denoting the object of comparison (*mushabbah bihī*) is explicitly stated.
isti'nāf commencement, recommencement, to start afresh, esp. of a sentence (*grammar*).

J

jadal debate, argument, rebuttal.
jahl ignorance, lack of knowledge or awareness.
jahl basīṭ simple ignorance, not knowing something and acknowledging the ignorance thereof.
jahl murakkab compound ignorance, not knowing something but claiming to know it and claiming to be correct about it.
jawāb reply, response, answer; apodosis, complement.
jawāb al-qasam apodosis, or complement, of an oath (*grammar*).

jawāb ash-sharṭ apodosis, or main consequent clause, of a conditional sentence (*grammar*).
jazā' consequence, reward, recompense; apodosis of a conditional sentence (*grammar*).
jumlah clause (*grammar*); complete, holistic.
jumlah fi'liyyah verbal clause or sentence, which in Arabic is one that begins with a verb (*grammar*).
jumlah inshā'iyyah performative clause or sentence, one that conveys a command or prayer etc. rather than information; affective statement (*grammar*).
jumlah ismiyyah nominal clause or sentence, which in Arabic is one that begins with a noun, and the first part of which is the subject and the second part is the predicate (*grammar*).
jumlah khabariyyah declarative/informative clause or sentence, one that states facts (as opposed to *jumlah inshā'iyyah*).

K

Kalām the science of the rational statement of *'aqīdah* and its evidences.
khabar predicate in a nominal clause or sentence; it is preceded by the subject (*grammar*).
khāṣṣ specific, particular, restricted, qualified.
khuṭbah speech.
kināyah (*pl. kināyāt*) indirect expression (*see ṣarīḥ*).

L

labbah low point of the neck, pit at the top of the breast-bones between both collarbones where camels are stabbed for slaughter.

M

maddah elongated, stretched, esp. pronunciation of the Arabic vowels in an elongated manner and rendering them corresponding quiescent letters; ا *alif* (equivalent to the English letter 'a'), و *wāw* (equivalent to the English letter 'u') and ي *yā'* (equivalent to the English letter 'i').

madhhab school of thought; in Islamic law, the legal school one adheres to in practising Islam.

majāz metaphor.

majāz 'aqlī conceptual or cognitive metaphor.

majāz lughawī linguistic metaphor, a figurative expression that is linguistically based.

majāz mursal a division of linguistic metaphor (*majāz lughawī*) – a word used for other than its original intent; metonymy.

majrūr genitive (*grammar*).

makrūh disliked, repugnant, offensive, abhorrent (*fiqh*).

mandūb recommended (*fiqh*).

manṣūb accusative (*grammar*).

mansūkh abrogated Qur'ānic *āyah* (*see nāsikh, naskh*).

manṭiq speech, logic.

marfū' raised up, held high; nominative (*grammar*).

marfū' ḥadīth that which has been elevated, i.e. traced back to the Prophet Muhammad ﷺ.

ma'rifah knowledge and recognition [of Allah ﷻ], gnosis (*dīn*); a definite noun (*grammar*).

ma'ṭūf conjoined word (i.e. the word that follows 'and', 'but', 'or', etc.) (*grammar*).

ma'ṭūf 'alayhi conjoined to (i.e. the word that precedes 'and', 'but', 'or', etc.) (*grammar*).

mawlā al-muwālāh the 'client' who enters Islam at the hands of another man. The latter inherits from him and his tribe or kin pay any compensatory payments for injury he inflicts on a third party or homicide.

mawqūf — stopped; *mawqūf ḥadīth* – that which has stopped at a Companion without his ascribing it to the Prophet Muḥammad ﷺ.

mawṣūf — something described, noun qualified by an adjective, quality or an asyndetic relative clause (*grammar*).

mawṣūl (ism) — relative pronoun.

millah — religious community.

mīzān — balance; scales of Divine Justice that will be established on the Day of Rising and Judgement (*Yawm al-Qiyāmah*).

mu'āmalāt — transactions with others – such as contracts of sale and renting; those parts of the *sharī'ah* apart from *'ibādāt* – acts of worship.

mubāḥ — permissible.

mubtada' — subject in a nominal clause or sentence; it is followed by the predicate (*khabar*) (*grammar*).

muḍāf — the first or governing noun of a genitive construction (*grammar*).

muḍāf ilayhi — the noun that is governed in a genitive construction (*grammar*).

muḥaddith — expert in Prophetic *ḥadīths* who profoundly knows and narrates *ḥadīths* with the chains of their narration, and who knows the original and famous narrators.

muḥkam (āyāt) — *āyāt* of the Noble Qur'ān that are unambiguous statements on the *'aqīdah*, provide decisions on legal rulings and clear distinctions such as between truth and falsehood, that require no further explanation.

mujtahid — a *faqīh* who is qualified to practise *ijtihād* (*leg.*).

mukallaf legally responsible person, someone to whom the law is applicable (*leg.*).
mukhāṣamah dispute, debate, antagonism, polemic.
mukhāṭab addressee; second person (*grammar*) (*see hāḍir*).
munāfiq hypocrite, in the sense of someone who makes his *īmān* public but conceals *kufr*.
mushabbah something compared, the subject of comparison.
mushabbah bihī the thing compared to, the object of comparison.
mushrik someone who associates partners with Allah.
muta'allaq related (*grammar*).
mutakallim speaker; first person (*grammar*); scholar of *kalām* (the science of *'aqīdah*).
mutashābih (āyāt) *āyāt* of the Noble Qur'ān open to multiple interpretations. They refer to something known only to Allah ﷻ and, according to some, "*those firmly grounded in knowledge*"; allegorical.

N

nafs self.
nafs ammārah the commanding self that incites evil and the pursuit of base instincts.
nafs lawwāmah the reproachful self, the person who reproaches himself when he commits a wrong action.
nafs muṭma'innah the peaceful self, the tranquil self that is at peace because it has pleased its Lord ﷻ.
naḥw grammar, syntax; the science that deals with the nature of speech and its rules.
naḥwī grammarian, philologist, someone who adopts or is an expert in *naḥw* (*grammar*).
nakirah rejection, rebuttal (*leg.*); indefinite noun (*grammar*).
nār fire, the Fire of Hell.
naṣārā Christians.

nashīd	song, often to do with the *dīn*.
nāsikh	one that abrogates; an abrogating Qur'ānic *āyah*. (*see naskh, mansūkh*).
naskh	abrogation, esp. of one Qur'ānic *āyah*, or any of its aspects, by another.
naṣrānī	Christian, of or pertaining to Christianity.
nifāq	Hypocrisy (*see munāfiq*).

O

P

Paraclete	comforter, advocate, taken by Christians to be the Holy Ghost, and by Muslims to be "the '*Periclyte*' which precisely signifies 'Aḥmad' in the sense of 'the most Illustrious, Praised, and Celebrated'"[648] i.e. the Prophet Muḥammad ﷺ.

Q

Qur'ān	Recitation; the Speech of Allah سبحانه وتعالى revealed to the Prophet Muḥammad ﷺ as a comprehensive revelation abrogating all previous scriptures.

R

radīf	rhythmic ending of two or more verses, with one or more words (*poetry*).
rajaz	partly metrical form of Arabic poetry, a discourse in rhyme used to push the limits of lexicography; classical Arabic musical poetry with a simple metre that is often recited in military/war chants (*poetry*).
rawī	the last quiescent letter of a rhyming word (*poetry*); the rhyming consonant.

648 Abdulahad Dawud, *Muhammad in the Bible.*

riwāyah transmission, narration.
rukn (*pl. arkān*) integral, essential aspect; foot in a verse (*poetry*).

S

sā'ah hour, watch/clock, the Last Hour when all creation will perish preceding the Day of Rising.
sabab (*pl. asbāb*) cause, reason, circumstance (*lit.*); tent-rope; an Arabic word composed of only two letters (*grammar*).
ṣadaqah voluntary giving.
ṣadaqat al-fiṭr incumbent *ṣadaqah* paid per head by the financially well-off to the deserving on the day of 'Id al-Fiṭr.
sā'ibah an animal consecrated by *mushrikūn* by being released in the name of an idol.
ṣalāh the rite of prayer, which includes standing, bowing, sitting, and prostration, in addition to specific words and phrases.
ṣarf word morphology, etymology; the science of the forms of words (*grammar*).
ṣarīḥ explicit, the clear and unambiguous meaning of a text, be it written or spoken.
ṣawm abstention, to refrain from; fasting.
sa'y hastening; the rite of hastening between two specific points between the Mounts Ṣafā and Marwah in Makkah during *ḥajj* and *'umrah*.
sharṭ precondition; the conditional clause (*grammar*).
shirk association of partners with Allah.
ṣifah description, adjective (*grammar*).
sunnah (*pl. sunan*) custom, manner, mode; the practice of the Prophet Muḥammad ﷺ; not to be confused with '*ḥadīth*' which is an account of his practice, words and tacit confirmations of the words and

deeds of his Companions.

sūrah (*pl. suwar*) a large section of the Noble Qur'ān, sometimes translated as 'chapter'.

T

tafsir interpretation, explanation, hermeneutics, commentary, exegesis (esp. of the Noble Qur'ān).

ṭahārah purity, purification, particularly *wuḍū'*, *ghusl* and *tayammum*.

taḥrīf alteration, distortion esp. textual distortion.

tahrīf lafẓī textual distortion, alteration of actual words.

taḥrīf ma'nawī alteration of meaning.

talbiyah the *ḥajj* chant of the pilgrims during *ḥajj* in Makkah.

ta'līl seeking, forming, discovering or explaining the effective cause (*'illah*).

taqwā derives from *wiqāyah* 'protection' and 'safeguarding'. It comprises avoidance of acts of disobedience, fulfilment of the acts of obedience, and contains the sense of fear of Allah.

ta'rīḍ (*pl. ta'rīḍāt*) allusion.

taṣawwuf is the Islamic behavioural science of *iḥsān* and is based on sincerity of intention and honesty of action according to the teachings of Islam, with overwhelming awareness of the omniscience of Allah ﷻ.

tashbīh to compare, to liken one thing to another (*linguistics*); anthropomorphism (*kalām*).

tayaqquz alertness, vigilance, awareness.

ṭawīl is a compound metre used in classical Arabic poetry. It has one short syllable and two long syllables (*poetry*).

ta'wīl esoteric interpretation, esp. of the Noble Qur'ān.
tawjīh understanding something in a given context; resolving an apparent contradiction.
Tawrāt *see* Torah
Torah Divine scripture revealed to the Prophet Sayyidunā Mūsā (Moses) ﷺ.

U

'ulūm insāniyyah human sciences, humanities.
ummī untutored by anyone; of or pertaining to a community.
'umrah lesser pilgrimage made to the Ka'bah in Makkah, consisting of verbal and physical rites.
Urūz measures in poetry, esp. in Urdu poetry (*see 'Arūd*).
uṣūl *see aṣl*
uṣūl al-fiqh Legal Theory, Principles of Islamic Jurisprudence (*leg.*).
uṣūlī expert in *fiqh* (esp. Islamic) or its principles, legal theoretician (*leg.*).
Uwaysī someone who benefits or acquires blessings directly from a spiritual doctor or even from the Prophet Muḥammad ﷺ, i.e. the transmission of spiritual knowledge without physical interaction.

V

W

waḥy revelation.
wājib incumbent, something one is obliged to do; an act or omission whose binding nature is proven by non-definitive evidence (*Ḥanafī fiqh*).
walī guardian, friend, assistant, helper.

watad (*pl. awtād*) wedge, stake, tent-peg (*lit.*); an Arabic word of three letters whereof the first is voweled and the second or third is quiescent (*grammar*).

wazn (*pl. awzān*) weight (*lit.*); metre (*poetry*).

wilāyah guardianship, friendship.

wird (*pl. awrād*) any *dhikr*, *du'ā* and *āyāt* of Qur'ān that a person undertakes to recite regularly (*dīn*).

wuḍū' minor purification in order to touch the Noble Qur'ān, circumambulate the Ka'bah and perform *ṣalāh*; ablution (*leg.*).

X

Y

yahūd Jews.

yahūdī Jewish, or pertaining to Judaism, a Jew.

yawm a day.

Yawm al-Qiyāmah Day of Rising [from the dead] – a name for the Day of Judgement.

Z

zakāh obligatory tax on held wealth that is taken by Muslim authorities from the Muslims' livestock, crops and cash. On the latter, Muslims pay 2.5% annually on the surplus of their wealth for the poor and needy and the other categories who may legally receive it (*leg.*).

Zaqqūm a tree in Hell, sometimes identified with the Indian Fig, barbary fig or Sweet Prickly Pear (Opuntia dillenii or Opuntia ficus-indica), part of the Cactaceae family.

ẓarf adverb of time or place (*grammar*); receptacle.

ziḥāf a non-uniform or non-regular change, esp. in poetry.

Bibliography

Abū Dāwūd, Sulaymān ibn al-Ash'ath ibn Isḥāq al-Azdī (202 AH/817 CE – 275 AH/889 CE). *as-Sunan*. Riyādh. Dārussalām. 3rd Edition. 1421 AH/2000 CE.

Al-Bayhaqī, Abū Bakr Aḥmad ibn al-Ḥusayn (384 AH/994 CE – 458 AH/1065 CE). *Shu'ab al-Īmān*. Beirut, Lebanon. Dar al Kotob Al-'Ilmiyah. 1st Edition. 1410 AH/1990 CE. Vol. 2.

Al-Bukhārī, Abu 'Abdullāh Muḥammad ibn Ismā'īl ibn Ibrāhīm ibn al-Mughīrah ibn Bardizbah (194 AH/809 CE – 256 AH/869 CE). *al-Jāmi' aṣ-Ṣaḥīḥ*. Riyādh. Dārussalām. 3rd Edition. 1421 AH/2000 CE .

Al-Būṣīrī, Muḥammad ibn Sa'īd (607 AH/1211 CE – 693 AH/1294 CE). *Qaṣīdat al-Burdah (al-Kawākib ad-Durriyyah fī Madḥ Khayr al-Bariyyah ﷺ).*

Al-Khafājī, Shihābuddīn Aḥmad ibn Muḥammad ibn 'Umar (d.1069 AH/1658 CE). *Nasīm ar-Riyāḍ fī Sharḥ Shifā' al-Qāḍī 'Iyāḍ*. Beirut. Dar al-Kotob al-'Ilmiyah. 1st Edition. 1421 AH/2001 CE Vol. 5.

Al-Muḥaddith ad-Dihlawī, Shāh Waliyyullāh (114 AH/1703 CE – 1176 AH/1762 CE). *Qaṣīdah Aṭyab an-Nagham fī Madḥ Sayyid al-'Arab wa'l-'Ajam (Arabic/Urdu)*. Karam Shāh al-Azharī, Pīr Muḥammad (1336 AH/1918 CE – 1418 AH/1998 CE), trans. Lahore. Ziyā' al-Qur'ān Publications. 1405 AH/1985 CE.

Al-Qārī, Al-Mulla' 'Alī (d.1014 AH/1605 CE). *Sharḥ ash-Shifā'*. Beirut. Dar al-Kotob al-'Ilmiyah. 1st Edition. 1421 AH/2001 CE Vol. 2.

An-Nasā'ī, Abū 'Abdurraḥmān Aḥmad ibn Shu'ayb ibn 'Alī ibn Sinān (215 AH/829 CE – 303 AH/915 CE). *as-Sunan aṣ-Ṣughrā*. Riyādh. Dārussalām. 3rd Edition. 1421 AH/2000 CE.

Ar-Rūmī, Dr. Fahad ibn 'Abdurraḥmān ibn Sulaymān. *Buḥūth fī 'Ilm Uṣūl at-Tafsīr wa Manāhiju-hū*. s.l. Maktabat at-Tawbah. Fourth Edition. 1419 AH/1998 CE. p.186.

Aṣ-Ṣāwī, Aḥmad (1175 AH/1761 CE – 1241 AH/1825 CE). *Ḥāshiyat al-'Allāmah aṣ-Ṣāwī 'alā Tafsīr al-Jalālayn*. s.l. Dār al-Fikr. Vol. 1.

As-Suyūṭī, Jalāluddīn 'Abdurraḥmān ibn Abū Bakr (848 AH/1445 CE – 911 AH/1505 CE). *Ad-Durr al-Manthūr fī at-Tafsīr al-Ma'thūr*. Beirut. Dār al-Fikr. 1414 AH/1993 CE. Vol. 7.

——— *Jam' al-Jawāmi'*. Beirut. Dar al-Kotob al-'Ilmiyah. 1421 AH/2000 CE.

Aṭ-Ṭabarī, Abū Ja'far Muḥammad ibn Jarīr (224 AH/838 CE – 310 AH/923 CE). *Jāmi' al-Bayān 'an Ta'wīl Āy al-Qur'ān*. Beirut. Dār Iḥyā' at-Turāth al-'Arabī. 1421 AH/2001 CE. Vols. 23 – 24.

At-Tibrīzī, Imām Abū 'Abdullāh Muḥammad ibn 'Abdullāh al-Khaṭīb (741 AH/1340 CE). *Mishkāt al-Maṣābīḥ*. Beirut. Dār al-Kotob al-'Ilmiyah. 1424 AH/2003 CE.

At-Tirmidhī, Abū 'Īsā Muḥammad ibn 'Īsā ibn Sawrah ibn Mūsā as-Sulamī (200 AH/824 CE – 279 AH/892 CE). *al-Jāmi' al-Mukhtaṣar mina's-Sunan 'an Rasūl Allāh* ﷺ. Riyādh. Dārussalām. 3rd Edition. 1421 AH/2000 CE.

Az-Zarkashī, Badruddīn Muḥammad 'Abdullāh ibn Bahādur (745 AH/1344 CE – 794 AH/1391 CE). *al-Burhān fī 'Ulūm al-Qur'ān*. s.l. Dār al-Fikr. 3rd Edition. 1400 AH/1980 CE. Vol. 1.

Haywood, J.A., Nahmad, H.M. *A New Arabic Grammar of the Written Language*. London. Lund Humphries Publishers Ltd. 7th Edition. 1984.

Ibn al-'Arabī, Abū Bakr Muḥammad ibn 'Abdullāh (468 AH /1076 CE – 543 AH/1148 CE). *Aḥkām al-Qur'ān*. Beirut. Dar al-Kotob al-'Ilmiyah. 1424 AH/2003 CE.

Ibn Kathīr, 'Imāduddīn Ismā'īl ibn 'Umar (700 AH/1301 CE – 774 AH/1373 CE). *Tafsīr al-Qur'ān al-'Aẓīm (Tafsīr ibn Kathīr) (Urdu)*. Lahore. Ziyā' al-Qur'ān Publications. 1424 AH/2004 CE. Vol. 4 .

Ibn Khallikān, Shamsuddīn Abu'l-'Abbās Aḥmad ibn Muḥammad (607 AH/1211 CE – 680 AH/1282 CE). *Wafayāt al-A'yān wa-Anbā' Abnā' az-Zamān (Deaths of Eminent Men and History of the Sons of the Epoch)*. De Slane, McGuckin (1801–1878) William, trans. London. Oriental Translation Fund of Great Britain and Northern Ireland. 1257 AH/1842 CE.

Ibn Mājah, Abū 'Abdullāh Muḥammad ibn Yazīd (209 AH/824 CE – 273 AH/887 CE). *as-Sunan*. Riyādh. Dārussalām. 3rd Edition. 1421 AH/2000 CE.

Karam Shāh, Pīr Muḥammad (1336 AH/1918 CE – 1418 AH/1998 CE). *Ziyā' al-Qur'ān (Urdu)*. Lahore. Ziyā' al-Qur'ān Publications. 1399 AH/1978 CE. Vol. 5.

——— *Ziyā' an-Nabī (Urdu)*. Lahore. Ziyā' al-Qur'ān Publications. 2nd Edition. 1415 AH/1994 CE. Vol. 1.

Lane, Edward William (1801 – 1876) *Arabic-English Lexicon (online version)*. London. Williams and Norgate. 1863.

Muslim, Abu'l-Ḥusayn Muslim ibn al-Ḥajjāj ibn Muslim al-Qushayrī an-Naysābūrī (206 AH/821 CE – 261 AH/875 CE). *al-Musnad aṣ-Ṣaḥīḥ al-Mukhtaṣar min as-Sunan*. Riyādh. Dārussalām. 3rd Edition. 1421 AH/2000 CE.

Shipley, Joseph Twadell [ed.]. *Dictionary of World Literature: Criticism, Forms, Technique*. London. George Routledge & Sons Ltd. 1943.

Al-Baghawī, Abū Muḥammad al-Ḥusayn ibn Masʿūd ibn Muḥammad, al-Farrā' (436 AH/1044 CE – 516 AH/1122 CE). *Tafsīr al-Baghawī (Ma'ālim at-Tanzīl)*, in the margin of *Tafsīr al-*

Khāzin (Lubāb at-Ta'wīl fī Ma'ānī at-Tanzīl) by al-Khāzin, 'Alā'uddīn 'Alī ibn Muḥammad ibn Ibrāhīm al-Baghdādī (678 AH/1278 CE – 741 AH/1341 CE). 4 Volumes. Beirut. 1399 AH/1979 CE. Vol. 3, Part 4. commentary on Sūrat al-Kahf (18:60)).